THE SOMBER SIDE OF A
SCIENTIFIC
MIND

CHRISTIAN TYODER

AND

LYNN TYODER

Fulton Books, Inc.
Meadville, PA

Published by Fulton Books 2020

Cover Art Credit to Ghost Writer Media

ISBN 978-1-64654-197-3 (paperback)
ISBN 978-1-64654-198-0 (digital)

Printed in the United States of America

Editorial Formal Review

This is a historical fiction novel based on real-life events. It's the story of a brief but unlikely friendship between Hans Reinberg and Abdulai Rasulov. The two find themselves waiting out a snowstorm in a café in Paris. From this moment on, they are basically stuck with each other, and by the time they say their goodbyes, the young Hans has become deeply fond of his old friend.

It's a sad but casual goodbye as the two part ways, and Hans is quite surprised when Abdulai makes a request asking him to one day write the memoir of his life. This he accepts. It is revealed later on that he wasn't the only one who missed an opportunity to say a proper goodbye to Abdulai, hence the relevance of the book's title.

Given the vast amount of detail contained in this book, it's not one to be rushed through. I was fully invested in the characters. It's inspiring how consistent his character traits are, and I picked up valuable lessons on hard work and compassion from him.

Amidst the reality of Abd's life, themes of war, friendship, religion, discrimination, depression, family, and cultural values are well tackled. I especially liked how the authors painted an accurate picture of the various scenarios. From the flow of the story, I could envision the life of an Afghan refugee, challenges faced by an Arab immigrant to Europe, the pain of a divorced, single dad, a conniving ex-wife's evil plot, and the obstacles faced by a young woman trying to get in touch with her roots.

There were several moments when I paused to reflect on my own relationship with my family members.

This being a poignant and reflective read, I would recommend it to students of psychology, immigrants and anyone seeking to strengthen the bond with their family members.

—Mercy Bolo, OnlineBookClub.org member,
07 March, 18:23

INDEPENDENT REVIEWS

"This book is an engaging and often 'page-turning' account of the saga of a multicultural family and its heartaches. The descriptions of locations and landscape are often enchantingly beautiful."
—Alfred D. Heggie, MD, Cleveland, Ohio, USA

"This novel makes me think of the intercultural world we are living in. I think that such stories are always welcome in the fight against racism and discrimination."
—Cristinaro, OnlineBookClub.org member

"*The Somber Side of a Scientific Mind* is a fascinating story that will have you hooked from the start. Tyoder convincingly provides the reader with touching insights into a legacy full of ups and downs. Intelligently and intriguingly written, the reader will find him or herself dramatically immersed in the memoir of a man that you will feel like you have known your entire life. Highly recommended!"
—Leni Scholl, Esq., Heidelberg, Germany

"This is a complex but captivating memoir-based novel dealing with intertwining lives. Readers will find in this intriguing story topics that arouse their personal interest."
—David S. Pearlman, MD, Denver, Colorado, USA

"What really got me intrigued was your description of how these two characters initially meet and then the story shifts into revealing the past through this idea of a memoir. Very interesting!"
—Camille Turner, OnlineBookClub.org member.

"This sounds like an interesting read. The topic is certainly very timely in many parts of the world."

—Kislany, OnlineBookClub.org member (previous Member of the Month)

"This sounds like a fascinating and lifelike story! Abd seems to be a character one can look up to."

—Jkhorner, OnlineBookClub.org member

In memoriam of Abdulah Rasulov whose legacy is marked by endurance, resiliency, compassion, tolerance, and love.

CONTENTS

ACKNOWLEDGMENTS

Our deepest gratitude to Martine in La Rochelle, France, for fully entrusting to us the ambitious task of keeping her husband's legacy alive through this book.

PROLOGUE

Destiny brought two individuals of different ethnicity, culture, background, age, and education together during a house-bound snowstorm. Their short and direct personal contact ended with the blizzard, but their genuine friendship outlasted the death of one of them. Unexpectedly, the memory of the deceased was revived through this book after more than thirty years of complete lack of contact between the surviving family members of the deceased and his young friend. Mystery interrupted this silence when the fortuitous recovery of a handwritten document was found at an unexpected place and time. The revelation of the deceased's extraordinary life is the subject of this writing.

CHAPTER ONE

Fortuitous Encounter

Exhausted after running almost half a mile from the main entrance to the Icelandic airport counter at Boston Logan Airport, Hans was the last passenger who entered the old plane before the baby-faced young male flight attendant closed the front entrance door.

He extricated himself from the carry-on that had been banging on his left hip for the last five minutes. Hans squeezed his leather suitcase and his heavy winter coat into the overhead bin, then slumped into the window seat 28A, panting. The DC-6 was already at least fifteen minutes in the air, yet the rhythmic rattle of the fuselage had not subsided. The copilot announced that the plane was at 16,000 feet altitude at a speed of 250 knots. The rattling sound kept Hans awake even though he had not slept for more than thirteen hours, counting from the time he left Bronx, NY City, early that morning on a sardine-packed Greyhound bus. Hans's mind was wandering from an ice-cold, wind-swept Reykjavik airport tarmac upon disembarkation, to a three-hour refueling overstay, then the final landing at the snowy Luxembourg Findel International Airport, where he would have no difficulty catching a public bus in the early morning hours, heading for the city railroad station. His imagination ended only at the completion of his six-hour train trip to Buchs, a Swiss town a few miles west of the border; then a twenty-minute bus ride to Vaduz, his hometown.

Even though still suffering of an aching body, tired arms and legs, Hans already rejoiced over the prospect of viewing from the train the snowy landscape that he had been familiar with from the past. The joy of a reunion with his parents and sibling and that of rejoining a childhood friend pervaded his imagination. Three long years in the US for his postgraduate education followed by the two-semester vocational training in the banking business, interrupted by a couple of return Christmas visits, was then regarded as an eternity by people in a tightly knit community like Vaduz.

The plane's vibration gradually became less perceptible and eventually was replaced by a perpetual humming. Hans's breathing was getting heavier. The elder lady sitting at the aisle threw him a quick look, expressing her annoyance. Suddenly the lights on the ceiling turned off, leaving the travelers with spot illuminations shining down from the bottom of the overhead luggage bins. Passengers quieted down. The majority of them prepared for a night's rest, while an elderly man dragged his feet back and forth on the aisle. Otherwise, there was no noticeable human activity. Almost the entire cabin plunged into a light sleep, frequently interrupted by the presence of a quiet female flight attendant walking up and down the aisle. Here and there one still noticed a spotty but bright shining light over an opened book or a magazine. The monotonous engine sound pervaded the cabin. Several resting hours had passed when the wake-up light turned on.

The captain's rattled voice was heard, "Good morning, ladies and gentlemen. We are approximately forty-five minutes from Reykjavik. The weather there is partially cloudy, and the temperature is thirty-four degrees. The visibility is over two miles, and the wind less than twenty-five miles." Two blond female flight attendants, each with one hand carrying a tray and the other, forceps, were offering hot facial towels. Human activity slowly resumed in the cabin. The captain announced the preparation for landing. The fuselage front end slightly tipped down. The usual noise of the landing gear was heard, and then the plane made a quick, shallow left turn. Within a few minutes, the plane was on the runway. After the smooth landing, hand clapping, rejoicing, the uneventful flight broke the anxious silence.

Awakened by the commotion, Hans lifted up the porthole cover and looked out into the distance. Everything on the ground was white except for a few ragged mountain peaks toward the north side of the airport. He gathered his two pieces of luggage and his coat and then followed the disembarking crowd. A sensation of cold, numbing fresh air invaded his floundered body as he stepped out onto the movable staircase. He smiled to himself, thinking that the three-hour stay over at the Reykjavik airport shouldn't be too hard as by now he had regained some badly needed sleep.

Once Hans passed the custom and immigration checkout point, he looked for the sign Connecting Flights guiding him to the in-transit passengers' waiting room. He sat down at the far corner, stretched his legs, rested his tired body against the leather couch, pulled the pieces of luggage close to his feet, and then fell asleep. Suddenly he was aroused by a loudspeaker announcement that he could not distinctly hear. He was somewhat disoriented, probably because his sleep was at stage 4 of its cycle. The only word he heard was *boarding*. He dashed to the nearby gate desk where a friendly Icelandic Airlines agent confirmed that was indeed the second call for the reboarding at gate 2B for Luxembourg. He had exited that same gate three hours earlier.

After showing his boarding pass, Hans reoccupied his 28A seat. When he was about to settle down, ready for another nap, a deep voice from a tall, bearded man was addressed to him, "Is this seat taken?" In his half-sleep state, Hans nonchalantly replied no, then slumped back into his seat. The plane was now up in the air, but the same rattle didn't seem to keep him awake this time. He went into his deep sleep, and once again he skipped the hot meal served by two different female flight attendants. Suddenly the background music stopped. A clear female voice came on, "Ladies and gentlemen, the captain is about to make an announcement." Within approximately fifteen seconds of total impatient silence, a deep male voice came on, "We were just informed by the ground control tower that a severe snowstorm is presently affecting air and ground travels over South UK, Northeast France, Belgium, Southwest Netherlands, and entire Luxemburg. We are advised to divert our landing to Paris or to London. You will be kept informed of our final decision as soon as we get further instructions from the ground control agent."

Conversations between passengers resumed, interrupting the silence in the cabin. They noted that the plane was slowly climbing to a higher altitude. Several overhead dim lights calling flight attendants became lit one after another, possibly an indication of passengers' anxiety. Then the background music stopped, followed by a few seconds of complete silence. The captain's follow-up announcement was back on loudspeakers: "We have been given instructions to make an early landing in Paris at Orly Airport as we are now almost over London airspace. Please fasten your seatbelts. We might encounter air turbulence soon. Thank you for your patience."

Flight attendants were seen walking up and down the aisle. Occasionally they bent down listening to questions from passengers while keeping a friendly voice and a pleasant facial appearance while discreetly having their eyes on the seatbelts.

Hans slept through the commotion, then finally opened his eyes, looked around then at the empty seat next to him. Slowly he leaned over it, turning his head in the direction of the gentleman sitting at seat 28C. "Sir, please explain to me what is going on."

"The captain has announced that a heavy snowstorm is developing over the entire area, including Luxemburg."

"Thank you."

Right after Hans's inquiry, the air turbulence became very noticeable. Some passengers were trying to locate the air sickness bags that were supposed to be kept in the pouch behind the front seat. Hans checked his seatbelt, adjusted it, and abruptly placed his left palm over his mouth, hiding his yawn he often experienced after having a sleep of several hours. After a few minutes of resting his neck over the headrest, he unfastened his seatbelt, stood up, excused himself, got out of his seat, and assumed a stretching position while standing in the aisle for a few seconds. He tightened his loose right shoelace then proceeded to slowly walk toward the back of the carrier.

On his way, he had to stop when facing the brunette ponytail of a female wearing a green flight attendant uniform. The latter turned around when she heard, "Please inform me of what has been going on since the plane left Reykjavik. Sorry, I missed what the captain had said a few minutes ago on loudspeakers."

Not exactly on purpose, but for sure with this approach, Hans had the chance of taking a glimpse at the face of the young and slim descendant of Norse origin. She gave him the same answer as the one he received a few minutes earlier from the man sitting at seat 28C; but this time he got, in addition, a friendly smile.

"Please return to your seat as soon as possible and be sure to fasten your seatbelt. The turbulence is likely getting worse."

The plane was coming down fairly fast. Hans heard someone in the next front row saying, "We are in Orly." At the same time, he looked out the window and saw the words "Orly Airport" on one of several hangars. The landing of the aircraft was relatively smooth despite the low clouds hanging over the region. Once beyond the disembarking gate, Hans looked for the in-transit waiting room. He sat down on an empty seat adjacent to the main walkway, took out the pocket-size address book from his suitcase, turned to section "N," then marked it by folding back its right upper corner. Hans's stomach growled. He missed the two meals and the two snacks in the plane. He was hungry. Leaving his belongings on the seat, he walked to the food stand across the walkway, stared a few seconds at the handwritten menu on the wall, and sat down again at an unoccupied table. Now Hans decided not to waste his time waiting for the plane to resume its flight to Luxemburg. He decided to pay a short visit to his old friend Norbert living in Paris, Quartier Latin, then to take ground transportation all the way to Vaduz. He remembered they exchanged Christmas letters last year.

Suddenly he heard someone just pull the chair behind him. He turned around. To his surprise, he saw the same ponytailed brunette he talked to earlier in the plane. She smiled to him. "Well, here you are again. Are you going to continue your flight to Luxemburg once the weather permits?"

"I don't know yet, and you?"

"I will continue my route to Luxemburg then return to Reykjavik on the next day."

"Would you like to have something to eat?"

"No, thank you. I am not hungry."

"How about a cup of coffee or a glass of juice?"

"A glass of apple juice, if they have it."

She sat down on a seat next to his. He stood up, went to the counter, then came back with a glass of juice and a cup of coffee for himself while discreetly admiring her beautiful young body wrapped in the tight green uniform.

"Thank you."

"You're welcome. Where is your home?"

"Reykjavik."

"How long have you been with Icelandic Air?"

"Almost three years."

"Have you frequently encountered this type of weather and the flight had to be diverted away from the destination airport?"

"Rarely, fortunately. And what is your final destination?"

"Vaduz, Liechtenstein. Have you been in Liechtenstein?"

"No, but I heard it's a charming city with so much history."

Hans was curious about this attractive young lady. He was thinking that perhaps the unexpected circumstance might give him the opportunity to spend some time with her at the airport while waiting for the resumption of the final leg of his plane trip. He suddenly realized once again that he had finished his schooling, his apprenticeship, and ready to be self-sustainable from now on. As a matter of fact, Hans was awarded the PhD degree in economics last year at New York University and had just completed his internship at Chase Manhattan Bank in the Bronx. He thought he was on vacation, so to speak. He had plenty of leisure time to spend anywhere and at any time. He noted that the flight attendant had no rings on her fingers and she was not accompanied by anybody. He felt quite safe for not infringing on somebody else's property.

With a smiling face, she glanced at him with an inquisitive expression. "I note you don't have the Germanic accent."

"I had my college then postgraduate education in the US."

"The Yankees must have made you very much an American."

"Have you known about the American continent?"

"No, I was born and raised in the suburb of Reykjavik, then spent my entire childhood and teenage years there until I was eighteen when I had the first chance to get away from an eight-month-a-year snowy and icy landscape. I spent that three-week vacation in Corsica with my British girlfriend. What are you going to do in Vaduz?"

"I am going to rejoin my parents at least for a few weeks. I haven't decided where I will eventually make my permanent home, possibly in America, in Liechtenstein, or in another German-speaking European country. I want to take a whole year traveling, being still single and free...would you like to spend a few days next month sometime, visiting Liechtenstein? I'll be happy to show you around."

"Thank you. But my boyfriend and I have made plans to go on vacation next month in Tuscany."

Sensing that the chance of getting to know the gorgeous Icelandic lady had completely dissipated, Hans looked at his wristwatch then at the large wall clock. It was almost noon.

The flight attendant grabbed her luggage handle, stood up, then stretched her right arm to shake Hans's hand. "Thank you for the juice. I am going to take a rest at the airline flight attendants' club while waiting for a call to resume the flight to Luxembourg. Good luck with your career."

Hans reciprocated the same while directing with relish his look at the back of the graciously moving beautiful and sexy female body leaving him. It was a real treat as he had been for the last several months tired of having, day in and day out, to frequently look at overweight customers and employees alike at the bank in New York. A couple of minutes later, Hans went to the nearby public telephone booth. He dialed his friend Norbert's telephone number he read out of his address book. There was no answer.

Outside the heavy snowstorm was raging; at times sheets of snow noisily lashed at the tall glass-paneled walls facing the deserted snow-covered runways. One could barely discern slow-moving heavy snow-removal equipment and parked planes. Hans left the food stand and returned to the seat occupied by his two pieces of luggage. He slumped back into an adjacent vacant one. With his arms stretched out over the backs of the seats and his eyes staring at the ceiling, Hans tried to figure out what else he was going to do during the next twelve months besides travels and visits with friends and relatives. He had decided to do the job search in the fall. He was looking for opportunities to meet well-dressed, beautiful young European ladies, and who knows…it was time to seriously think about a stable career, a family, and children. He rejoiced at these thoughts while passengers were walking up and down the corridor and incessant loudspeaker announcements kept him in a semi-sleeping state.

A few hours passed. Enough rest by now, Hans stood up, went back to the food stand, and ordered a plate of fish and chips. While enjoying the hot food, his eyes fell on an abandoned local newspaper dated December 12, 1968, left on the next table. He quickly glanced through the business section, stood up, discarded his empty paper plate and cup, and then walked to the public phone booth. He placed another call to his friend Norbert, but again there was no answer. By this time the storm had calmed down substantially. After gathering his two pieces of luggage, Hans walked to the custom and immigration checkpoints, showed his passport, and headed for the main airport exit door. Cold and wet snow flakes were still falling, but not heavy enough to deter Hans from walking to the metro entrance less than a block away. He saw a phone booth a couple of buildings down the street. He stopped at the booth and dialed Norbert's number the third time. But there was still no answer. He descended the subway entrance and approached the agent at the counter to purchase a one-way ticket for Gare de l'Est station. He gave up the hope of seeing Norbert this time. After a few minutes, a train packed with commuters arrived. He managed to squeeze himself in one of the cars just before the automatic door closed. He got off at Gare de l'Est, stepped down three stairs, and here he was in a huge noisy building with railroad SNCF cars lined up in rows. A large board suspended several feet off the floor and electronically powered with frequent changing train departure and arrival schedules was facing him. Hans looked at the "Arrival" column on the left side of the board. He saw the word *Buchs* on a horizontal line that read, "19:15, Paris–Basel–Zurich–Buchs–Salzburg–Wien." He directed his eyes to the railhead posted with the sign Paris–Wien. There was no car on the tracks. The big clock's handles on the far wall indicated 7:21 p.m. Hans mumbled, "Six minutes late," then let out a deep sigh.

Exasperated, he walked in the direction of the information desk. A man wearing a black uniform and a hat with embroidered letters *SNCF* was standing behind the counter talking to a middle-age woman facing him. Their pure Paris French accent impressed Hans, who took three steps forward after the woman left the counter with "Merci, monsieur." The man heard Hans's broken French, "Destination Liechtenstein." He replied with distinct words, "The next train for Buchs will depart from gate 9 at six fifteen tomorrow morning. Be sure to make a connection in Basel. It might be with some delay due to the snowstorm." Hans thanked the man and then directed his regard toward the opened end of the train station.

Paris was plunged into a dreary day of late December, but the fall of snowflakes had ceased. Now that he was stuck for the rest of the night in an unknown ward of Paris, Hans had to figure out what he would have to do to kill time until the next morning. He remembered having seen a few minutes earlier the sign "Café de la Gare" about half block away from the metro entrance. Hans decided to go there, get a cup of cappuccino, read the remaining business section in the *Le Monde* newspaper he picked up earlier, and then return to the SNCF building. He stopped under the café's canopy and wiped the foggy glass-paneled door with his winter coat's sleeve. There was light inside.

After pulling up the door's rusty lashing handle, Hans shook off a few snowflakes from his coat, opened the door, and entered the store. Hans was facing a short-statured middle-age man standing behind the counter who looked at him. "Please come in. We are still open."

Those words in English were spoken almost without the typical French accent. Hans thought it was very likely the bartender had a good number of foreign customers. A second man, in the midsixties, bearded, with gray skin, sunken dark eyes, and sunken bony cheeks, sitting at the counter, slowly turned his head toward Hans. "Hello there. Don't bring us any more snow."

Hans approached the counter, sat down two seats away from the man, took his coat off, and then ordered his cappuccino and a cognac. The man continued, "What are you doing here at this time of the day and in this city ward?"

The man's English had a faint Arabic accent to Hans's ears. As his hand reached the tiny cup of condensed coffee, Hans gazed at the man. "My plane had to be diverted to Orly. I presumed this unusually heavy snowstorm wouldn't end for another day or two, so I have decided to get to my destination quicker by train."

"Where is your final destination?"

"Liechtenstein."

"Several years ago, my two older boys and I took a vacation trip to Austria. We stopped in Liechtenstein. We stayed at a B&B in Moëliholz bei Vaduz for a few days before heading for Salzburg. I vaguely remember those quaint little towns in that minuscule country."

"And you? Since you ask me what brings me here, can I ask you the same question?"

"You would be surprised when I tell you that I came to Paris by car. I got lost several times while driving through snowy suburbs. So, I decided to wait until the storm is over, then to hang around in this gem city for a few days before resuming my long and tedious journey."

"Where will be your final destination?"

"Let me offer you another cognac, and then I will talk about it, okay?" The man extended his right arm to Hans while ordering two cognacs. With his gnarled hand, he gave Hans a tight shake. "My name is Abdulai Rasulov. They call me 'Abd' for short. And yours?"

"Hans Reinberg. The Americans call me Hansi."

The new acquaintances continued their conversation for a while longer. In the meantime, the café owner Louis was cleaning up the place, ready to be closed for the day. "Do you want any more drinks?" Abd handed the owner a ten-frank bill after looking at Hans, who shook his head, saying, "No, thank you. Please keep the change."

"Thank you. I am about to close the shop earlier today. But from what I overheard, you seem to have no place to go for the night. Have you noted that the heavy snowfall has resumed? If you don't mind, I will go upstairs and leave you two down here. You are welcome to stay as long as you like. I'll see you tomorrow if you will still be here by then. But one thing I want to be sure of…no more customers for the day. If you decide to leave, just pull the door tight and make sure it is locked. You may move to the parlor and make yourselves comfortable." He turned the outside front lights off from the under-the-bar-counter switch and walked toward the back of the room. "Good night, gentlemen."

"Thank you for letting us stay here for the night. See you tomorrow," gratefully replied Hans.

Abd reached over to the seat where he was sitting, grabbed his old-looking black beret with his left hand, stood up from the creaking barstool, and trudged over the worn, creased green carpet, bending slightly forward, in the direction of the parlor. "Hans, would you be willing to keep my company until the snowstorm shows some letup? We might well finish the almost empty bottle of cognac Louis purposely left on the counter for us."

Glancing at Abd's stiff gait then directing his regard to the streets covered with deep snow, Hans audibly sighed. "Precisely, we both are café house-bound for the moment until at least tomorrow. We are better off staying put for now."

"It seems that we are reading each other's mind," said Abd.

Each man plunged into brown upholstered large chairs, separated by a round glass-topped table on which stood a tall ceramic vase with silk flowers. Hans looked tired and somewhat depressed even though he had taken a few catnaps here and there since he boarded the plane in Boston. Abd, on the other hand, still quite awake, remained fairly talkative. He reached into his shirt pocket, pulled out his smoking pipe, filled its bowl with sweet, aromatic tobacco shreds, packed them down with his index finger, and then looked at Hans. "Do you mind if I smoke?"

"By all means, please go ahead. I don't smoke, but I can stand the tobacco smoke a short time until I start to cough."

"Thank you. It's a bad habit, but I need to smoke my pipe every night before I doze off."

Hans was in a half-sleep state. He had no desire to carry on further the conversation; he wanted to be polite to a stranger being about the same age as his father. "You had not finished telling me from where you drove to Paris."

"I left my home in Tarbes, Midi-Pyrenees region, a week ago. I drove to Toulouse, my favorite university town, then from there to Pays de la Loire, where I stayed overnight with my friends' family in Nantes. From there I continued my route to Paris through Le Mans, Chartres, and Versailles. I stopped at Chartres to spend a few hours at the cathedral. I had planned to spend a few days leisurely sightseeing Paris, perhaps for the last time. I will be heading for my first destination, which is Vienna, then eventually my second and final stop in Bamyan, Afghanistan, where I was born."

Hans was somewhat surprised, trying to reconcile the two notions, i.e., a man's Arabic background and his Christian faith. He found this quite interesting. He promised himself to learn more about this unusual combination. Furthermore, he noted that Abd had not mentioned anything about his wife, even though there was a wedding ring on his left fourth finger, but Hans wanted to remain politely discreet. He refrained from being regarded as a nosy individual; therefore, he listened to Abd with a great deal of interest but without asking questions. "Why two destinations?"

After a dry cough, then what appeared to be a gasp for air or a shortness of breath, Abd proceeded to say, "I don't know whether I will make it to Afghanistan, but hopefully to Vienna, where one of my brothers lives in exile."

Hans realized that Abd was definitely not well. He quickly developed a deep sympathy for the old man. Annoyed by the flickering floor lamp, Abd got up from his comfortable stretching position on the chair. He ran his fingers along the electric cord from the lamp socket all the way to the wall. He then firmly pushed the cord's two prongs into the outlet. The flickering stopped. In the poorly lit parlor, but with the light shining directly over the middle section of Abd's body, Hans saw bruises with various discolorations from dark red to light green colors on both forearms. For a moment, the thought of being in the company of a drug addict came to his mind, but he acted as if he had not seen these skin marks pending further observation. Abd continued with the story of his last week's trip by car. His lively description of all what he had seen along the way kept Hans awake. Hans listened attentively to Abd, but he still refrained from asking for details, especially about his new acquaintance's personal matters even after the latter had spontaneously, and on several occasions, mentioned these to him. Abd continued to talk to his evening companion, who gradually showed no reaction. The latter slowly fell asleep. Abd took two sips from the cognac bottle. Gradually his eyes became dull and finally closed. Complete silence permeated the parlor, occasionally interrupted by the usual rhythmic Hans's breathing noise. The quietness of the night persisted when suddenly Louis's heavy footsteps pounding on the wooden stairs just a few minutes before the grandfather clock chirped six o'clock woke the two men up. Outside the snow was tapering off. There was practically no human activity on the snow-covered dark streets. That was a Sunday morning on a dreary day that enticed even the most active person to leisurely stay in bed.

Abd lit his pipe, took two puffs then turned to Hans. "I am hungry. How about you? Should we ask Louis whether he still has some leftover bread? I have two jars of jam in my car. The bakery stores remain closed until eleven on Sunday in Paris."

Hans nodded his head, showing his approval. As Abd had the intention of going to his car parked on a side street, he opened the entrance door, stepped out onto the platform, but quickly got back inside, shivering. "It's colder than last evening. I hope I will be able to start my car."

Through the tiny side window's glass panel, a barely perceptible quivering moonbeam slowly swept over one of the round tabletops. The outside weather was bleak and cold. The temperature in the room had dropped significantly during the night, forcing Hans to put on his winter coat, lamenting, "It's too late for me to catch the train for Basel at 6:15 a.m. Perhaps I should go back soon to the railroad station to find out whether there is another later on that has connection in Basel with trains going in the direction of Liechtenstein."

He was quite astonished when he heard Abd say, "Don't worry, Hans. Unless you are in a real hurry to rejoin your family, I would be most happy to have you travel with me by car at least to Basel. I prefer to go through large cities before arriving in Vienna anyway."

Intrigued by Abd's route preference, Hans remained silent for a brief moment then directed his eyes to Abd. "Thank you for your offer. It's very kind of you. But I am curious. You must have a definite reason for choosing the heavy traffic of the large European cities."

Abd heaved a deep sigh. "My health problem is the reason. Specifically, my leukemia is for the moment in remission, but it could flare up at any time, even though I have just finished a full course of chemotherapy plus radiation and I am going through a maintenance treatment plan. Therefore, during my trip I am trying to stay closer to medical centers that have a leukemia treatment protocol."

Hans's earlier suspicion of a drug addict had evaporated. He felt very reassured and without hesitation responded, "I would be glad to accompany you if you think I could be of some assistance in case you need an extra set of hands."

"You certainly could be very helpful to me. I will further explain to you once we are on our way to Basel."

After their breakfast, consisting of croissants left over from yesterday, marmalade, and coffee, Hans placed in Louis's hand a twenty-frank and a ten-frank bill folded together, saying, "Thank you very much for your hospitality. This is from both of us and for the cognac you left on the counter last night and the breakfast. Please keep the change if any."

After retrieving their possessions, the men put on their heavy coats, walked to the door while turning back their heads, and waved goodbye to Louis. They strode out of the café house in the bitter morning cold, heading for Abd's car. All of a sudden, the wind shear at a street corner blew Abd's beret away, exposing his bald and shiny vertex. Carefully, step by step, he waded through the wet snow, deep to above his ankles, crossed the narrow cobblestoned street, and freed his head covering stuck between the two twirls of a window wrought iron ornament. Against the forceful glacial penetrating wind blasting his frail body, Abd struggled to reach his Citroën hidden under a thin sheet of snow. The vehicle was parked on Rue Le Favre, half a block away from Café de la Gare. Abd pulled out of his wrinkled shirt pocket the car key, opened the trunk half full with what appeared to be a small camping tent, a transparent plastic bag containing aluminum connecting rods, a medium-size worn-out brown leather suitcase, steel chains, thick coiled ropes, an opened carton box holding half a dozen jars, and a clear plastic four-gallon container two-thirds full with a clear liquid. A large neatly folded green blanket occupied the remaining trunk space. He lifted it up and placed it over the suitcase, making room for Hans's belongings, and cast a friendly look at his travel companion. "Place your valise and your handbag in the trunk's empty space, but bring your coat inside and leave it on the back seat. You might need it later."

Hans gently opened the squeaking door on the passenger side, waiting for Abd to slide over the front seat behind the felt-wrapped steering wheel, before he placed his left leg on the car floor to get himself inside. Abd looked straight ahead and put the key in the ignition. The motor started at once. A dark cloud of smoke ejected from the exhaust pipe. Turning his head toward Hans, Abd uttered, "Are you ready?"

Hans calmly replied, "Yes, Abd. I have a permanent international driver's license. When you are tired, please don't hesitate to let me take over, okay?"

The Citroën squeaked and rattled over the cobblestone-paved streets. The dashboard clock time was 7:18 a.m. and the fuel tank less than two-thirds full. Paris was quiet at this time of day on the weekend. Off and on in the suburb Chateau de Vincennes, freshly baked French bread aroma smelled in the air, giving the men an insatiable appetite for an oven-fresh French baguette. But no stores were opened and the men kept driving. At this point, they were out in the countryside. Houses were no longer conglomerated.

Hans cast an inquisitive look at his driving companion. "I am curious. What route are you going to take from here on, and what cities are we going to drive through?"

While keeping his eyes on the roads covered with a thin layer of snow free of vehicle tracks, Abd responded, "From my past experience, the most direct way to Basel is through Troyes and Dijon. The roads, for the most part, are fairly wide, well maintained, and the attractive landscapes are dotted with old churches of all shapes and ages. However, we might encounter some black ice, especially in the vicinity of Dijon. If you are not in a hurry, we can make a stop at Troyes Cathedral to admire the multicentury-old cathedral, ornately decorated with over sixteen thousand square feet of stained glass windows and the flaming gothic facade. After that, if you still want to see one more national monument of France, we can make another stop at Dijon Cathedral, a masterpiece of Romanesque art."

Hans did not immediately respond to Abd's suggestion, as the thought of letting his parents impatiently wonder of his present whereabouts during this snowstorm haunted him. The Citroën passed a couple of small villages with scattered modest snow-roofed houses lined along and on the south side of the road. After a few long minutes of silence, Hans lifted his set of road-watching eyes from the snow-slushed winding pavements and turned his head toward the driving companion. "If there wouldn't be too much inconvenience, I would like to make a call to my parents at the next public telephone booth. I should allay my folks of their anxiety for not knowing where I am and what mode of transportation I will take to get to Buchs."

"Of course, I will stop when you want me to. Besides, we need some provisions for the day. I will try to find a corner store within the next couple of hours when stores are opened for business. Any food you don't care for or you are not supposed to eat? I will look for a two-day supply while you make your phone call."

Hans took a glance at the dashboard clock. It was almost 10:30 a.m. Due to time zone changes since he boarded the plane in Boston and the lack of a regular sleep pattern, Hans had completely lost his sense of time and space. Bewildered somewhat by the absence of human activities on both sides of the deserted streets, he astonishingly uttered these words, "Is it Sunday today?"

Abd looked at him, amazed. "Yes. As you probably are well aware, in Latin European countries, people take very seriously Sunday as the day of rest, just like the seventh day of the week as the day of worship for Christians. Only food stores are opened and just for a couple of hours on Sunday."

By this time the two men were about halfway to Troyes. The snowstorm of yesterday minimally affected this region. Plowed wheat fields were bare, dotted here and there by small snow-spangled, gale-spared spots. The sun was playing peekaboo with the dark low clouds to the east. There were hardly any cars on the wet roads, except for rare snow-splashing overtaking semitrailers. About three hours after leaving Porte de Vincennes, the two men saw from a distance the usual red-yellow Shell logo hung high on a tall post.

Abd slowed down the car to a complete halt, right in front of the lonely vintage gas pump carrying a hand-written instruction: "No out-of-town checks. Pay first inside." Both men got out of the car about the same time. They felt the gusty wind that rattled the loose Cinzano sign over the entrance door. Quickly both put on their winter outerwear, then walked to the store with their hands in their coat pockets. One kilo of ripened bananas, two loaves of French bread, three cans of corned beef, three cans of sardines, and six oranges constituted the twenty-four-hour provision they had in mind earlier. While Abd nonchalantly picked food items from the shelves, Hans got into an outdoor phone booth and made his call to Vaduz. He reappeared from the freezing outdoor call box smiling. Abd returned to his car carrying two heavy plastic bags after paying for the food items and eighteen liters of medium-grade gasoline. He filled the gas tank, opened the hood, and checked the oil level with the bent oil rod.

Hans interrogatively cast a regard at his travel companion. "Sorry, I am of little help to you. The telephone call to my parents was longer than I had anticipated. They worried about my whereabouts. How much do I owe you for food and gas?"

Abd slammed the hood and looked at Hans with his deepseated eyeballs beneath the frosty eyebrows, smiling. "Don't worry. I didn't spend a lot of money. With or without your company, I would have to use some of my savings to get to my destination anyway. But if you insist, I will keep all receipts and we will share the expenses on food. How are they, your parents?"

"Thank you for asking. They are fine and glad that I have decided to finish my homeward trip by car then train and bus. To be expected, they cautioned us about winter driving hazards."

Abd started the car, turned on the windshield wiper to remove the melting snow, then glanced at his travel companion. "Are you ready?"

Hans replied. "Do you want me to drive?"

Abd added, "Not yet. Will let you know, or ask me again when you see that I am getting sleepy."

With melancholy Abd sang along with Edith Piaf's ballad "La vie en rose" he heard on an AM station as the Citroën 1961 model, visibly getting old with areas on the trunk lid showing paint discolorations and bubbles, then they pulled away from the gas pump, going east in the direction of Troyes. Occasionally rare small wet snowflakes fell on the warm glass windshield surface then melted into streaks of water running down to the immobile wiping blades. Abd looked at the dashboard clock and realized that he had been at the steering wheel for over three hours. Even though slowly getting tired, Hans's heavy breathing kept him fully awake since they left the gas station. Finally, the long-awaited sun came out and the blue sky appeared, spreading westward.

Suddenly Abd yelled, "Ouch."

Awakened abruptly from his deep sleep, Hans, frightened and bewildered, turned his head to the driver. "What's the matter?"

With his right hand rubbing his right calf, Abd uttered again, "Ouch, ouch, charley horse in my leg."

"Pull over, quick."

"Would you like to take over the wheel for a while?"

"Gladly."

The shrieking car brakes ended with a full stop on a narrow strip of asphalt shoulder. The two men exchanged their seats. A few yards ahead of them stood a road sign that read "Troyes–Chaumont–Mulhouse (Belfort)–Basel." Once at the steering wheel, Hans, almost a head taller than Abd, adjusted the rear and side mirrors, the seat, and then released the foot brake, turned on the turn signal, and the Citroën started to slowly go back on the fairly dry intercity road to Troyes. The car was climbing the northeastern plateau. The immense wheat fields to their left, extending to the horizon, were draped with a thin white snow blanket. The northwest wind raged the hill, swaying the fully loaded car. Gusty wind tossed sprinklings of fine snow across the newly asphalt-resurfaced road. Frequently Hans had to forcefully take control of the steering wheel with both hands to keep the car from getting too close to the mushy shoulders. The windshield wipers, in constant motion, scraping the icy snow partially attached to the glass, produced a pulsing noise suggesting that the outside temperature was dropping to the freezing point.

Unable to clear the snow smeared over the glass windshield with the blades, Hans pulled over to a stop, got out of the car, lifted up the ice-frozen blades, and started scraping off the built-up ice sheets, while Abd turned on the defrosting knob, yelling, "Hans, you have been at the wheel almost three and a half hours. Let me take it over. I am no longer tired. I am fully awake. I have been reading the milestones along the road. Chaumont is only about ten kilometers from here. We might be able to find a café still opened on Sunday afternoon. It wouldn't be a bad idea to grab something to eat, a cup of coffee, get warm, then back on the road. What do you think?"

Getting back to the passenger seat, Hans, looking very tired and exhausted, replied, "Okay with me, but take it easy. We are over the pass, going downhill, and the winding road appears to have several hairpin turns, looking at it from this elevation."

Abd got back in the driver's seat. The car slowly rolled down the steep hill. Half an hour or so later, the travelers arrived to a valley with scattered clay-tiled small dwellings.

"It must be the outskirt of Chaumont," Hans mumbled. Within a few minutes the two men were in the middle of a much denser settlement with chimneys spewing out smoke from dark brown to light gray colors.

Abd pointed to an age-worn metal post with the inscription "Chaumont Centre," saying joyfully, "We are indeed in town. Let's look for a café."

With his searching eyes, Hans announced suddenly, "Look, Abd. To your left is one with the lights still on and some moving human shadows."

Abd immediately pulled over across the street and right in front of the café. The entry door slowly opened from inside. A bundled-up person strode out into the windy outdoor, slowly walked away, and then disappeared behind the tall courthouse building. Hans crossed the snow-sprinkled narrow street, gently turned the handle of the same entrance door, looked back at the direction of the car, and then waved at Abd to follow him. Once inside, the two men, one after the other, pulled the high chairs out from under the counter and sat down facing a chubby man wearing a white apron and holding two wine glasses. In fluent French with a mild rolling *r* of the Midi-Pyrenees region, Abd ordered, "Two mochas and two croissants please." While discreetly looking at two persons sitting at a table adjacent to the foggy window panes, he added, "It is nicely warm here, cold and windy outside."

Freshly brewed coffee aroma permeated the entire room. A weak winter sunray, penetrating the partial ice-covered window glass panes, shone on the hollow-cheeked face of the dark-haired motor-mouth woman in the white sheath dress. The two travelers finished quickly their coffee break, generously tipped the café owner, and then in a hurry got on the road.

It took Abd three ignition key turns to start the engine. Chaumont's chimneys, one after another, disappeared from the rear window as the car was going downhill, leaving behind the Sunday afternoon, semi-dormant city. The road became more winding as the Citroën descended the steep hill partially covered with a thin layer of fine snow. Hans abruptly grabbed the dashboard with his two hands and worrisomely uttered, "Watch out! Black ice. Be cautious, Abd."

Instantaneously, Abd manually locked the low gearbox ratio to better control the car and increase its running smoothness. Suddenly the front wheels slid and the car forcefully swayed to the right, hitting the end post of a low-cabled guardrail and emitting a scraping noise. The rear right side of the car slightly tilted down over the snow-powdered grass of the road shoulder. The two men abruptly got out of the Citroën, put on their winter coats, and then anxiously examined the chassis and all four wheels. Abd sighed. "We are lucky, no visible damage, thank God."

With their gloved hands applied to the right end of the front bumper, they tried to move the front wheels back on the asphalt surface. Because of the lack of strength caused by his illness, Abd was not able to effectively assist Hans in pushing the wheels toward the center of the road. Their feet kept sliding over the wet grass of the road shoulder. Finally, with Hans's feet applied to the guardrail's end post, they managed on their third pushing attempt to move the front of the Citroën in the right direction. The sun reappeared but with its lower half hidden behind the darkening horizon. Both men got back into the car. Abd, at the wheel, let the vehicle smoothly run downhill in the "N" gear. Before it reached the bottom of the pass, a sharp snapping sound was heard toward the back and under the trunk of the car. Within a couple of seconds, the rear of the car dropped lower on the passenger's side. This was immediately followed by a grinding, chattering, teeth-grinding rasp that appeared to be generated by the scraping of a metal object over a rough and hard surface. Abd applied the brake and then pulled the car over to a complete stop.

Hurriedly, the men, without putting on their winter coats, jumped out of the vehicle. Almost simultaneously they ran toward the rear of it. Horrified, they saw the right rear wheel leaning against the inside of the splashboard and the right end of the rear axle, broken off from the wheel, resting in a slanting position. Abd reached into the glove compartment and took out a black marking pen, opened the car trunk, tore a cover off from one of the two used cardboard boxes, then placed it on top of the car hood. A few small snowflakes landed then melted on the dorsum of his left trembling hand while he was writing "Voiture en panne" (disabled car).

After inserting the sign between the blades and the glass windshield, Abd looked at Hans. "I am sorry for putting you through all these inconveniences." By this time the sun had completely disappeared, projecting upwardly its last golden haze of the day over the shadows of faraway bluish flat-topped hills. Farther to the east and from a distance, houses appeared as dark dots on a blanket of white snow left behind by yesterday's snowstorm. Abd heaved another deep sigh. "The rear axle, I believe."

"I think you are right. The axle is broken," Hans replied.

"It is getting late and colder. What do you think we should do next?"

"I am afraid we have to try, first of all, to find a place to overnight in the middle of nowhere until tomorrow. The next hurdle to overcome will be the task of finding a mechanic who can replace the axle."

The travelers grabbed from the car trunk enough loads to carry on their shoulders, and they started cautiously walking along the icy road in the direction of these faraway houses that, one after another, straggled along their passage. They were getting nearer. After a long, exhausting good hour, the two companions were in front of an old square brick dwelling, standing alone a few yards from the main road. The men searched for the walkway to the house with their eyes, as the ground around it was covered with at least a foot of undisturbed fresh snow. Hans trudged through the deep snow, approached the entrance platform, wiped off the wet glass door panel with the right sleeve of his coat, and looked in. Suddenly the light that indicated earlier the house was inhabited turned off, plunging the inside of it in darkness. Timidly Hans knocked at the glass doorframe then silently listened. The light turned on again. The inner paneled wooden door was opened just enough for a man's head to stick out halfway. Then slowly a wraith-thin body, with its back facing the dim light of a wrought iron rustic chandelier, showed up, face-to-face with a stranger. His wilted and mussed gray hair over a tired-looking visage indicated that the man was about to quit for the day. Toward the back of the room, the wall clock chirped nine o'clock.

With a quivering voice, Hans glanced at the forwarding head. "Our car broke down. It had to be left at the roadside a couple of kilometers up the road. Would you please inform us whether one will be able to find an inn, a B&B, or even a private home in town where we can stay for the night."

The man pushed the door wide open, making a quick sign with his hand. "Please step in. It's too cold to stand outside." Hans and his companion shook off the snowflakes from their winter coats and then entered the house. The tenant of the dwelling closed the door behind the unexpected but reassuring visitors while adding, "There is no commercial lodging around here, but there is an old lady living alone in a three-bedroom house just a couple of hundred meters behind our house. Occasionally, she rents out a spare room to tourists when her son is not in town visiting her." The man glanced at his wristwatch then stared at Abd. "Let me make a quick call to find out whether the room is available for rent. In the meantime, please warm yourselves up at the fireplace and help yourselves with a cup of hot cider if you wish." The man trudged forward, picked up the wall-mounted phone handset, and then dialed. A rattling voice answered. He listened and then said a few words that were almost inaudible. Less than a minute later, he returned to the fireplace where the two visitors were soaking themselves in the warmth of the dying embers. He smiled. "Yes, the lady is willing to rent the vacant room to you. She will leave the porch door light on for you to see her house from a distance."

The man proceeded to show the travelers how to get to the pedestrian bridge bringing them to the other side of the river where the lady's house was located. Pleased with the unexpected arrangement, the two companions put their coats back on, thanked the host, and then cautiously stepped down from the doorsteps into the darkness of the night. The two men were gradually adjusting their sight to the pitch dark outside. Unlike the ships that keep a certain distance from the lighthouse, Abd and Hans walked directly toward the only dim spot of light that appeared off and on behind a clump of densely grown trees. It was getting brighter as the men were getting closer to the house's silhouette. The chimney smoke swirls illuminated by the porch light could now be seen.

Abd loudly sighed. "It must be the house!"

Exhausted after trudging through the deep snow on the path, he was at some distance behind his companion. Short of breath, he suddenly stopped walking and let Hans approach the house first. As the latter reached the doorsteps, a five-foot-tall lady with a slouched posture was standing at the door. With the same rattling voice the men had heard earlier, she friendly greeted them as Abd was now a few feet behind Hans. "If you are the folks who are looking for a place to stay overnight, this is it."

Hans politely replied, "Yes, ma'am, we are the stranded travelers."

"Come in please, but be careful with the slippery doorsteps. My name is Louise Bojeau, but they call me 'Madame Jo' in the area."

The men took off their heavy outer coats, wiped their shoes, and then entered the living room. The hand of the circular thermometer hung next to the outside window frame was at two degrees Fahrenheit (–16.7 Celsius). The old lady continued, "Please pull that couch closer to the fireplace and warm yourselves up quickly while I am going to heat some cider for you."

Hans looked at her hospitable face. "Yes, lovely. Thank you."

A few minutes later Madame Jo returned, carrying a tray with two large cups and a thermos. After pouring the steaming liquid into the cups, she showed a glass jar of cinnamon powder to the guests. "Yes, or no?"

Both men said yes. They also looked at each other, very content and satisfied with the outcome that followed the unlucky event of the day.

Still standing near the left side of the fireplace's brick mantel, Madame Jo glanced at the wall clock. "It's getting late. You must be very tired. Let me show you your room upstairs with a private bath."

Abd replied with a weak voice, "Indeed, I am very tired. We left Chateau de Vincennes almost fourteen hours ago." He surely looked pale and exhausted, ready to lie down for a rest. The men followed Madame Jo, climbing up a steep squeaking wooden staircase. Once on the stair platform, the lady opened the door of the room with two double beds and turned on the ceiling light. "Here is your room with the window shades already pulled down. Two glasses and a water bottle on the night table in case you are thirsty. Please don't hesitate to knock at my door if you need something during the night. Sleep as long as you wish. I presume you know how the chain-operated shower works. Breakfast will be ready for you when you are up for the day. Good night."

Abd, very fatigued and weak, slumped into one of the beds. Hans came down to the living room to retrieve Abd's belongings as well as his. Both slept like the bears in hibernation. Hans's heavy breathing didn't seem to disturb his companion. Toward the morning of that Monday, occasional cocks' crows from a distance woke them up. Looking through the partially foggy windowpanes to the west, Abd and Hans saw shadows of neighboring houses projected on sparkling bright snow-covered backyards and realized that they started out the week with a sunny day. Slowly the men got out of their cozy, warm beds, took turns to wash themselves up, and quickly got dressed. One after the other, the travelers came downstairs and sat at the dining table.

Madame Jo came out of the kitchen wearing her usual apron made in Normandy. "Today is Monday. Local convenient stores will open only at noon. Can I offer you an omelet with mushroom, salted butter, strawberry jam, slices of bread, and coffee this morning?"

The two hungry men, having not eaten for over eighteen hours, gladly looked at Madame Jo. "Thank you. That is more than we can bargain for."

Before finishing his first cup of steamy coffee, Abd turned to the old lady. "Do you know any auto mechanic in town?"

"Yes, Monsieur Langvin is a very popular mechanic in this area. His shop is on the other side of the river. Every year and about this time, he takes a couple of weeks off and goes to Provence to visit his daughter. Let me make a quick call to see whether he is still here at the moment." Mrs. Bojeau walked to her antique oak bureau placed against the wainscoting kitchen wall, picked the white phone handset, and dialed while the two men were looking at her anxiously. She returned to the dining table with a chirpy voice. "You are lucky. Mr. Langvin is still in town until the coming Sunday."

Looking at Hans, Abd's facial expression instantly changed from anxious to relief.

"I think both of us will take a walk to his shop in a few minutes. May we temporarily leave our travel gear with you until we know exactly when we might be able to get our car repaired?"

"Certainly." Perhaps at the moment she was thinking of her only son Jacque, a sales rep of Nestlé Company, who traveled by car all year round, covering almost the entire eastern third territory of France. If so, she must be imagining that similar misfortune could happen to him at any day. The two men stood up from the table, gathered the empty plates, cups, saucers, and dirty silverware, and then carried them to the kitchen sink while Mrs. Bojeau looked on. "You don't have to help me clean the table. I am used to doing it myself to show to my son each time he comes for a visit that his mother is still capable of taking good care of him. Thank you anyway. Go to see Mr. Langvin. I will be here for the rest of the morning." A couple seconds after, she added, "If you don't mind the deep packed snow, I'll show you the shortest and easiest way to get to his shop. The footpath starts behind my neighbor's house to the right. It crosses the frozen creek, over a narrow ten-meter rusty steel bridge, then veers slightly to the left. Keep walking straight ahead until you approach a Virgin Mother shrine on your right. Make a quick stop there for a few seconds. Look slightly to your right, at about one o'clock on the watch dial. You will see a junkyard full of rusty automobile bodies and parts. This is Mr. Langvin's property."

The men thanked Mrs. Bojeau then got on the road. Twenty minutes or so, they were at the shop after wading through the deep snow that caused some shortness of breath to Abd. The only human in the large shed presumably was Mr. Langvin, they thought. He was in the middle of getting the woodstove going.

In a shivering voice, Hans asked, "Are you Mr. Langvin?"

"Yes, I am the person Mrs. Bojeau talked to on the phone earlier. What can I do for you? But first please take a seat on that bench. You will quickly warm yourselves up once the stove burns efficiently."

The travelers replied almost in duet. "Thank you." Abd clearly described to Mr. Langvin what had happened to his Citroën. He meticulously and sequentially went over in detail the various events leading to the automobile being out of commission.

The mechanic listened to him attentively. Not able to control his yawn revealing wide-gapped, malaligned teeth that he tried to hide by placing his hand nonchalantly over his care-neglected mustache, he cautiously uttered, "I have to see your car in order to know whether it has to be towed to a Citroën dealership or alternatively I could repair it myself."

Mr. Langvin got up from his squatted position in front of the stove and signaled the visitors to follow him. They got into an old half-rusty and hastily repainted open-back truck and managed to navigate through the deep snow-covered unplowed roads, heading toward the Chaumont direction. Suddenly, Hans pointed to a lonely snow heap off the road on the driver's side. He barely recognized that the Citroën was completely covered with fresh snow since they left it at the roadside last night.

Mr. Langvin parked his truck behind the abandoned vehicle, walked back to the rear of his truck, and picked up two shovels. He handed one of the two tools to Hans while keeping a calm face. "Would you mind giving me a hand? We will take turns to dig out at least the rear of the car before we can determine the problem."

Approximately half hour later, the back of the Citroën was freed of the white stuff, but the bottom end still needed to be cleaned out in order for the mechanic to thoroughly examine the axle and the attached wheels. This was accomplished without much trouble by the youngest of the three, Hans. With his bare hands, Mr. Langvin wiped off the remaining thin snow layer on the axle and pointed out to the two men the abnormal position of the right rear wheel in relation to the axle. He asked Abd to try starting the engine. After a couple of key turns of the ignition, the motor started. Mr. Langvin attentively listened to the motor noise and took a deep sigh. "You are lucky. Only the axle and the right strut are broken. I can handle the problem without difficulty. But let's get back to the shop. It is too cold here to discuss about the repair process."

Once back at the shop, the three men warmed themselves up in front of the stove, now burning hot with glowing embers. Mr. Langvin reached over a small desk to get his fingerprint-oil-stained Rolodex. He found the telephone number he was looking for and made the call. He talked with someone for a few minutes then returned to the anxiously waiting visitors with the following explanation. "I have showed you the problem with your automobile that you are fully aware of. In order for you to safely get back on the road, the rear axle and the two struts, also known as lower control arm toe rods, need to be replaced. The car is an old model of Citroën sedan. I just got in touch with a junkyard owner. He agreed with me, it wouldn't be easy to find a used axle and two compatible strut rods, but he will call back to let me know where he might be able to locate these parts, used but still usable. It might take a day or two to get a definitive answer, especially because the snow covering the parts needs to melt out a little before they can search for these suitable ones. Excuse me for a moment. I will be back in a few minutes and then you let me know whether you will opt to wait for the call or you would prefer to have the car towed to a dealership. The closest one is in Troyes. As you probably know, the towing is not cheap, and the repair cost at a dealership is more expensive. I have no problem repairing your Citroën as long as I have the right parts. Please think it over. Either way is fine with me. I realize that you need to have the car running as soon as possible." Then he walked to the car he was working on yesterday afternoon.

In the meantime, Hans leaned his head toward Abd and murmured, "It looks as if he knows how to repair and service French vehicles of all ages and models. Hopefully, he will live up to his local reputation."

"It is fine with me. I don't think we have another choice."

While waiting for further discussion with Mr. Langvin, the two large color frameless posters stapled to the sidewall near the shed's entrance attracted Hans's attention. He smiled when he recognized that he had seen identical posters in a New York car repair shop. The only difference was that these subtitled in French. One depicted a brunette girl in a bikini sitting on a Harley-Davidson motorcycle and the other in her high heels, also in a bikini, leaning to the driver's side door of a Chevrolet Impala coupe.

As the mechanic was walking back to the stove, Abd looked at him, settled in his decision. "We talked over the situation and have decided to wait until we hear from the junkyard's owner before we decide on another option."

Mr. Langvin poured a freshly brewed cup of coffee to Abd and Hans, who patiently were waiting for the phone call. A complete quietness reigned inside and outside of the shed. Abd slowly dozed off while Hans was doing mental planning with his pocket calendar. Suddenly the phone rang. Mr. Langvin picked up the handset, listened, smiling. "Are you serious, Henry? What? I can hardly believe it. Are you really hopeful in finding the third piece? Is it too late to get these two pieces on this afternoon courier? Thanks so much for your effort, and my best to you and Olivia."

The mechanic went back to sit near the stove, facing the two travelers. "The junkyard's owner that I mentioned to you earlier has successfully located the axle and one of the two strut rods we are searching for. The second one remains to be found, but Henri reassured me that, one way or another, he should be able to find it, very likely from the yard of steel scrap one of his friends owns. The first two components will arrive here in two days at the most, and if the second rod could be located within a couple of days, you two should be able to get back on the road by Thursday or Friday this week."

Abd immediately replied, "Thank you very much for all the troubles. We would prefer that you do the repair."

"Fine, I will be able to give you the final figure once I receive all the parts. My guess is that the total cost would be less than 80 FF [the exchange rate was $1.00 US for 4 French francs approximately]. Is it acceptable to you?"

"Certainly, it is very reasonable." Abd knew he still had plenty of cash to pay Mr. Langvin. But the next urgent step was to find a place to stay until the car was repaired. He asked the mechanic the permission to use his phone. He called Mrs. Bojeau, who told him that both of them were welcome to stay at her place until her son's monthly visit in two weeks. He informed the mechanic that they were going to stay at Mrs. Bojeau's place.

Hans and Abd stood up, ready to leave, when Mr. Langvin reassured them, "I will give you a call as soon as the first two parts arrive. You are welcome to come and see how I will start the repair process, but I want first to know whether you want me to tow your car myself."

"Of course! Please go ahead at your convenience. Is there a bank in town? I want to cash a check to pay you for the parts."

"No rush! The local branch of Banque de Lyon is located on the south side of town. If you don't need cash right away, I will take you there in a couple of days when I'll go there myself to make a deposit of my customers' checks."

Abd and Hans left the shop, returning to Mrs. Bojeau's house. At the door, Abd looked back and said, "Please give us a call when you get the news on the second strut rod."

Walking back on the same path, the two visitors were shivering in the cold gusty wind but very content with what had been accomplished so far. Mrs. Bojeau brought to them two steamy cups of freshly brewed coffee then turned to Abd. "Well, any luck with Mr. Langvin?"

"Yes, we are very lucky indeed. He seems to know how to solve our problem. With a little more luck, we should be able to get back on the road by the end of this week."

Hans asked Mrs. Bojeau about the daily meals. Since there was no restaurant within walking distance, she explained to the men that she only cooked twice a day for herself, and if they didn't mind to have only two simplified hot dishes each day, they were welcome to be at the dining table with her until they would be back on the road. The men accepted her offer to cook their meals with pleasure.

While waiting for the men to return from Mr. Langvin, she called her daughter-in-law Natalie, with whom she got along very well. She found out that her son Jacque might not be able to stop by her house in two weeks. He was sent to New York City for business by his company and would not be back until the first week of next month. As a matter of fact, three days ago, Natalie drove him to Le

Havre where he boarded the Transatlantic Crossing Queen Elizabeth of Cunard Line that took five days to get to the destination instead of less than a day by propeller planes. Jacque had flight phobia.

After finishing their coffee, Abd slowly climbed up to their rented room. He showed evidence of exhaustion and had to lie down. Just at the moment when Hans was about to go upstairs, Mrs. Bojeau, with napkins and silverware in her hands, gently called out, "It's already five to one. Would you like to have lunch in about thirty minutes?"

"Yes, thank you. Abd told me on our way back from Mr. Langvin that he was also hungry."

Once in the room, Hans noted that his travel companion had a gray facial look with his eyes closed. He worried about Abd's overall health. "Are you okay, Abd?"

"I am very tired, possibly because my red blood cell level has come down to below the normal count or simply because I am hypoglycemic."

Hans could not hide his worry about Abd's health, as he knew of Abd's serious illness. The idea of taking Abd to the hospital for an urgent evaluation came to his mind. He slowly and gently closed the door behind him and tiptoed down the staircase. Mrs. Bojeau, hearing the wooden squeaking sound, reappeared at the end of the dining table then looked up. "The *dejeuner* [lunch] is not quite ready yet. I will call you in about fifteen minutes."

"I am not trying to rush you. I just want to ask you whether I can use your phone to make a long-distance call to my parents in Liechtenstein."

"Absolutely, Hans. By the way, can I call you by your first name?"

"Of course! How do I know how much the call will cost?"

"Very simple, dial zero. The local operator in Baumont will come on, and you dial the number you want to call. At the end of the call, she will tell you the total cost with federal and departmental taxes included. She will also ask whether she could bill our telephone number. It's that easy. I will close the kitchen door so that you would have some privacy."

Hans did exactly what Mrs. Bojeau had told him. He informed his parents where he was staying and the reason why his trip with Abd had to be temporarily suspended. He was reassured that his parents were fine, even after shoveling the deep snow for hours. He reopened the kitchen door to thank her for letting him use her phone and to let her know that everything was okay with his parents. By this time their look at each other inspired reciprocal trust and good feeling.

After lunch, Abd thanked Mrs. Bojeau for the nice meal then excused himself and went back to their room for a nap, while Hans remained downstairs to help the host clear the table and clean the dishes. While working side by side at the kitchen counter, Mrs. Bojeau and Hans exchanged information on their family, background, hobbies. At the end of their conversation, she thanked him and then, with utmost discretion, she softly uttered, "Is your friend well? He looks pale to me."

Without going into details about Abd's general health, Hans, in a discreet manner and with his regard vaguely directed to the kitchen floor, responded, "Abd is not used to a long walk in the snow, especially when the gusting wind was strong enough to blow a frail body away."

Abd woke up a couple of hours later feeling somewhat better. The two men spent the most part of that afternoon in their room mapping their travel route on a Michelin road map. They decided to enter Switzerland at the Basel border checkpoint. Since Hans knew fairly well the international trade and circulation agreements between European states, he asked Abd whether he was a French citizen. Showing a sad facial expression, Abd informed Hans that he was a legal war refugee and had been living more than twelve years in France; but because of his personal family problem, that he was going to explain later, and his illness, he had not come around to apply for the French citizenship. However, as a law-abiding person, Abd had carefully prepared his trip. It took him more than two months to obtain passport visas of all the countries he had anticipated to drive through until he reached Kabul. Being a citizen of Liechtenstein, Hans could freely travel between Western European countries with his driver's license. He was not required to have a visa.

Hans continued to be concerned about Abd's health. With utmost discretion, he found out that his companion was going to have a "repeat blood count" once they arrived in Basel. Sensing that Hans was a trustworthy individual, Abd started to gradually confide in him his illness, his boyish secrets, his successful career, his personal sentimental past, and then eventually his family problems. The two men continued their conversation on many personal matters such as ethnicity, religion, family, education, health, and job. Remarkably, Hans noted that Abd seemed to dwell on subjects dealing with his spouse and his children.

Hans quietly listened with sympathy to his companion, who seemed choked at times when the latter went over the events that occurred during the years after his divorce. On one occasion, just a few minutes before Mrs. Bojeau announced that dinner was ready that evening, Hans was the witness to a great sob that rose in Abd's throat. He quickly placed his arms around his friend for sympathy and consolation.

It was getting dark outside. The grandfather clock in the living room chimed at the stroke of six. Mrs. Bojeau called out from the foot of the staircase, "Gentlemen, dinner is ready in a few minutes."

"Do you need help to set the table, Mrs. Bojeau?"

"No, thanks, Hans."

Abd hurriedly got dressed. The two men then joined Mrs. Bojeau for supper. Abd complained that he was still tired. He ate very little, excused himself, and then went back to his room for an early night's sleep. Mrs. Bojeau's earlier observation was now confirmed. Abd was definitely ill. She quickly cleared the table and then suggested to Hans while unwrapping a thermometer she took out from the dining table drawer. "You should take his temperature and his pulse."

Hans went upstairs and found Abd dressed in pajamas, sleeping. He did not want to disturb his companion. Occasionally the latter's raspy cough broke the silence of the night. Abd woke up a couple of times to take his medicine and to go to the bathroom.

After more than eight hours of sleep, Hans slowly got up. He found his friend sitting in the upholstered chair with his drooping head between two sunken shoulders. Hearing the squeaky noise of the bed, Abd slowly directed his look at Hans. "Did you have a good sleep last night? I am feeling much better. My cough is subsiding. It is an indication that I don't have anything wrong with my lungs. Probably it was caused by the cold air I breathed while walking to and from Mr. Langvin's shop."

Being a doctor, Abd was aware that his asthmatic diathesis predisposed him to develop reactive airway disease when he subjected himself to strenuous physical activities or a lengthy inhalation of cold air. After a long yawn, Hans replied, "I am glad you are feeling better. Mrs. Bojeau and I were worrying that you were getting sick."

It was still quiet downstairs. Only the monotonous sound of water dripping from melting icicles hanging on the roof edges was heard. The sun was just over the hills. The packed snow surface was sparkling in Mrs. Bojeau's backyard. In soft words, Abd continued, "During the night I heard footsteps downstairs, and the living room light was on for a while. Off and on a barely audible recitation of Hail Mary caught my ears. I presume Mrs. Bojeau was up and saying her nightly prayer."

Quite surprised, Hans was asking himself whether Abd was a Christian Arab, as the latter seemed very familiar with the Catholic Hail Mary prayer. "Good guess, Abd. Last evening, before I went to bed, I noted that a worn-out black leather-covered Bible was on the kitchen table next to a half-empty cup of coffee. She must be devotedly religious. Do you note that she is not only trusting but also motherly in dealing with us? She lives alone and has no nearby relatives. Her only son and his family are almost six hours away by car."

Abd finished his routine morning washing and shaving. He emptied the soapy washbowl water into the toilet and then looked at Hans still sitting at the foot of the bed. "Your turn, Hans. By the way, how old are you? I was sixty-nine last July."

"I just turned twenty-eight this past month."

"At your age, I completed my residency in internal medicine specialty. But I didn't want to set up a private practice. So, I decided to stay in academic medicine."

"Where?"

"At Karolinska University Hospital." Thinking of his thirty-seven-year-old son, Emal, who didn't want to go on past his bachelor's degree, Abd went on to say, "I would like to hear more about your education and your professional achievement."

"I didn't have as much education as you did. Briefly, I finished my high school and then college in Vaduz, completed my postgraduate in economics at Ecole Des Hautes Etudes Commerciales du Nord in Paris [a top-ranking business school in France], where I received my PhD in business. From there, I went to Brussels where I had my internship in banking. My last two years were spent in Brooklyn, New York, as a junior executive banker."

As the conversation on their life became more intense, the men stayed up into the early morning hours of the following days. Due to the subfreezing outdoor temperature and the all-day-long gusty wind, they stayed in their room after each meal. Religion was another subject Abd spent a lot of time on, besides the social issues that covered not only Europe but also the entire world. Much of the religious topic was centered on Islam versus Judeo-Christian culture, even though Abd was brought up in a Buddhist environment.

On the fourth morning at Mrs. Bojeau's house, the penetrating freezing wind had died down and the sky was cloudless. The two men decided to take a walk to Mr. Langvin's shop.

The latter, well bundled-up, was sitting at the doorsteps with an unlit cigarette hanging from his mustache-embellished mouth. With a smile, he looked at the returned visitors. "The axle and one of the strut rods were delivered a few minutes ago. I carefully examined them. They are in good condition. My contact still has not been able to locate the second strut rod. I have known him for years, and I am confident that, one way or another, this man will find the remaining part through one of his many connections. Just give him a couple more days." All three men went inside. Mr. Langvin showed Abd and Hans the parts he received that morning.

Anxious to breathe the outdoor fresh air, the travelers bade goodbye and then went out for a continuing walk. The wind was calm. The bright but cool sunlight shone on Abd's hollow face that looked to have a better color this late morning. Walking side by side on a partially snow-melting path leading to a denser conglomeration of dwellings, the two travel companions continued their intense conversation, interrupted occasionally by Abd's dry cough. Due to his young age with an uneventful youth, highlighted only by his delivery of the valedictory high school address at the commencement exercises and a brief sentimental relationship with a young American lady in the Brooklyn bank last year, Hans didn't have much to tell his friend about his life. On the other hand, Abd's life story went all the way back to his mother's home birth sixty-nine years ago in a small village located in central Afghanistan. He went on and on, talking about the civil war affecting his childhood and his youth. This period was followed by the separation from his parents at an early age then his relocation as a war refugee in another country, his education and professional achievement, and finally his family. At times the recount of each phase of his life appeared to be unending.

Hans's first thought was that Abd, due to his current illness that could cause mental depression, just wanted to get off his chest the hardship of the life he had endured for seven decades. Frequently, Abd repeated the same details about his life, narrated the same events, raised the same questions at least twice within a day of conversation. Eventually, Hans started to suspect that Abd's tendency of repetition must have a special purpose and therefore he didn't mind to patiently listen. Occasionally Abd choked on giving an account of quite remarkable events of his life. This indicated to Hans that his friend was genuine in his storytelling. They became more trustful and more intimate by the fifth day of their stay at Mrs. Bojeau's home. That evening, before saying good night to his friend, Abd revealed that he was married twice and explained to Hans the reason for his current trip to Istanbul.

On the next morning, the phone rang when all three were having breakfast. Mr. Langvin announced that the second strut had finally arrived and the travelers should be able to get back on the road no later than tomorrow midmorning. Bundled up warmly, Abd and Hans went to the local branch of Credit Lyonais Bank in town and had a check of eighty French francs made out to Mr. Langvin. They also got additional cash to pay Mrs. Bojeau for lodging and meals.

Upon their return, Mrs. Bojeau served her guests an elaborate dinner comparable to a sumptuous small-scaled banquet. The meal was not complete until she opened a bottle of robust, sturdy, and earthy red wine, from France's Languedoc region, that played well at the dinner table. After the "adieu dinner" (as Mrs. Bojeau called it), the men went upstairs. One could hear them conversing for a few more hours until the host turned off the lights on the first floor. Hans gradually realized that Abd was not only beset by his chronic granulocytic leukemia but also by some sort of family feud. Abd remained very discreet in telling his story, and Hans, in trying to understand his companion's state of mind, not through delicate questions but rather through mind reading. Bit by bit Abd revealed to his, by now, intimate friend numerous remarkable experiences of his life, while Hans patiently and considerately listened to his companion with compassion. The two men had spent time together for only seven days, yet their friendship appeared as if it was decades long. They carried their conversation into the late part of the night. The response to Abd's last word about his two sons was the usual Hans's heavy breathing. A complete silence pervaded the entire house.

Next morning, before the sun shone its first rays on the convex silo top, the two travelers were already up and about. They had their breakfast in a hurry. They paid Mrs. Bojeau and then Hans asked her whether they could leave their possessions in the living room until they returned with the Citroën. At the entrance of the Langvins' property, they noted that the freshly washed car was parked a few feet from the shop's main door, waiting to be picked up.

Handing the car key to Abd, Mr. Langvin took a puff from his cigarette. "Please go ahead and make a test run. Pay attention to the repetitive uneven tire rubbing sound against the smooth asphalt surface. I didn't hear any such a noise this morning when I drove for more than ten minutes."

Abd and Hans were able to start the motor within a fraction of a second and drove toward the main road, heading for the direction of Mrs. Bojeau's house. Abd accelerated and then decelerated the vehicle on purpose, carefully listening, but the noise described by Mr. Langvin wasn't there. They turned around and slowly reentered the driveway littered on both sides with rusty large auto parts. They parked the car again at the same place and then entered the shop. Abd took out the eighty-eight FF bank check from his shirt pocket and handed it to Mr. Langvin. "Thank you very much for your outstanding service. The car ran smoothly. We didn't hear a single abnormal noise."

"You are welcome. I am glad I was able to help you. If you ever come back this way, please stop in to have a drink."

The travelers bade goodbye and then drove back to Mrs. Bojeau's house to pick up their belongings, which were orderly rearranged in the trunk and the back seat of the car. They both leaned toward Mrs. Bojeau and deposited a kiss on each of her cheeks to express their thanks and say adieu. As soon as they got into the Citroën, Mrs. Bojeau ran out with a large bag in her left hand, waving at the men when the car started moving. "Wait, wait. Here is your provision for the day."

Hans rolled down the window glass, grabbed the bag, then said thanks to the old lady. He could barely hide his emotion. Slowly the car got back on the main road in the direction of Basel. It was a sunny but cold day. By then it was a couple of minutes before 9:30 a.m. on Hans's wristwatch. Abd increased the speed once the car passed the last house in Chaumont. The Citroën continued to perform flawlessly. Abd resumed his unfinished personal story. Hans patiently listened to his travel companion. To be sure that he understood correctly what Abd meant to say, he occasionally raised a question. Otherwise, he was rather quiet but attentive to each of Abd's words.

In the early afternoon, they arrived in Mulhouse. They stopped for a break and filled the gas tank after eating the sandwich Mrs. Bojeau had sent along. Abd drove to Mulhouse regional hospital, showed to the receptionist his oncologist's instruction letter, and then went to the hospital's lab for the blood tests recommended. The travelers almost fell asleep in the emergency department's waiting room. Finally, the lab technician who drew his blood earlier came out with the results, which were within the expected ranges one month after he received his first blood transfusion.

The two men arrived to the outskirts of Basel in the late afternoon of that day. After going through the Swiss border's custom and immigration station, they headed for Basel's main railroad station.

They parked the Citroën just a few hundred meters from the main entrance, entered the building, and looked at the train departure board. Hans mumbled, "Basel–Olten–Zurich–St. Gallen–Vaduz–Feldkirche 19:30." With a facial expression of sadness, he snuffled discreetly then tendered Abd a ten-Swiss-franc bill. "It has been a great pleasure to be your travel partner during the past week. I hate to see you by yourself from now on until you arrive in Vienna. You had promised to let me help you partially defray some of the travel expenses. Please drop me a note once you reach Kabul."

"Thank you for being so helpful during the entire trip and for putting up with all inconveniences."

They embraced, and they were at the brink of shedding tears. Hans cast a somber regard at Abd, turned around, and walked to the exit door. Just at that moment, one by one the century-old, gas-powered street lamps lit up. Quickly he reentered the hall where Abd, woebegone by the inevitable separation from his companion, was slowly heading back to his car. Facing his friend, Hans emotionally uttered, "It's getting late. You are not going to drive through the night, are you? I come to think that it would be very late in the night when I arrive in Vaduz with the next train and I don't want to disturb my parents unnecessarily. Why don't we stay here in Basel for the night?"

"It's a good idea. I am tired too."

They approached the station information counter and got the address of an inexpensive hotel located a few blocks from the station. Afterward, the two men had their fast dinner at a food stand next door. They returned to the car, drove a few minutes, and then checked into the hotel. After taking their showers, Hans sat on one of the two double beds with his back against the headboard and Abd on the only upholstered chair. They slowly drank the still very hot tea Abd had just finished preparing using the portable electric water boiler. Both men were thinking of the next day's personal activities but remained quiet for the moment. Suddenly Abd somberly looked at Hans. "Can I still say a few more words to you about my future plan after we separate tomorrow?" Concomitantly he thought about his two estranged grown-up sons and silently wept.

"Of course, Abd. You should know by now, I am good at listening, but clumsy and shy at expressing."

"As you probably have correctly guessed, I don't have too many months left to live. With my rapidly declining health, realistically I wouldn't be able to leave behind any written chapters of my life for my beloved ones. Now that I have confided to you during the last few days my true story, would you be willing to write my own memoir after my death? I am asking you to do me this big favor. I realize this is a colossal undertaking. You may write it in any form you choose, as fiction based on a real story or as a deceased's memoir. If you accept to do it, please take time to do it leisurely. It doesn't matter when you start writing, before or after you have a family with a loving wife and well-mannered children."

Hans got off his comfortable bed, came to sit next to Abd, and gently stroked his back as a gesture of consolation. "I'll do it with pleasure, as long as you are aware, I am not born to write, but rather to play with numbers. I cannot promise you the exact date when the book will be completed, but you can be reassured that it will be written in your honor."

"Thank you very much for accepting this time-consuming task. Once arrived in Vienna, I will drop you a note giving you my home address in France where my wife Martine lives. I will instruct her to let you know of my whereabouts during the next few months if I will still be alive that long."

Next morning after a light breakfast at the hotel, the men drove back to the railroad station. The next train for Buchs via Sargans was about to leave in a few minutes. From Buchs, Liechtenstein buses go to Vaduz. Hans took this route many times in the past. In a hurry, he bade a tearful farewell to his travel companion. "Be reassured, Abd. I will complete your memoir in a published book form. Future generations will learn a great deal of your life so rich with teaching experiences." Those words, trembling with emotion, were heard on Abd's left shoulder as Hans tightly embraced his friend for the last time. In a hurry, he climbed onto the platform with his luggage. The train started to move. Abd slowly walked in the same direction while directing his sad regard to Hans. Suddenly Hans, while descending one step from the platform and with his right hand holding on the opened door's handlebar, yelled, "I almost forget to give you my business card." Abd quickly grabbed the card from Hans's outstretched left arm. They waved to each other as the train sped up. Hans went inside of the passenger car, sat down, then looked at his wristwatch. It was Sunday, January 8, 1969, the day he saw his affectionate friend for the last time.

CHAPTER TWO

Twenty-Eight Years Later

It was Wednesday, February 26, 1997, a sunny but fairly cold day for the season in Queens Borough, New York. Hans, a bank manager, came home from work earlier than usual today. His American-born wife, Shelly, sitting in the den near the window, was typing on her newly acquired Apple a report to the school board on ways to improve the school children's behavior.

As Hans was hanging his cashmere garment in the coat closet, Shelly approached him and deposited an affectionate kiss on his dry lips. "Are you all right? You came home early today."

"The annual meeting of Manhattan Bank Managers in Bronx ended a few minutes after four, and I decided to come home directly from there instead of going back to my office and having to fight with the traffic."

Shelly poured two cups of jasmine tea kept warm since 5:00 p.m. under an ornate red thick fabric cozy their son brought back a few years earlier from Sweden. Husband and wife sat down on two Queen Ann-style chairs near the bay window. They were enjoying the fragrant tea. Hans reached out to his wife's gorgeous, slender, long-fingered hand, cheerfully uttering, "I love you."

"I love you too, darling." Both turned their head toward the window glass panel and looked down onto the traffic-jammed streets of Queens from their comfortably warm twelfth-floor, two-bedroom apartment. The desk phone on the narrow kitchen table rang. Shelly quickly got up to answer. She placed the handset to her right ear. It looked as if she was frowningly trying to figure out who was calling and where the call was coming from. She quickly handed the handset to her husband, saying, "Honey, all I could make out was that some-one wants to talk to you."

Hans said to the caller who continued to jabber in English with a strong foreign accent, "Hallo, hallo." Sensing that the lady on the phone had perhaps French as her mother tongue, Hans politely sug-gested. "S'il vous plait, parlez votre propre langue" (please speak your own language).

Hans finally realized after a few seconds that it was Martine, Abd's wife, whom he never met. She was calling him from La Rochelle, France. They spoke in French, and their conversation lasted over an hour. Hans mentioned that he had not heard from Abd since their separation at Basel main railroad station in January 1969, even though his address and his phone number were given to Abd at the last minute. He also told Martine that he had tried several times during the subsequent four years to locate her in Tarbes, Midi-Pyrenees district, but his attempts by phone calls and letters were in vain. Martine explained to Hans that she had moved back to La Rochelle to be near her family after Abd passed away on February 14, 1969. Hans quietly listened to her while jotting down a few details of the story that went like this.

At the end of January 1969, Martine received a telegram from Ali, her brother-in-law who lived as a war refugee in Vienna, notify-ing that Abd had finally arrived in Bamyan, Afghanistan, and that he was very sick with his leukemia in exacerbation. She managed to get a visa for that country and then for Pakistan within seventy-two hours; she then flew to Islamabad. From there she switched buses three times to arrive a week later at the house in Bamyan where Abd was born and now occupied by his oldest brother, Zekirullah. Martine found Abd moribund to the point that he could barely recognize her. She went into details about the remaining thirty-six hours she spent at his bedside, weeping.

A month and a few days earlier, Ali was quite surprised to see his brother show up in Vienna alone, without announcement. Apparently, around the time Abd arrived in Vienna, his illness took a fast downhill course. He had to be admitted urgently to the university hospital for several days. He received blood transfusions that had helped him regain some strength. Instead of taking a convalescing rest at Ali's home, he stubbornly made the most difficult trip of his life to Bamyan by trains then by buses less than a week after he was discharged from the hospital. The interaction between him and Abd was rather limited during the short visit, probably because of the latter's illness. But at the inspection of the plastic bag containing items belonging to Abd that one of the nurses at the hospital handed over to him, he found, among others, garnet-colored rosary beads with crucifix and a validated Linz-Vienna train ticket. From subsequent rare and brief conversations with Abd, Ali learned that his brother did not dare to drive alone anymore because of frequent episodes of headache and dizziness by the time he reached Kirchdorf am Inn in southeast Germany. He abandoned his car there. From there he hitchhiked all the way to Linz, then finished the rest of his trip by train.

"I am curious. How did you find out that your husband and I met in Paris?"

"Are you ready to hear the real but intricate circumstances leading to this call to you? I will not be surprised if you are befuddled by what I am about to recount."

"Please, continue."

The French lady thanked Hans and went on to tell him the long story with each episode in detail and in chronological order. Abd arrived in Bamyan sometime at the end of January 1969. He became weaker by the day. His brother Zekirullah sent an urgent request to their uncle Faisal, a general medical doctor, to make a house call. The latter lived three hours away by donkey transportation or two hours by bike on rough country roads. Facilities for blood transfusion, commonly used in Western European countries as a supplement in the care of patients with leukemia, were out of the question. Zekirullah reported that Faisal could only give Abd injections of "bismuth for his relentless bloody diarrhea," of "vitamins to maintain his waning physical strength," and of "antibiotics to ward off hidden infections."

Being the only Catholic in the whole county of Bamyan, Martine had to administer the last rites to her dying husband just before he took his last breath. The funeral was quite simple. The day after he died, his body was placed in a hard cardboard box, as coffin, and then carried by an ox wagon to the ancestral cemetery where a freshly dug grave lay next to his father's tomb. Her brother-in-law Zekirullah, his wife, and their two sons were at the burial site. The silk flower from Martine's coat was placed on the casket. Zekirullah recited a Buddhist prayer, and silently Abd's remains were slowly lowered into the ground. On the next day, painfully bereaved by the loss of her companion of thirty years, Martine returned to France to find solace through close contacts with her family in La Rochelle.

Hans, noting that she became extremely emotional at times, with sentences repeatedly interrupted by audible sobbing sounds, interjected, "I am very sorry. I should not have asked you to go through your suffering again. Perhaps it would be better that I call you in a couple of days and then you can tell me the rest of the story."

"No, no, please let me finish it now. It shouldn't be much longer. I need your sympathy and your help, as you will know why in a moment." Then Martine continued to keep Hans interested in her unfinished story.

After the death of Abd, she remained in touch with his surviving siblings and their family for years, in particular with Zekirullah and Ali. They exchanged letters and occasional phone calls. Not able to take risky trips back to Bamyan during the subsequent years to visit her husband's tomb, she wanted to be certain that it was well marked and well taken care by Zekirullah, his wife, and their two sons. To express her gratitude, twice a year she sent them financial assistance that had undoubtedly helped improve their living condition, as Afghanistan was, during the period preceding the Russian

War, impoverished by interminable battles between warlords. Depressed and feeble by his illness, Abd had been very little communicative after he returned to his parents' home in Bamyan. He spent the most part of the day indoor, either in bed or on the upholstered couch, writing off and on in his tattered notebook. Neither Ali nor Zekirullah knew what was going on with Abd once he left Tarbes for Afghanistan.

Then in March 2004, a shocking surprise startled everyone in Rasulov's family. The oldest son of Zekirullah was about to move out of his parents' home with his newlywed wife to live in the neighbor town Dokani. The only couch in the house was given to them as a part of the dowry. During the moving process of this piece of furniture, Hans's business card was found stuck between the springs and the cushion-protecting canvas. On the back of the card were these words in Abd's wobbly and splotchy handwriting: "Please get in touch with Hans and give him my diary." Martine told Hans that the word *diary* was not fully written and that the *y* is represented by a long backward slash. She said she and the Rasulov brothers believed that Abd became unconscious at that point. He was found with the head drooped, the ballpoint tightly held in his hand, and the notebook by his side.

The search began for the person with the name Hans, whom nobody on both sides of the family had ever met or heard of. Given the turmoil in the country, Zekirullah knew that it would be a very lengthy and difficult task of honoring Abd's request. The telephonic communication between Afghan cities was most of the time interrupted and that from the country to the outside world for personal use practically nonexistent. Afghanistan was ravaged by skirmishes between warlords on one hand and the Soviet annexation attempt on the other. Soviet-supported government military planes' bombardments of tribal encampments were not infrequent. Zekirullah sent the retrieved business card and the notebook to Ali, who lived in a Western European country that had a much better telephonic system of communication, asking him to actively try to locate Hans's whereabouts. It took almost two months for the message to arrive in Vienna. Ali started out with a phone call to Vaduz, Liechtenstein, using the telephone number printed on the recovered business card. The occupants of the house, whose address was listed on the card, informed him that nobody by that name was known to them and that they had been living in the dwelling for almost ten years. Ali got in touch with several bank managers and the high school superintendent in Vaduz, and also with the local chamber of commerce, but there was no trace of Hans. In the meantime, Martine received from Ali a package containing Abd's notebook and Hans's business card. She locked these items up in her safety box and hoped that someday this mysterious person would show up.

Several years had passed. Martine continued faithfully to keep in touch with the Rasulov brothers. Then in the early part of January 1997, the unconfirmed news that Hans had moved to Sweden came as a total surprise. The railroad section of Vienna transportation department just hired a trilingual office clerk who happened to be a citizen of Liechtenstein and had his office desk just a few feet away from that of Ali. The latter quickly found out that the man knew someone who might have known Hans years ago. After all, Liechtenstein is a tiny nation. A week later Ali learned from this man that Hans's parents had passed away, and their house was sold and resold a couple of times and finally to the current Austrian couple. Hans's sister Karolin got married then left town soon after. But the most important bit of information obtained from the third party was that they had lunch together before Hans left Vaduz for Stockholm where he was supposed to be hired by a bank. Ali called Sveriges Riksbank, one of the main banks in Sweden. They confirmed that Hans was indeed employed by the institution's suburb branch but had left for another job with Rusam Company Ltd., Copenhagen, a few years ago. Further telephone inquiries led Ali to successfully locate Hans at his current employment in the Bronx.

Without being asked, Martine explained to Hans why she could not succeed in advising her husband not to make the trip back to his homeland. "Abd is a self-denying man who has tremendous willpower, resolve, determination, and especially self-discipline. Once he makes up his mind, nobody can change his plan. In retrospect, I think he had tried to play down the severity of his illness in order to spare me from suffering. He knew that the lymphocytic type of leukemia that he had been diagnosed with was incurable. Therefore, in his opinion, it would have made no difference whether he received treatment in a developed country like France or no treatment at all in his homeland. A few months of prolonged life through repeated blood transfusions would do nothing more than just prolong his family members' agony and suffering. In addition to his untreatable illness, the relationship between him and his two sons became the last straw that broke the camel's back. So, he chose to leave us behind, as little as possible affected by his ailment, to return to his homeland and spend the remaining few short weeks there. The following words found in his notebook truly reflect his intention. 'Out of sight, out of mind.' Furthermore, he had on several occasions expressed the desire, when the time came, to have his body buried in his homeland, next to his parents' tombs."

At the end of their telephone conversation, Martine asked, "Do you know why my husband wanted us to give his diary to you? Knowing Abd, I am convinced that he must have had a solid reason to leave behind such an instruction just before he became unconscious."

"Please let me quickly relate to you events that took place after I met Abd at the Café de la Gare in Paris, and then you will find the answer to your legitimate question." Hans went on in length, recounting the activities of each day he was in the company of Abd back in January 1969. Very touched by Hans's story, Martine occasionally interrupted him to ask for more details, in order to find out whether Abd had suffered with his terminal illness.

"Thank you, Mr. Reinberg, for having accepted to keep my husband's legacy alive through your writing of his memoir. I am too old [Martine would be seventy-eight years old two weeks from that Wednesday to undertake such a demanding task]. I will mail my husband's notebook to you the first thing tomorrow morning." She slowly and clearly, letter by letter, spelled out to Hans her mailing address in La Rochelle and then said adieu to him after they agreed to stay in touch frequently.

Three weeks later Hans received Abd's notebook and a copy of the business card he gave to his travel companion twenty-eight years ago. The cover of the journal was partially tattered; but there were no missing pages, except a small part of the last page was torn off. He spent that same weekend deciphering the handwritten contents of the diary and was very pleased to find out that the essence of Abd's life was already known to him through the eight-day past conversations, except for some details from the diary which would certainly make his memoir writing more accurate and easier. Hans started to tackle the writing task the following week.

CHAPTER THREE

Challenging Preteen Years

The years following the Afghan independence from the British and recognition by the Soviet Union and other nations in March 1919, Afghanistan continued to experience social unrest and bloody confrontations between warlords. When fighting broke out in Bamyan and other large cities,  Afghan men went into hiding in isolated mountainous hamlets with their family for weeks or even months. The Rasulov family made no exception. Then, barely nine years of age, Abdulai's father took him, his mother, his fifteen-year-old adopted sister Omira, his ten-year-old brother Zekirullah, his eight-year-old brother Faiz, his six-year-old twin brothers Ali and Aamir, and his four-year-old baby sister Nabeela to a small and narrow, rocky unnamed strip of rugged land and with hidden caves in the southwestern part of the Hindu Kush Mountains. It took them about a day and a half from Bamyan, first on foot then by rowboat on the Helmand River's upper stream, to get to this site. Animals were usually escorted on foot by young boys or old men to the hiding place. The Rasulovs were familiar with this hideout from similar trips they had made in the past several years. Being members of small Buddhist remnants from the Mauryans' era still living in the Bamyan province and frequently persecuted by Sunni Muslims, the location of this secret hideout was passed on from one generation to another. The preparation for the evacuation was made precipitously the night before. At dawn on the next day, with already packed belongings, including warm clothing, rice, flour, light cooking utensils, and everything else they could carry on their backs, the whole family set out on foot in the early hours of a cold late winter morning. Abd's father and two of his brothers carried fishing rods with them.

Once reaching the foothills, they still faintly heard the sounds of gunfire and explosions. As they ascended the narrow steep path, Abd looked back toward their corrugated-roofed, single-room house made of sundried mud bricks, wondering whether it would still be there, in the outskirt of Bamyan, upon their return or burned down after looting by armed bandits. By midday the whole family arrived at the river site where their twenty-foot-long partially covered boat was moored next to a half-sunken one. In addition, a couple more wooden rafts attached side by side to a pointed rock made up the improvised marina. Abd volunteered to continue on foot, escorting the three goats. He insisted on looking after the animals, whose milk was the only source of protein for the family, himself and continued his journey alone. He arrived to that decision after giving himself the following thoughts: His father, the sole bread and butter provider for the family, would risk being kidnapped by the bandits. Zekirullah had a bad left hip diagnosed last year as slipped capital femoral epiphysis by his uncle Faisal; he was still wearing a body brace and could not walk long distances. Mother and Omira, if not carefully hidden in the boat, could be gang-raped by roaming bandits. And the remaining male siblings were too young to handle three lively goats.

The rocky footpath ran very much parallel to the river. After a short rest and having something to eat, everybody stood up, ready to continue their journey. Abd's mother, fearful for his defenselessness and safety, approached him, pulled him to her khaki burka-wrapped waist, held him tight for a few minutes, and softly murmured to his ear with tears running down her cheeks, "Stay alert and pay attention to human noises while walking. Don't resist when someone tries to take away the animals. Let him have them. I love you." Each member of the family took turns to hug Abd before getting in the boat. Abd's mother and father wiped their eyes welling up with tears.

Abd started walking with the three goats on leash. He waved at his family, and they quietly waved back. The mountain's echo could attract bandits, a risk the Rasulovs didn't want to take. Abd had to make several stops along the walking path to let the animals graze the grass very much burned by the past summer's heat. Frequently the goats had to descend the steep sloped riverbank to get to the stream. Likewise, Abd filled up several times his gourd with crystal clear Helmand River water. Intense midday heat could cause exhaustion. Once in a while well bundled up large Afghan families with several children, silently walking in the same direction, hurriedly overtook this lonely nine-year-old boy with his three goats. Abd wondered whether they also were on their way to a hiding place. Off and on, he was able to watch his family's boat floating downstream from his roadside vantage points, as the footpath ran alongside the river. The rough current combined with multicolored ragged and dangerous rocks jutting out of the water slowed down the boat with Zekirullah at the helm.

Once the sun was behind the highest peak, Tirich Mir, Abd was still only a little more than halfway to the hiding place. Before a few first stars appeared to the east side horizon, Abd settled down for the night between two large boulders off the beaten path. The temperature dropped to almost the freezing point. Crouching on his side, the boy was encircled by the three goats. He covered himself with a sheepskin and kept himself warm by the body heat of the animals. On the next morning, the young shepherd resumed his journey at the first sunrays of dawn. The family boat was at some distance downstream but still clearly visible. By noon, the whole family arrived at the hideout. Ali and Aamir took over and guarded the goats while Zekirullah, Abd, and their father inspected, then cleaned up the two nearby caves to be used as family dwellings. Abd's mother, in the meantime, rekindled a leftover dead fire by adding a few dried twigs, and then used an aluminum pan to cook the first away-from-home meal.

During the two and half weeks spent at the site, the Rasulovs subsisted on fish caught from Helmand River and flour they brought with them. Occasionally Abd's father walked to a few neighbor refugee campgrounds to get news of Bamyan City from latecomers. Finally, the words reached the dislodged people that fighting between various rebel groups had moved to Maymana province and calm had returned to the city now occupied by Afghan government troops friendly to the Russians. The Rasulov family was waiting for the confirmation of the good news from people who came to these camps to bring their loved ones home.

On that sunny morning in late March, the whole family left the hideout, heading home. Abd volunteered once again to accompany the animals on foot. The rest of the family returned home by boat. They had to move the vessel upstream, in countercurrent, with long wooden poles. Abd's parents instructed him to be as often in sight as possible. They feared of bandits still possibly roaming around in the area. Quietness reigned on all fronts except for the flapping noise of water waves against the boat's hull.

Suddenly, on the left riverbank and at some distance appeared, in front of Abd and approaching him, three fast-walking men carrying rifles and bandoliers. Abd's father recognized immediately that these men were bandits. He and Zekirullah, with all their arm strength, quickly moved the boat to shore. He jumped off the boat, ran toward Abd and the accompanied animals, hoping to deal in person with the bandits. Trying to prevent his son from further beating, he squeezed himself between the attackers and Abd still lying on the ground bleeding. Unfortunately, the bandits had already inflicted a great deal of damage to Abd before his father could get to the scene, and the robbers had already seized all three on-leash goats. The boy had a deep gash on his left temple and an oozing cut on his vertex. He was groaning in pain. Abd's father saw traces of fresh blood on one of the attacker's rifle butt, and his face cringed. At the very moment appeared another much taller man dressed in some sort of green-tan uniform, wearing also cartridge-loaded bandoliers, but with a head-gear similar to sea captain hat instead of white Islamic turban.

This newly arrived man stepped forward, facing Abd's father, who was fearfully trembling and having a staccato voice in his mother tongue Dari. "We are poor and displaced refugees." The man kept looking at Abd's father, failed to reply, and showed no change in his facial expression. Realizing that his interlocutor did not understand what he had said, Abd's father then tried to speak in Pashto, the other main Afghan language.

The tall man smiled and then replied in Pashto, "Sorry for your boy's injuries. These rascals shouldn't have done that to a little child. Can you speak more than these two languages?"

"I can speak five more Afghan dialects."

The tall man appeared to have the three robbers as subordinates, for he abruptly yanked the three animals' leashes off the hand of one of them and then handed them over to Abd's father. At the same time, he reached into his pocket for a card with a mailing address. "If you are looking for a well-paying job, we can use your service. You are free to go, and you can have the animals back."

At that time, Afghan warlords were recruiting educated individuals they could trust to be used as middlemen for liaisons between friendly tribal groups. Turning around, the tall man sternly looked at the robbers and loudly talked to them while pointing his finger to the direction where they came from. All four men walked away in a hurry while Abd's father pulled him up from the ground, cleaned his wounds with water from his gourd, and then put pressure on the injured areas to stop the bleeding. Still very frightened by the attack, Abd clung to his father, sobbing and groaning from burning pain. Both stayed in the same place for a while until there was no more bleeding. Abd's father offered to release him from the goats-escorting task, but Abd declined, insisting that his visible injuries would spare him from further attacks by bandits from here on. Father and son continued their way home separately.

A few hours later, Abd's father moored the boat once again to its marina and the whole family was back on foot before dusk. From the hilltop, they rejoiced on seeing their home still standing and illuminated by the last sunrays of the day. The double-dosed aspirin Abd's father gave him right after the incident had minimized the burning pain, and his uncle Faisal, who happened to make his weekly house call in town on that day, stitched the wounds on that same evening.

During the next five months, routine activities returned to members of the Rasulov family. Bamyan schools were reopened. The head of the household resumed his daily out-of-town school inspection trips by bike, and the children went back to half-day school sessions. Omira tended the three goats with the help of her brothers after school. Abd's mother made her routine twice-a-week pilgrimage to the local Buddhist shrines and her daily firewood gathering and additional house chores. Life went on without being affected by still ongoing wars between warlords' soldiers in the neighbor provinces.

It was mid-August. The scorching heat was already felt by nine in the morning. After the boys left for school and after washing and clothing Nabeela, Omira went to the back of their house to get the goats. She then escorted them to the public land for grazing. The soil was sandy and dry, barely supporting the growth of scarce sagebrush. Hay was nonexistent, yet the Rasulovs had to keep the goats alive and well enough to provide milk, which was the only source of animal protein necessary to nourish the entire family. The three goats had been grazing for over three hours under the watching eyes of Omira.

The burning sun was over her head. She fell into a deep sleep with her back leaning against a large standing, erect, flat boulder a few yards from the walking path. Suddenly an unusual commotion with increasing intensity was heard coming from the south side. Omira stooped low down behind the rock for fear of being seen by fighting rebels or bandits. She saw two bearded men coming in her direction. Both carried cartridge-loaded bandoliers and grenades. Trembling, she held her breath and lay flat on the ground when the two men walked past the rock. They didn't see her. She got up a few minutes later when the men's footsteps were no longer heard. With her fearful eyes, she looked for the dispersed goats. Frantically, she ran in all directions looking for them, but they were nowhere to be found. The sun was about to disappear behind the clouds covering the mountain peaks.

Omira was supposed to be back by this time. Mrs. Rasulov started to worry about Omira's whereabouts. She sent Abd to the scene to find out what was going on and to look for them. He saw the animals scattered in the gulley on the other side of the walking path, at some distance. He knew right away that none of them was watched for quite a while. He ran fast, dashing through bushes toward the frightened animals that kept wailing instead of grazing. Finally, brother and sister managed to keep the three goats again on leash. But neither could stand up. They were exhausted from running. Omira lay down first on a patch of dry grass. Abd sat down a few feet away, facing Omira, who looked pale. While still trembling, she directed her weeping eyes to Abd: "Thanks for saving me from being harmed by these uncontrollable dangerous bandits who roam around looking for women. The idea that you might be shot at by these criminals, every moment they see some sort of movement in tall grass, frightened me. Thanks God, the danger is finally over."

All of a sudden, with his eyebrows raised, his eyes and mouth wide-open, Abd worrisomely directed his regard toward the right side of Omira's dust-stained cloak where a two-inch broken thorn lay horizontally at the center of a wet-looking area. "Are you having pain somewhere?"

"On my side," replied Omira, who lifted up the right half of her apparel to show her brother where she was experiencing pain. The white blouse she wore under the cloak showed a large wet bloody area. Immediately she turned her lying body away from Abd and pulled up and freed the right flap of her garment tightly tucked to her skirt.

"A deep cut with oozing blood. It is burning and very painful."

"Where exactly?"

"Above the nipple."

Without hesitation, Abd took his dirt-spotted plaid shirt off, shook it vigorously, and then handed it to Omira. "Lay the inside of it over the wound, and then place your left palm firmly over it."

Omira did exactly what her brother had instructed her while keeping her back facing him. As Omira turned to her left side and flipped back the headpiece attached to her cloak, Abd spotted another horizontal cut, approximately one and a half inches, on the right side and at the root of her neck. Fresh blood was oozing out of this second wound. Omira worrisomely looked at her brother. "It stings there."

"Where?"

"Between my right ear and my shoulder."

Abd knew right away that she was referring to the same place he was looking at. He moved close to her, grabbed another section of the shirt, placed it over the nuchal wound, and then firmly applied pressure over the area with his left palm. This was the first time this eleven-year-old boy saw wounds and fresh blood. He got scared but could remember what he had recently learned in school on how to handle bleeding in case of emergency. He also remembered that his teacher taught the students the danger of having a deep cut on the sides of the neck. While sister and brother continued to apply pressure over Omira's wounds, Abd kept the three animals on leash in order to prevent them from wandering away again. Calmed down from the initial fright, they recounted to each other the whole event, and both realized that Omira's wounds were inflicted by nasty thorny bushes when she ran aimlessly looking for the scattered goats. Abd freed the gourd off Omira's neck and gave her some water to quench her thirst. They stayed on the ground, exposed to the scorching early-afternoon heat. Afraid of being scolded by their parents for leaving the goats unattended, Omira asked Abd not to say anything to them about her falling-asleep incident while she was supposed to tend to the animals. She didn't want to lose her parents' confidence in her, being the oldest child who assumed a large part of many in-house responsibilities. But most importantly, she didn't want her status of an elder sister caring for younger siblings to be questioned. Abd agreed to her request. In order to hide the whole story, she sent Abd home, instructing him to look for a clean garment and return to the site with it without letting Mother Elaha or anybody else see what he did. He did exactly what his sister had figured out and brought back a clean cloak, which was soaked in a pile of dry dirt before she put it over the blood-tainted dress.

Abd had the animals on leash and walked behind Omira, who slowly strolled back to the goats' open stall. That evening, Dr. Faisal made a trip on camel's back to take care of Omira's wounds. Before saying goodbye to the Rasulovs, he left ten tablets of penicillin for the girl to take every day for the next five days. Fortunately, the wounds healed uneventfully.

During the next two years, life was going on as usual with the Rasulov family. Zekirullah turned thirteen. He needed to find an evening job and hoped to go to high school during the day.

Uncle Faisal's medical practice was getting too busy, even though he already had five full-time employees. He was thinking of hiring someone to assume the office's cleaning job at the end of the working day. He thought about the oldest Rasulov boy, who had the hip disease three years ago and was now fully recovered. The week after, he came to talk with Abd's father and offered the job to Zekirullah, who was delighted with the prospect of being able to continue his schooling in Kabul area while earning a small wage. Abd's parents saw this arrangement as the very first opening for their children to be potentially educated and exposed to employment opportunities beyond the suburb of Bamyan. They counted on the traditional Afghan custom that the oldest sibling would help the younger ones to be successful in their education and career.

Within a couple of weeks, Zekirullah left home. He went to stay with the Faisal family. Five days a week, he had to get up before 5:00 a.m. and bike to the high school in Tuti Koshteh, a town located approximately twenty kilometers east to Bamyan. After five in the afternoon, he returned to work at Dr. Faisal's office in Tupchi, another small village ten kilometers west to Tuti Koshteh. He was allowed to have two weeks off per year when Dr. Faisal's medical practice was closed for vacation. At the end of the first year, Zekirullah's report card was "excellent" in all subjects. His parents were very pleased. But the uneventful life in the Rasulov family was short-lived.

In the fall of that year, the Rasulov family was struck by a calamity. When the weather turned cold, Abd's mother started to cough and seemed to have a persistent low-grade fever. She had no appetite and felt tired all day long. At first, she and her husband didn't make much out of it. They thought they were dealing with a common cold that she couldn't shake off. A couple of weeks passed. Her symptoms got worse. Dr. Faisal finally was asked to check her out. After carefully examining her, he concluded that she had some sort of lung disease that needed to be investigated further. He wrote a note on his prescription pad to the radiology department of Kabul City Hospital requesting a chest x-ray as soon as possible. Not able to walk, Abd's mother had to be transported on the back of a donkey borrowed from their neighbor. Husband and wife left for Kabul on the next day. They went directly to the hospital, handed Dr. Faisal's note to the receptionist, got registered, and then waited in a small room packed with coughing and sneezing patients for her turn to be called. Abd's parents returned the same night to Bamyan. They anxiously waited for the x-ray report. Five days later Dr. Faisal came to their house with bad news. The radiologist's note to him read: "There appear to be some parenchymal shadows with possible cavitation on the lower half of the left lung, suggesting mycobacterial infection. Gastric aspiration for culture is strongly recommended to rule out active tuberculosis." In the meantime, Abd's mother's symptoms got worse and the skin test on her left forearm, done three days earlier by Dr. Faisal, showed a circular redness with central induration. This finding together with the radiological abnormal reading was in those days considered a solid proof of acute TB infection. That meant she had to be isolated from direct contacts pending a long stay in a sanatorium for treatment. Dr. Faisal performed skin tests for TB on all members of the Rasulov family. He came back three days later to do the reading which was "negative" on every member of the household. Within a few more days, Abd's mother was admitted to the sanatorium in Charikar. The children were told that her disease was very contagious; therefore, they were not allowed to visit her in the hospital until three weekly repeated test cultures of her stomach juice became "negative." Since the TB germ grows very slowly in artificial lab culture medium, the waiting period for results could be as long as three to four months. It could take even longer for the final lab report, because occasionally the culture had to be sent to London School of Hygiene and Tropical Medicine, UK, or Pasteur Institute in Paris, France, for further examination and confirmation. The sanatorium chief medical doctor anticipated an average stay in isolation and away from home of at least one and a half years if Abd's mother responded well to treatment with anti-TB medication.

The separation of Abd's mother from her family was heartbreaking. Zekirullah got permission to come home to give his father a hand in bringing his mother to Charikar Sanatorium. In the early hours of that Wednesday, the pony-drawn wooden cart was parked in front of the Rasulovs' house. The animal was fed and given drinking water by Zekirullah. Two thick blankets were placed at the bottom of the cart, barely long enough for his mother to lie down on her back.

Abd's father was inside of the dwelling trying to explain to the children that Mother had to be hospitalized for a "catching" disease that takes several months to recover and that they needed to be protected from acquiring it. He elucidated why they wouldn't be allowed to see her while she would be on strict isolation at the hospital. The children were asked to say a prayer for their mother several times a day. Bursts of cries were heard by Zekirullah, who was checking one of the carriage's two wooden wheels. He stopped for a second, wiping off the tear running down his cheeks.

Abd's father helped his wife to get up from the kitchen table to go to the cart, when suddenly Nabeela cried out loud while pulling on her mother's khaki burka. "No, no, I want my mother. Don't take her away from me."

This was her first separation from her mother. All other siblings joined in, crying for their mother's leaving home. Walking to the cart, they all sobbed loudly behind their mother, who was leaning on her husband's right arm. They cried louder when Abd's father, Zekirullah, and Omira were lifting the sick lady up and placing her recumbent in the wooden box. After the children were told to say goodbye to their mother, the pony, led by Zekirullah on foot, was on its way.

Abd's father followed behind, having his eyes constantly watching his wife. The crying children kept waving at their departing mother until the pony and its passenger disappeared behind the village's largest boulder. After a while the children calmed down, except Nabeela, who was still clinging to her sister's cloak, weeping. She kept crying all day long, refused to eat and to drink, despite Omira's intense effort to console her. The calamity showed no letup at this stage.

Instead, it continued to intensify. At the dinner table, the nightly prayer often was followed by one of the twin's sobs. The children were unusually quiet. They all grieved the absence of their mother, who left an empty chair at the south end of the table. Abd's father's somber face at the end of a long workday didn't seem to give the children much reassurance. Every evening, the same questions came up: "When can we see Mom?" or "When is Mom coming home?" and the answer was always the same: "I don't know, but we can ask Uncle Faisal next week when he is to give us reports on her condition."

Abd had trouble concentrating in class. He kept thinking that his mother might never return. At night, he tossed and turned in bed. His midyear report card went from "good" to "failed" within a few months. The twin brothers argued incessantly with each other, requiring Omira's frequent intervention. Nabeela gradually showed developmental regression. Irritable and whiny, this youngest child's appetite dwindled drastically over the next several months. Bedwetting occurred practically every night. Having to assume all her mother's functions since she left, Omira was burdened with extra house chores in addition to the care for the three goats during the day. Fortunately, the milking of the animals was done every evening by Abd, the oldest son still at home. Omira's overwork made her overtired, and this gave her insomnia. Every member of the Rasulov family was profoundly affected by their mother's stay in Charikar Sanatorium. The most worrisome matter was Nabeela's weight loss and regression despite Father's necessary but unconfirmed verbal reassurance that Mother would recover soon. Like his son, Mr. Rasulov had often the grim thought that he might be a widower in a short time.

Once admitted to the sanatorium, Abd's mother was confined to a six-by-eight-foot room at the end of the corridor. The majority of the patients had acute tuberculosis, and all of them were in "isolation" mode. Patients' coughs were heard from one end to the other of the hallway of this three-floored old building. In those days, positive air pressure in the corridor was unheard of, let alone hourly air exchange or air recirculation through HEPA filtration to keep the saliva droplets within the patient's room or escaped through the ducting system. One could imagine how heavily the indoor air of the building would be contaminated with the germ *Mycobacterium tuberculosis*. Gowning and masking were the only means of minimizing the spread of the disease through caregivers. Children's visits were inarguably prohibited. Spousal visit was limited to only fifteen minutes once a month, and the contact between spouses was made through speakers installed at the room entrance next to a small glass window. Uncle Faisal, through personal contact with the sanatorium authority, managed to introduce only one item into Abd's mother's room: the black-and-white photograph of her family. Sadness continued to reign in the Rasulov family over the next several months.

One Saturday of that fall, Omira revealed to Father that Nabeela, just turned six the week before, had not been eating enough "to sustain the life of a cat" and had been having a low-grade temperature for the last two days. Abd's father realized that his youngest child indeed had lost quite a bit of weight since his wife left. He became very concerned and decided to get urgently in touch with his cousin Faisal through the mailman, another relative of his. The next day came Dr. Faisal. He checked Nabeela out, examined her urine with his naked eyes, and determined that she had a urinary tract infection.[5] Before leaving, he left twenty tablets of sulfa drug for her treatment. While Dr. Faisal was at his home, Abd's father asked him if he could suggest a way to let his children have a quick look at their mother at the sanatorium. On his next house call to Bamyan, this compassionate man introduced a workable solution that he had worked out with the director of the sanatorium a couple of days earlier. As a matter of fact, Dr. Faisal had gone to see the latter in person and had presented the dire situation going on with the Rasulov family. Moved by the doctor's plea, the director had agreed to make an exception to the standard isolation procedure. Mrs. Rasulov would be properly gowned and masked and then wheeled to a utility room on the first floor where members of her whole family, also gowned and masked, could see her while being kept a minimum of ten feet from her. To minimize the risk of being exposed to her germs, the visit was limited to a short duration of five minutes. A caretaker would be at the meeting site to be certain that rules governing isolation procedures would not be inadvertently violated.

At the dinner table and on the same day, Abd's father made the announcement of the prearranged first visit with their mother after eleven months by the day. One should see the sudden joy expressed on the children's faces. Omira didn't have to insist on Nabeela's amount of food intake anymore. The little girl started again to eat and drink adequately.

The day of visit to their mother came. Abd's father managed to borrow from his second cousin, the mailman, a large pony-drawn cart that could accommodate all children except him.

Zekirullah joined them from Tupchi. The Rasulov family arrived at the sanatorium around midday. Mrs. Rasulov was sitting in a wheelchair, against the back wall of the utility room, waiting to see her family. As the door opened, Nabeela quickly ran toward her mother, crying. The caretaker instantaneously stopped her; otherwise, the visit went well. The children sobbed when they had to leave the room. But they were somewhat relieved when a friendly guard at the gate said to them, "We'll see you in three months."

The mighty God seemed to have pity and a special love for the Rasulovs. After the visit, calm and hope seemed to have overcome grief and distress. The boys were doing better in school, and Nabeela had regained her normal weight. Still longing for her mother, she cried off and on. But overall, she became more manageable to Omira, who gave her the best maternal care one could imagine. By now Mrs. Rasulov had been in confinement for just over a year.

On one evening of that hot and humid summer, Dr. Faisal sorted out his mail as usual after a long working day. He was astonished to receive a letter from the office of the medical director of Kabul City Hospital. He read the letter twice to be sure that he understood correctly its content. The sender's note informed him that all the three initial cultures of gastric lavages taken from Mrs. Rasulov over a year ago, first kept incubated in the hospital lab, then subsequently sent to London for confirmation, as well as repeated cultures after the nine-month treatment period remained "negative for *Mycobacterium tuberculosis*" and that the case was under review. Dr. Faisal was invited to attend a conference convened a week later at the hospital to discuss the case of Mrs. Rasulov. The participants included the hospital administrator, a young radiologist trained at the University College London, Whittington Hospital, United Kingdom, the hospital-based internist, the hospital chief of lab, and the medical director of Charikar Sanatorium. In those days, the diagnosis of tuberculosis was strongly suspected if the patient had a chronic cough, night sweats, blood-tinged sputum, and weight loss. To minimize the risk of spreading this lethal disease, the patient must be isolated as soon as possible in a sanatorium, pending the results of initial cultures. Often the radiologist was relying too much on the appearance of the x-ray films to report as "suggestive" of TB if the patient didn't have all the above elements of symptomatology. The meeting was held in the hospital radiology department. The internist was asked as usual to quickly go over the patient's medical record, starting with present illness, going through past history, physical and lab findings, etc., to end up with the family socioeconomic status. He pointed out that Mrs. Rasulov had only a chronic cough, some sweating, and a mild weight loss but no other cardinal symptoms. The radiologist, replacing the one who initially read her x-ray films and recently retired, placed all these films chronologically and side by side on the view box; he then took the hand-held magnifying glass out of his white coat pocket and then meticulously went over each of these negatives.

He turned around, looking straight at the internist's eyes and then at the hospital administrator. "Very interesting case indeed. I have seen no more than three cases like this when I was still in training in London."

"What is it?" the administrator anxiously asked.

"We are dealing with a case of mycoplasma pulmonary infection mimicking tuberculosis on x-ray." Pointing his finger to the semicircular shadow on the initial film that was read as "possible cavitation," and then to the one taken three weeks ago, he continued, "Now you can see. That round shadow was not there anymore on the most recent film which appears almost normal except for a few small white streaks near the left hilum." Then within the same breath, he added, "TB leaves a permanent scarring, which can be readily seen on x-ray and fairly characteristic in appearance. Mycoplasma pneumonia infection also results in scars of the parenchymal tissue, but these clear up usually within six to twelve months if prompt treatment was instituted."

The internist interjected, "This germ is still very sensitive to tetracycline, and we currently use this drug to treat community-acquired walking pneumonia, which is predominantly caused by mycoplasma species." In the meantime, he scrutinized the patient's chart once again and read the following sentence from the Charikar Sanatorium nurse's note: "Mrs. Rasulov has been here barely two weeks and she already recovered her appetite, gained two and a half kilograms, and seems to have more energy." Abruptly his facial expression changed, and then he added, "In my opinion, this nurse's observation note supports your contention that we are dealing with an unusual case of walking pneumonia. This patient couldn't get better so fast if she had overt TB, but one question remains to be answered. Why is Mrs. Rasulov still not infected with TB after staying over a year at the sanatorium? It is possible that the three-drug regimen used for her therapy has prevented her from getting infected with TB. The reading of Mrs. Rasulov's TB skin test last year as reactive or positive could be explained as a false positive or a cross-reactivity with other nonhuman mycobacteria species, and it should not be taken into account. Repeated negative cultures are the real proof that she did not have human tuberculosis."

While listening attentively to the discussion, the sanatorium director, quiet until now, asked, "I surmise that the two doctors have come to the conclusion that Mrs. Rasulov has no TB after all. So, could she be discharged tomorrow?"

Almost simultaneously the internist and the radiologist responded, "Yes."

The hospital administrator looked at the two practicing physicians, saying, "Without your expertise, we wouldn't be able to come up with such a clear-cut diagnosis. Thank you very much." He then turned to Dr. Faisal. "Did you hear that, Doctor?"

The conference was adjourned around 3:00 p.m. The next evening Uncle Faisal arrived to Bamyan to announce the good news.

The day after, around noon, Abd's father, on pony back, came to Charikar Sanatorium with a mule to bring his wife home. One could imagine the children's joy upon their mother's return. Abd said a thanksgiving prayer to God then said to himself, "The mighty God is looking after my family and always miraculously transforms suffering into a happy ending, simply because he loves all of us so much."

Abd's life also took a new turn. He became happier and more relaxed. Visits after school to neighbors became almost a routine for Abd and his twin brothers, Ali and Aamir. Even though he hadn't grown much in height, Abd's interest in the opposite sex was noted by his parents and his sister Omira. After all, he turned twelve three months earlier, and a sparse fuzz, precursor of sideburns, was visible at a close look. One late spring Sunday afternoon, Omira was looking for Abd to help her milking the goats. She went to all three neighbors' sheds trying to find him. One of the ladies among them was Mrs. Rasulov's aunt, who told Omira that Abd was having a conversation with her daughter, Elaha, a few minutes earlier in her shed's living room. But neither of the two was anywhere to be found when Omira stopped in, looking for him. She went outside, circled the mouth with her two palms, and then called loudly, "Abdulai! Abdulai!" There was no human response, only mountain echoes to her call. Omira proceeded to walk in the direction of denser bushes interspersed between tall rocks. The whole surrounding was tranquil and peaceful. Suddenly she heard noise of dried leaves generated by a tiny crawling lizard in front of a large red rock to which she directed her attention. "Here you are. We were searching for you the last hour or so."

Abd was standing with his back against the rock while holding the little girl Elaha with his arms and hands encircling her waist. The young couple was shivering at the mountain breeze. Omira scrutinized them from head to toes then uttered, "You two should go home now. It's getting late, and the goats are waiting for your daily visit, Abd."

All three left the isolated site, heading toward the conglomerated dwellings down in the valley. Elaha was brought back to her mother's home. The lady was told that the two children were found in an intensive discussion while walking in the direction of the elementary school. Before getting into their shed, Abd said to Omira, "Please don't tell Dad and Mom that you saw Elaha and me together. Otherwise, I will reveal to them the incident of dispersing goats that happened almost two years ago. Is it a deal between us?"

"You are a clever guy. I will keep both incidents as our own secrets for life." It was customary to the Afghan Buddhist society that physical contacts between boys and girls were not permitted until they reached the age of fifteen. Afghan parents considered the violation of this rule shameful to the whole family.

During the next several months, Omira frequently reminded Abd that he must never violate the agreement between them. Probably she wanted to be assured that Abd's parents would never know anything about the runaway goats' incident, for she hoped that the trust and confidence the senior Rasulovs had in her remained unaltered. In Afghanistan, it was customary for an adopted female child to grow up with barely an elementary education, if lucky, while assuming all the routine household chores, no matter how hard or numerous these were. As a result of this devotion to her adoptive parents, Omira had no time to socialize. Consequently, she had no opportunity to be alone with a person of the opposite sex during her entire life and therefore her natural human instinct had never been gratified. She was completely illiterate at her early adulthood when her biological parents delivered her to the Rasulov family. Subsequently, Abd's mother taught her how to read and write, just enough to correspond by letter with the junior Rasulovs studying or living abroad.

CHAPTER FOUR

Sickly Infancy and Emotional Childhood

Abd's parents were devoted Buddhists, just like their ancestors. The people practicing Buddhism in Afghanistan made up a tiny religious minority, and the practice was in secrecy. The Islamic intolerance toward Buddhism was exemplified by the demolition in March 2001 of Bamyan's Buddha statues by Taliban leader Mullah Mohammed Omar. In the eyes of the

Taliban, these statues were idolatrous and offensive to Islam. Open practice of Christianity and Judaism was not tolerated.

At least twice a week, Abd's mother walked almost two kilometers to one of the Buddha cave temples for worship. She carried out the pilgrimage throughout her pregnancy, in company of her husband or without him. Her previous first pregnancy was normal, and Zekirullah was born full term. The current one was not as uneventful. Nausea, vomiting, fatigue, blurred vision during the first trimester followed by persisting headache and spotting during the early part of the third trimester had been matters of great concern to

Haleema, her midwife. These symptoms persisted despite bed rest, daily aspirin administration, and proper diet. Haleema visited her every week. At thirty-one weeks of gestation, Dr. Faisal was brought in for consultation. He checked her over, as usual, very thoroughly. Her blood pressure was abnormally elevated. He took a sample of her urine to his office to check for the presence of protein. It contained a good amount of it, an indication that she was on the way of developing preeclampsia, a serious obstetrical complication leading to maternal and/or infantile death if not properly treated. At the doctor's recommendation, Abd's mother was hospitalized and vigorously treated with antihypertensive drugs, sedatives, etc. She stayed two weeks in the Bamyan City Clinic, was spared from preeclampsia, and then discharged with these same drugs but at a much lower dosing. The baby Abdulai was born at home at thirty-four-week gestation. Haleema had no trouble getting him out, even though it was a footling presentation. He was blue at first but started crying right after receiving a few gentle slaps on his butt. He was much smaller than Zekirullah at birth. Haleema estimated that he must weigh around five and a half to five and three-quarter pounds. After a short rest of a few days, Abd's mother resumed her house chores as usual, releasing her daughter from overwhelming burden. The cold she caught the week before the birth of her second son had subsided. The newborn took to breast fairly actively but developed a low-grade temperature on the fifth day of age. Abd's father immediately got in touch with Haleema. She came and checked him over and concluded that the baby had caught his mother's cold. Fortunately, he continued to feed well on breast, and within a couple of days, the temperature was abated. For the next ten years or so, life was not easy for the young boy Abdulai.

A few weeks after his fourth birthday, Abd came home from a walk to town with his parents, complaining of being exhausted physically. His mother quickly washed his face and his feet, put a long gown on him, and then sent him to bed. He tossed and turned the whole night with a mild headache. On the next day, after her husband left for work, Abd's mother went to see him still in bed but quieter than usual. She touched his forehead and then turned him on his back. His cheeks flushed red. He was burning hot and didn't want to get out of bed. Abd's mother coaxed him to swallow half of an adult aspirin and a mouthful of water. He refused to eat during the rest of the day.

His father came home, exchanged a few words with his mother at the doorsteps, and then directly went to his bed. He lifted up his gown and found a few red skin lesions on his abdomen but many on his face. He turned to his wife and said worrisomely, "We shouldn't have gone to town yesterday with him. He must already have had a temperature the last couple of days. The rash was at the same stage of development, and it appears umbilicated to me. I think he has small pox. We need to isolate him from Omira, Zekirullah, and Faiz, as well as from neighbor children. You and I undoubtedly have been exposed to this disease in the past and will not likely catch it again."

Abd's father was right. As a matter of fact, small pox had been reported in local newspapers off and on in the last several years in Bamyan City. He had seen small pox several times before. As there was no medical caregiver in the suburb where they lived, often he had to assist neighbors that developed syncope caused by fever or by heat stroke. He used ether inhalation, a trick he learned from his cousin Faisal to pull the victim out of that transient loss of consciousness. Since Abd's father, one of the rare literates living in the whole county, was always ready to help the people settled in the area, he was very well liked and respected for his role as an educator, for his wit, his experience, his kindness, his humility, his meekness, his patience, and especially his compassion. Preparation was immediately made to isolate the four-year-old boy behind the shed's back wall and under the eave. In order to achieve this end, Abd's parents improvised two beds using wooden planks. Handsewn chiffons supported by branches attached to Abd's bed were used as a tent to keep the boy from flies and mosquito bites. Once carried to his bed, Abd's body was bright red and very warm to his mother's touch. After he was coaxed to swallow a few sips of water, he was left undressed for the night. He was moaning and groaning all night long. His body temperature remained hot despite Mother's repeated sponging with used rags soaked with tepid water every ten to fifteen minutes. Suddenly she heard, "The huge demons are chasing me. Please stop them. Please, please help!"

She never herself heard those frightening words before, but she assumed that her son had delirium, frequently associated with high body temperature. Instantly she got out of her bed, stuck her head inside of his tent, and then gently shook his right shoulder. "I am here with you. I will make sure that they are not going to harm you, my son." She stayed by his side for the rest of the night. A flapping sound of the shed's rear door panel, made out of dried palm leaves, abruptly woke her up, as she just barely closed her eyes for a quick rest. Abd's father appeared at the boy's bed with a kerosene lamp. He turned clockwise its knob to increase the light intensity. While sticking his head inside of the improvised tent to examine his son, his wife whispered, "Let me watch him alone. You need to sleep so that you are well enough to go to work tomorrow. I will stay home and will do fine with catnaps."

Abd's father absolutely wanted to share the care of their son with his dedicated wife. That night, he came in and out of the family shed several times, checking his son's stuporous mental status and the slow-evolving rash. The couple felt helpless. Not knowing what else they could do to hopefully keep their son alive, they burned incense and joss sticks while saying repetitive Buddhist prayers for hours. It should be noted that the devotion of Abd's parents to their children and their gratitude toward the couple were remarkable. Between members of the Rasulov family, the unconditional love for each other could be recognized in their tender eyes and discreet smiles. Once the disease was strongly suspected, Abd's father sent word to Dr. Faisal, asking him to make an urgent house call. The latter arrived in the late afternoon of the second day, examined the patient, and confirmed the diagnosis of variola, another name for smallpox. He left on donkey-back after instructing Abd's father how to look for delayed complications of the disease. Abd had a couple more episodes of hallucination during the next three days until the fever gradually abated and all the skin lesions had very much flattened out. Except for a couple of nights during the week when his father was at home, Abd's mother was practically the only person who cared for him from the beginning of the rash development to the time when all lesions scabbed and fell off several weeks later, leaving Abd's skin with a few deep scars on his chest. It took several weeks before Abd was fully recovered and able to go school.

Because of his petite size at birth, he was nicknamed "the runt" by his neighbor playmates. As a matter of fact, he was the smallest boy in his class when he started school at age five. Even though he was able to keep up with his friends in street soccer games, Abd tended to tire out quickly. This was not surprising, in view of his frail constitution. Abd's parents often wondered how he would be able to cope with the ongoing poverty experienced by the majority of the Afghan population. The subject of severe malnutrition among Afghan children was repeatedly brought up at United Nations organization's meetings; but foreign aid to the country was hindered by the ravaging wars between regional warlords. Because of the turmoil, farming peasants were unable to grow their crops and raise animals for domestic consumption. The country experienced a severe economic downtrend that had a profound effect on the nation's infrastructure. In spite of being the provincial capital, Bamyan's water collection and sewer disposal systems were to be desired. Diseases caused by water-born microorganisms were not uncommon. Being relatively undernourished and having a weak constitution, Abd came down often with bloody, painful, mucous diarrhea presumably due to *Entamoeba histolytica*, a parasitic protozoan infecting predominantly humans and other primates. The word *dysentery* was used by Dr. Faisal to label Abd's illness. Because the boy's guts, affected by chronic diarrhea, were unable to absorb food nutrients, he experienced profound malnutrition resulting in severe weight loss. Dr. Faisal treated his disease with painful deep gluteal intramuscular monthly injections of bismuth, the only remedy against dysentery at the time. Being frequently sick and constantly undernourished, Abd missed school several months a year. Homeschooling wasn't effective due to his persisting spasmodic abdominal pain. Consequently, Abd had to stay back twice during his middle-school years. He lost friends who used to be either classmates or neighbor playmates. He was ridiculed by boys a couple of years younger than he was. Abd became depressed and felt isolated. This emotional state affected further his schooling. Sadness was noticeable on all family members' faces.

The declining national economy affected directly and indirectly every working-class Afghan family. The unemployment rate kept climbing steadily. The layoff of teachers and school supervisors added additional burden to the already depleting nation's unemployment benefits reserve. Abd's father was forced to assume additional duties to cover for laid-off colleagues and subordinates in neighboring provinces. He came home later in the evening but had to go to work in the early hours of the morning. Often, he had to stay away from home two to three consecutive nights when the conglomeration of inspection sites were forty to fifty kilometers from Bamyan or when the dirt roads were not passable on bike. Abd's father, a school inspector, was salaried by the unstable federal government led by King Amanullah. Often, he failed to receive his wages for months on end. He had to rely on Omira, now seventeen, to assume the total responsibility in the care for her younger siblings and the goats while his wife was in the sanatorium. The children missed the presence of both parents, especially when Abd's father had to stay overnight away from home. Abd's life was frequently stricken either by diseases or by unpleasant events.

One Wednesday late afternoon, at age eleven, he was late in coming home from school due to abdominal cramps. Suddenly he heard bursts of gunshot sounds overhead while walking alone on the winding path of a steep hill not too far from home. The sounds were getting closer, blasting at his eardrums. He realized this must be a resumption of fighting between warlords' mercenary soldiers around the township of Bamyan. He quickly jumped into the closest shallow ditch for safety, landing on a grown-up female body dressed in a dark cloak he realized was his neighbor's teenage daughter. She murmured to his ears, "Abdulai, lie down and keep your profile as low as possible. Squeeze yourself tight between the rock and my body and hold your breath as long as you can when you hear footsteps or commotion getting closer to us. Try to stay still."

Both stayed lying facedown in the ditch for quite a while. They got up and then walked home in the dark once gunshot sounds were no longer heard overhead. That was the first time in his life that Abd's body was in contact with a female one, and he felt very uneasy about this event for months.

The love and respect among the Rasulov children for their parents was extraordinary. One early Sunday morning while the children were still in bed and his wife was in the sanatorium, Abd's father woke up to inspect his bike parked at the doorway, preparing it for the next day's long trip to schools in the neighboring Wardak province. He rotated the right pedal and found the chain overstretched and dry. "It needs to be lubricated," he thought. Crossing his bony legs, he let himself down on the dirt floor, removed the chain from the rear wheel, and then placed it in an old beat-up aluminum pan. He was pouring a dark petroleum-smelling liquid over the chain when Abd, not able to have a decent sleep due to his sister Nabeela's frequent crying spells during the night for missing her mother, lifted up his head, looking at his father. While frowning his brows and rubbing his red eyes, Abd let out, "Dad, you stayed up until past midnight working with your report on your typewriter for hours. You must be exhausted by now. You need more sleep, Dad. Leave the bike repair job to me. I have done this type of work a few times in the past, remember, Dad?"

The frail boy jumped out of the squeaky bed he was sharing with his twin brothers, Ali and Aamir, and then took over the maintenance work on his father's vehicle. He spent almost two hours working on the chain, meticulously checking each link. After thoroughly oiling it, he placed the chain back on the bike and adjusted its tension; in addition, he checked both brakes and finally the tire pressure. He then slowly stood up, mumbling to himself, "Hopefully, he will get some rest before his three-day inspection trip."

While his son was working on the bike, Abd's father, sitting at the kitchen table, perused the pages of the instruction booklet on his Remington typewriter that he purchased from a salvage store years ago.

Once the British influence started to wane, the anti-Buddhism sentiment became more widespread among fanatic Islamists. Killing of Buddhist minority was not uncommon. To avoid fanatic Islamists' suspicion, Abd's parents made a portable altar for the family worship. This revered hand-made tray carried a sixteen-centimeter Tibetan-made clay statue of Buddha and the two black-and-white framed photographs of two local Buddhist statues, the male *Salsal* ("Light shines through the universe") and the female *Shamama* ("Queen Mother").[7] In order to keep their religion unknown to the Islam majority, Abd's parents or Omira took down the relic from the two wall-mounted brackets in the dining area and then hastily hid it behind the dwelling's back wall upon the first signs of a visitor at the door. The Rasulov family and a few neighbors, making up the tiny Buddhist community in the northwest suburb of Bamyan, constantly lived in fear of being tortured or killed by the Islam government agents or their surrogates. They kept their religious belief in low profile, almost to the point of secrecy.

Before her stay at Charikar Sanatorium, at least three times a week, Abd's mother went to one of the cave temples on foot, carrying on her back fruits and incense as offerings. On special Buddhist commemoration days, she slowly walked uphill on a rough gravel path while reverently looking at the two massive statues of Bamyan carved into limestone cliffs sometime between the third and the fifth AD centuries. Due to the intolerance of Islam against Buddhism, there were practically no worshipers at the two Buddha sites on these religious occasions. Upon the sight of an oncoming human shape from a distance, Abd's mother, for fear of being taken as a worshiper, pulled down her veil to hide her face and then acted as if she was a beggar gathering firewood.

As the government in Kabul showed less interest in education and more in elimination of other religions, in addition to the weak economy, the number of teachers and inspectors was drastically reduced. The result of this unfortunate Islamic misconception had a dramatic effect on the country's formation of the cadre of elites. The idea of sending children abroad for education was born. Of course, the poverty-stricken Rasulov family's aspiration for their children's advanced education was out of question. But the mighty God could perform miracles to surprise everybody.

Uncle Faisal's wife could not conceive due to some sort of reproductive system anomaly. They had no children. Zekirullah, while living and working for them, excelled in school. He had been the top achiever in his class of forty-five and was expected to graduate from his high school one year earlier and to deliver the equivalent American valedictory address at graduation that summer. Uncle Faisal had been thinking all along these years of finding a successor who could take over his busy medical practice in less than ten years when he retired. The political and economic turmoil in the country wouldn't be suitable to the education of a future doctor in medicine in Kabul, the only city with a university. He read somewhere that foreign students matriculated in a Swedish postgraduate college and having a good grade could apply for scholarship for the next four years in a government-sponsored medical school. The idea of sending Zekirullah abroad for advanced education came to his mind. Dr. Faisal thought he could financially sponsor this young man to get a bachelor's degree in Sweden in three years, and being unusually bright, Zekirullah wouldn't have any trouble of getting a full scholarship to complete his medical education. The following Monday, during his weekly house call, he stopped by and visited with Zekirullah's parents. He proposed his idea to them. At first Abd's father wasn't too thrilled with the thought of having to forgo the monthly supplemental income his oldest son had been bringing home during the last three years. However, after a lengthy discussion of pros and cons, the Rasulovs accepted Dr. Faisal's offer. Zekirullah left for Sweden that fall. He would not see his parents and his siblings until he got his bachelor's degree three years later. This was a painful separation, but full of promise. He started out on donkey-back with his father to reach Kabul. From there, instead of flying, he took two more much less expensive bus trips to arrive in Vienna, where he boarded a biweekly plane to Stockholm.

When there are many children in a family, there is the likelihood that one of them is an oddball who conducts himself in whimsical ways. All the Rasulov children got along well with each other. The older ones helped their younger with schoolwork assignments at the end of the day before supper. Faiz seemed to make the exception. After Zekirullah left home and stayed with the Faisals, this third child's behavior was disturbing for Abd's parents. He was bright enough to finish high school but showed his arrogant and condescending attitude at an early age. He looked down on his one-year-older brother Abd. Assuming simple house chores to help his parents and sister Omira was certainly not his forte. Arguments and noisy quarrels erupted between the twins and him several times a day. Abd was constantly teased and ridiculed by him because of his small size and frailness. Faiz, almost a head taller than Abd at age of ten, readily burst into rage when things didn't go his way. Thinking that the boy possibly had attention-deficit hyperactive disorder, either of Abd's parents patiently took him aside when he became intolerable, and then tried repeatedly to calm him down and to reason with him, but he remained incorrigible. For the Rasulov children, the spanking form of punishment for misbehavior was unnecessary. A stern look at the culprit followed by a quiet authoritative nonthreatening ruling was all that was needed.

Faiz's impulsiveness made him prone to accidents. He dropped out of school at fourth grade and ended up working as a farm boy in Tuti Koshteh. At the beginning of his farming career, he had some difficulty with the farmer owner due to his short attention span and concentration. But within a few years he managed to carry out the majority of husbandry tasks except field plowing using animals. Gradually he settled down and stayed at the community housing provided by his boss. Abd exchanged letters with him regularly. They came to understand each other much better in the next several months. Subsequently, Abd managed to visit with his brother three to four times a year in the company of his parents and siblings.

After she was discharged from Charikar Sanatorium, Abd's mother, without delay, resumed her wool carding work at home to earn a few Afghanis a week. Abd's father continued to cover an expanded area of school inspection. The total income from the couple was barely enough to make ends meet. Happiness returned to the Rasulovs family members, but not to Abd. Even though his chronic diarrhea with related unpleasant gastrointestinal symptoms was almost completely abated on his eleventh birthday, he remained very thin and tired easily. He could hardly keep up with his school home-work assignments. Being runty from birth, he was especially sensitive to borderline malnutrition for lack of basic micronutrients in the family diet. As a matter of fact, during that period of Afghan hunger, the Rasulovs' diet consisted mainly of *quroot* (dried yogurt) made out of their scanty three goats' milk and *naan* (bread). Two to three times a year, on special Buddhist commemoration day, the family was able to afford a nice meal of *qorma* (stew or casserole) made with lamb and herbs. The children were taught to bite on a wedge of lemon or drink half of a teaspoon of vinegar to satisfy their hunger when there was no food left in the house. Due to the country's poor economy, the Rasulovs were forced to live in near penury with limited amounts of starchy food to subsist. Not infrequently, roots and wild berries were parts of their diet. Sugar made out of beets was the main source of carbohydrate needed for the Rasulov children's growth when their parents could afford to buy. Priority to food went first to young children. Being the oldest child still at home, often Abd went hungry. Occasionally, through the mailman, Faiz sent home dried *naan* and *quroot* left over from the farm.

Despite near destitution, the family bond was remarkable. Here was one example among several to illustrate the reciprocal love and sacrifice among the Rasulov family members. One of two of Abd's maternal aunts came to visit with his mother a short time after Nabeela was born. The lady brought a small cooked carp as a present. Her intention was to add some animal protein to the diet of Abd's mother, who was breastfeeding her newborn. Since Abd's father was on a three-day school inspection trip, Abd's mother decided to save the fish untouched until her husband came home. In order to safely keep it from being spoiled by the summer heat, salt and water were added then recooked every other day. The fish was passed around at the table on that evening when the head of the Rasulov household returned. But nobody wanted to eat a small piece out of it. Father contended that Mother should take advantage of this rare source of animal protein being introduced into the family. Mother argued that Father needed better nutrition to cope with his strenuous biking trips necessary to make a living for the whole family. Abd, the oldest son still at home, pretended that he had no appetite for fish on that day, declined his parents' insistence on sharing the tasty dish with the twins. These two youngest children fell asleep at the table and had to be carried to bed for the night. In the end, the dish of fish remained untouched and had to be recooked for the third time. The twins finally finished it on the next day.

The feeling of being behind in school was of great concern to Abd's parents and to himself. His lack of basic principle knowledge in sciences including math, physics, and chemistry precluded him from making progress in school. Being an educator, the Rasulov head of the household strongly believed in education. Often, he tried to convince his children that a high school diploma was a small insurance policy and a community college certificate was a much better one that almost could guarantee a lifelong employment. He also taught them that their personal treasure didn't lie with monetary wealth but rather with education. Abd's parents were very responsible Afghans. They knew where the parents' duty lay. Therefore, they had been having a plan B for him since his tenth birthday. Not knowing for sure how he was going to make a living with persisting poor performance in school, they had negotiated with one of their neighbors to eventually lease a parcel of land at the foothill for Abd to cultivate crops. This project would be implemented in case he had to drop out of school within a couple of years.

One day Abd's father came home from a two-day trip with an unusually smiling face as he greeted his family. He turned to Abd. "Would you like to spend a year away from us in boarding school, learning over subjects that will prepare you for your future years in high school?"

Abd trembled with joy. "Certainly, Dad. But how can we afford to pay the tuition and lodging?"

"Don't worry about that. We have made plans for your future."

The night before, while on his school inspection tour, apparently, Abd's father went to see one of his old friends living in Panjab, a good-sized town southeast to Bamyan. This man ran a special school for underachieving students of upper-income families. They agreed that the one-year boarding school expenses for Abd would be paid in installments over the next five years without interest; and if not fully paid by then, Abd would be responsible for the balance of payment after he found a stable job. The agreement was made with a handshake. In the later summer of that year, instead of returning to the local school, his father took him on donkey to Panjab. The separation from his family for the first time was very painful. He sobbed with sadness as he mounted the animal and sat behind his father.

The first week in Panjab boarding school was not easy for Abd. As expected, he was teased by schoolkids for his petite stature and for his inexpensive clothing. Missing his parents and siblings made him feel lonely and isolated, despite the kind attention he received from the school director, his father's old friend, and the teachers. But Abd had shown to be a child with determination at an early age. Within three months, all his teachers were surprised to see him among the top five in his class. Then he scored the highest exam rating on all subjects at the end of his first semester. He was allowed to come home for the spring break of that year. He quickly gained respect from classmates and even students who used to tease him. Now with self-confidence, Abd finished the remaining semester with an "Excellent Student, ready for the first-year high school" certificate. In the coming fall, he attended his first year of high school in Tuti Koshteh while staying at Uncle Faisal's home, replacing Zekirullah for the after-school office cleaning job.

CHAPTER FIVE

Schooling, First Priority

E ven though there
was a high school
in Bamyan, Abd
entertained the idea
of attending the one
in Tuti Koshteh for
several reasons. The
latter was much larger
and therefore had
more teachers and

more facilities. Each teacher was assigned to a specific subject he had
the expertise on and was certified in. As a result, he had more time
to prepare the lecture and to work more closely with his group of
students. The learning process would be more challenging at this
school but also more rewarding for bright students like Abd. Staying
at and working for Dr. Faisal after school and having the same job
Zekirullah had would not only be more practical logistically but also
enable him to earn a monthly wage that could in part supplement
his parents' meager income. They let him choose the school of his
liking. Finally, he opted to attend Tuti Koshteh High School despite
his trepidation of being away from home most part of the year. He
entered the school that fall well prepared academically.

The first year in school was relatively easy for Abd. The subjects he liked the most and excelled in were, as expected, math, physics, organic chemistry, and English. He had little interest in social science, for too much emphasis was placed on the teaching of Islam and Sharia law. Being raised in a Buddhist environment, Abd was much more tolerant of other cultures and religions. It took him almost half of a year to detect who among the students that participated in soccer games with him were Buddhists. He used this game that he became very good at as the vehicle to get to know those who shared his culture and the value of humanities. At this early age, Abd's parents noted—and the teachers concurred with them—that their son already had a variety of aspirations for becoming a well-rounded person hoping to live in a "civilized society." But it was not at all easy for Abd to hide his religious belief and be friendly with Islam kids at the same time. In order to create friendship with them, he tried to be very helpful to everyone, not only in the classroom but also on the soccer field. Having gone through a spurt of growth of over eleven centimeters in height during the last two years, Abd stood out as the tallest boy who showed signs of leadership. Everybody liked him, teachers and students alike. Neighbors and playmates at home no longer nicknamed him "the runt." Now they called him "the late bloomer," in view of his sudden rapid physical growth and accelerated academic performance in school.

Three top students in his class were summoned to the principal's office at the end of the school hours on one afternoon in the spring of his fourth year at Tuti Koshteh High School. Abd was one of them. They were told that the British government's Foreign Affairs Services, Education Department, had announced through the government in Kabul that a dozen scholarships were made available to outstanding Afghan students of the last high school year who wanted to pursue advanced studies abroad. If their parents or caretakers wanted to take advantage of this rare foreign assistance, they should inform the school in writing within one month. Abd's parents received the notice from school within a few days. They realized that the departure from home of another child, of who knows how long, would not only deprive them from an extra source of income but also bring about a dent in the family bonding. However, for them the education and the future of the children should supersede over all other concerns and sacrifices that must be made in appropriate circumstances. The office of the principal sent without delay the students' applications, accompanied by their three-year school transcript, to the British embassy in Kabul. The Rasulovs learned of the good news that same summer: Abd was chosen to go. The British embassy offered to pay for all transportation expenses from their hometown to Manchester, England, where all twelve scholarship recipients would have to take a three-month crash course in English. That was another painful separation from his family. He thought about the many years he would be away from them.

He stayed awake for the most part of the night preceding his departure date. Abd's parents couldn't sleep either. Mother's sob in bed saddened Abd further. He promised himself to return home and to live near them as soon as possible once he finished his education, but he had no idea then what was going to happen in the next several years. His father's cousin, the mailman, loaned the family workhorse to take them to Kabul. Like it was with Zekirullah, father and son were on their way to the capital. Everyone shed tears until long after the horse carrying him disappeared behind the massive boulder. On his way to England, he realized that the other two classmates were not among the twelve scholarship recipients. He felt bad, as they were good friends having the same purpose of life and the same dream.

Once they arrived in Manchester, the twelve scholarship recipients were placed in scattered suburbs around the city and they were lodged in private homes of British families. The three months spent in Prestwich, a small town a few kilometers northwest of Manchester, at the "Moelfre" (the grandparents of Mrs. Ormerfryn had moved from an area east to Mt. Moelfre in Scotland to the Manchester district four decades earlier) residence, remained memorable for the young Afghan student. Abd's experience took place a few years after the WWII. Moelfre owners, named Ormerfryn, a middle-age couple, were living with their teenage daughter Gwen in this house they inherited from the girl's maternal grandparents a few years earlier. Food rationing in the United Kingdom had eased up considerably that summer, but meat, such as mutton, pork, and especially beef, was still not readily available on the market, even with priority coupon books reserved for infants and children. The Ormerfryns could use some extra income from the government as monetary compensation for lodging and English teaching of foreign students, as the household head was the only breadwinner. His wife, a schoolteacher, afflicted by a chronic migraine headache, had not been able to work for over three years, and their daughter was too young to find a job, as the unemployment reached 22 percent during that postwar period. As a result, the only food stuff they could provide to their young guest were white bread, jam, lard, and tea. Petrol and kerosene were also included in the commodity rationing program. Every morning except Monday, Mr. Ormerfryn took the train to go to a shoe store in Manchester where he worked as a sales assistant manager. His salary was so little, barely enough to buy the abovementioned food stuff and pay monthly utilities. Quite often he went to the train station after a cup of tea as his breakfast. No one should be surprised when each of the four tenants at Moelfre residence had one to two slices of bread, a quarter cup of strawberry jam, and a cup of black tea as breakfast and then the same menu at lunch. At suppertime, again bread, jam, and tea were served, but an additional two-finger-size piece of lard seasoned with salt and pepper was offered. Abd was still in the early phase of fast physical growth. His voracious appetite could not be satisfied by the available amount of food, but he knew how hard the British population from the low middle class down was affected by the rigorous food rationing during the previous five years, and therefore he did not complain. Instead, Abd was very impressed with the way the Ormerfryns thanked the Lord before supper. Around the table, while holding each other's hands and bowing their heads, they remained silent for a dozen seconds then reverently recited the daily short prayer.

In the evening, after supper, the young student, under the dim light of a kerosene lamp, learned how to pronounce English correctly with the help from one of the Ormerfryns. Abd received here and there a gentle tap of encouragement on his shoulder from Mrs. Ormerfryn. A few days before the end of his three-month stay, right after the practice of English poem reading, she pulled him close to her and rubbed his hair, saying, "English pronunciation is not easy for foreigners to learn quickly, but it's marvelous that you have mastered it without noticeable effort within a short period of time. Congratulations."

Daily, Abd helped Gwen set the table and clean then arrange the dishes in the cupboard after each meal. He conversed with her, and she corrected his English while working in the kitchen. He swept the floor every morning and did other chores such as taking the garbage to the street curb on Friday evening without being asked. He even volunteered to do what they called "aerendes"—"messages," "missions," or "errands" in old English—during the day when Gwen was in school. He assumed the household work a boy in a peaceful and loving family is supposed to do. The Ormerfryns loved him dearly. The lady and her daughter cried when he left, and they exchanged letters for many years thereafter. Fifteen years later, on her honeymoon trip to Bearitz, Gwen managed to locate Abd in Foxeline. Unfortunately, Abd was attending a medical conference in Toulouse on that day and they could not see each other. However, they exchanged letters during the subsequent few years until Gwen and her husband moved to Australia.

After the three-month stay in Prestwich, Abd was sent to Oxford University where he was supposed to obtain his bachelor's degree in liberal arts in three years, but still had to spend at least three more years of basic sciences study before applying for medical or dental school studies.

Once arriving in Oxford from Manchester, Abd's first concern was to find a quiet place to stay, as he was very sensitive to noises. That morning in August the weather in Southern England was too misty and cold for someone who grew up with the arid desert climate of a Middle Eastern country like Afghanistan. Abd entered a convenience store on Castle Street. Behind the entrance door was a bulletin board attached to the paint-peeled wall. As he pulled the doorknob to close it, another person about his age, standing on the outside doorsteps, pushed it in the opposite direction. It was another student. Both young men side by side were scrutinizing attentively the few ads of apartment rental. They ended up signing a one-year rental contract sharing a one-bedroom flat with a den located a couple of blocks from the store.

Proficient in English, Abd enjoyed his first year at Oxford University where he befriended a few foreign students. Among those were two male German students with whom he practiced his self-taught German through the French Assimil system of teaching foreign languages. On weekends, as a pastime, they taught him German student "Lieder" and Austrian/German folk dances. Abd had a hard time learning the various dance steps, being by nature too clumsy. He caught on quickly with the music, but he had a real difficulty with the rhythm. They had a lot of fun with the "Sauerkraut tiroler polka" dance and often had a good laugh when Abd, not able to rhythmically bend his knees, fell on his butt. Abd couldn't afford to buy the Assimil audio version. He had to be content with the much less expensive visual-phonetic one. It wasn't easy for Abd to learn the pronunciation of the German words and writing grammar by reading the instructions outlined in the book alone. Fortunately, with the help from his two German friends and his love for German arts and culture, Abd arrived to converse and write in German while still going to school in Oxford. As far as his study in basic sciences was concerned, he easily passed his final exams in June of three consecutive years.

After each school year, despite high unemployment, Abd managed to get a part-time summer job in the local industry of beet growing. Many British farmers liked to help poor foreign students. His duty at the farm included soaking of large batches of beetroots in water as a means of improving germination and thinning of beet seedlings on the field when they grew to two inches high. He was allowed to bring home thinned-out seedlings for consumption as salads or stew. Being frugal by nature, Abd succeeded in sending home almost one-third of the money he received as scholarship plus the entire pay he received from the farming job. He exchanged letters with his parents every two weeks. He was very happy with his schooling, the friendship with foreign students, and being able, after the first year, to pay for and live alone in a studio apartment on Bayswater Road, a couple of kilometers east of Oxford. He bought himself a used bike and a biking rain gear to go to school with. But he missed seeing his family in Bamyan and felt it every evening after he finished his school homework and daily German reading exercises. On weekends Abd read advance copies of lectures to be given by professors on subsequent weekdays and then, when the weather permitted, spent some time promenading in the nearby South Park. Once back in his apartment, he enjoyed listening to either classical music on the Netherland Hilversum II radio station, or world news on German broadcast out of Bonn. Often, he thought about his future back home and occasionally counted on his fingers the number of years and months left before he would be able to rejoin his parents and his siblings. He knew that there was no major illness at home, and with the extra money he sent home every three months, no one starved anymore. He felt not only reassured but overwhelmed by the unusual reality that the two Rasulov sons, even though still in school, were able to financially assist their parents. Last fall, Zekirullah wrote and informed Abd that a wealthy family in Stockholm had given him a free lodging in the furnished attic above their three-car garage; and in return, all he had to do was to trim the hedge in summer and shovel the snow then sprinkle sand on the short walkway to the main door in winter. By that time, Zekirullah had finished his premed years and was about to start his first year of medical school in Karolinska.

Abd's parents were very pleased that their two sons were doing well in schooling in foreign lands and would have a bright future when they returned home. The only worry still lingering in Abd's mind for his family was the political turmoil in his homeland. Indeed, skirmishes between Afghan warlords' soldiers were still going on, and there was no letup with the country's anti-Buddhist sentiment. Abd tried very hard to keep these two issues off his mind and concentrated on his education, longing for the medical doctor degree award, after a couple of years of residency in general medicine, and the final reunion with his family. The daily six o'clock bell toll of the Episcopal chapel, located one city block away, for some reason awakened his sentiment toward religions at the beginning of his second year in Oxford. There was no Buddhist temple anywhere in the UK at the time, but he continued to observe Buddhist teaching. However, he became more and more preoccupied with the general notion of deity. Quite often he omitted the word "Buddha" in his daily prayer and replaced it hesitantly with a vague, unnamed "entity," expressed by a silence lasting about a fraction of a second and eventually by the word "God." In a letter his father wrote to him at the end of his second year in the UK, Abd read this following sentence with a great deal of reassurance: "I am glad that you have decided to undertake the study of other religions. Take advantage of all library facilities available to students to acquire knowledge on human spirituality…" Not many days after, he started reading the Bible's book of Genesis. For a while, he was struggling with the understanding of the difference between the two words *religion* and *philosophy* in terms of spirituality, until one day when he attended a lecture on individual choice of religion given by the bishop of the Church of England. That was the first time in his life that he tried to extend his religious study beyond Buddhism.

Another unexpected circumstance brought Abd close to Christianity. At the end of his first year at Oxford University, Abd befriended his classmate David Osgood, whose mother lived a few blocks away from his studio apartment. Christmas was drawing near. Mrs. Osgood was a widow. Her husband, an army captain, died on the battlefield during WWII. There was no class on the twenty-third day of December at the university. David invited his friend over to his house to meet his family and to listen to Christmas music broadcast on several European radio stations. The family room of the townhouse was upstairs, on the second floor. The two friends sat on the cushioned sill of the only bay window looking down onto the deserted cobblestone-paved street separating the two rows of narrow old brick townhouses. The neighbor church bell ended its hourly toll at the stroke of six. The street lights lit up. A heavily bundled-up lady wearing a beige coat and a black skirt suddenly appeared at the street corner. The rhythmic sound of her shoes on the cobblestones when she crossed the passageway was muffled by frequent freezing gusts. A couple of minutes later, the house's main entrance door opened and Abd could hear the air draft gushing into the cold dark corridor. The lady seen earlier on the street turned out to be Mrs. Osgood. She opened the door with a key chained to her waist and then entered the house. She pushed the heavy wooden door against the outside blowing wind to close it behind her. She locked it from inside and quickly removed and hung her winter coat. Appearing somewhat languorous, slowly she entered the living room. While staring at her oldest son, Charles, sitting on the handed-down upholstered antique chair with a part of the yesterday local newspaper on his hands, she asked with her shivering soft voice, "Where are your brothers, Charles?"

"David is upstairs with Abd, and your baby [he meant Harry, her youngest child] is in the cellar trying to finish building his short-wave radio. I went over his homework. He did a good job with his school assignments. By the way, did you have a decent sleep last night?"

As she entered the living room, she looked straight ahead at Isabella, who was sitting with a notebook on her lap and a pencil in her left hand, completely absorbed by what she was reading or writing. Sensing the presence of another person in the room, Isabella lifted up her head, gazing at her mother. "Hi, Mom, how was your day at the bank? Glad you're home. Almost freezing outside. Come and sit next to me and Maria. I am going to prepare a cup of tea to warm you up."

The two girls were spending most of the late afternoon next to the only charcoal stove heating the entire three-floor house. Isabella slowly got up and walked in the direction of the kitchen. Mrs. Osgood sat down next to Maria, her youngest daughter, who glanced at her wristwatch that used to be worn by her father, saying, "Again you worked overtime today. We note that you have been waking up three to four times during the night, likely being overtired and couldn't sleep, right, Mom? We worry about your health, Mom."

Mrs. Osgood indeed looked somewhat exhausted but reassured, knowing that all her five children were accounted for. Maria leaned over to deposit a loving kiss on her mother's cheek. Isabella reappeared with a porcelain teakettle and a matching mug. She deposited them on the adjacent writing desk, moved closer to Mrs. Osgood, and then gently placed her lips against her mother's forehead before returning to the kitchen. "Take a good rest, Mother. I will pour you some hot tea in five minutes."

Slumped into the upholstered old love seat, Mrs. Osgood, with her two varicosed legs elevated, grabbed the newspaper and started reading. Within a couple of minutes her eyes closed and her breathing became audible. Watching her from the upper floor, Abd and David realized that a catnap would do a great deal of good to someone like Mrs. Osgood, who worked overtime in the office during the week plus four to five more hours at home. Having lost her husband who used to earn a decent salary, she was now the sole breadwinner. Often, she had to ask the bank manager to give her overtime work in order to make ends meet. She had no other income. Despite the heavy workload at the bank and at home, Mrs. Osgood managed to attend the daily evening Mass at the church just a few blocks from her house. Abd never heard a complaint nor had he seen a faint sign of unhappiness, discouragement, or depression on her face. Instead, she smiled frequently and exhibited a jovial mood to everyone. Abd thought about the similar reverence to Buddha every evening at home. While keeping Charles's company upstairs, Abd witnessed all of what was going on down in the living room through the open ceiling between the two floors. Abd was invited to stay for supper that evening. At the dining table, before food was served by Isabella and Mrs. Osgood, everybody bowed their heads while Maria recited her daily prayer. Subconsciously, he compared the Osgood family's bond and that of his family. Knowing that Abd had no place to go to on Christmas Eve, Mrs. Osgood asked Abd whether he wanted to spend the entire day with her children, celebrating the much-anticipated joyful birth of the Lord. He accepted with great pleasure before he went back to his studio that evening, enraptured.

The reverberating sounds of bells of a half-dozen churches in the distance interspersed with the much louder strokes of the single Catholic chapel in the area announced the birth of the Most High at the end of a few remaining sacred hours of the twenty-fourth of December. After the late supper, Abd asked David whether he could accompany the whole family to attend the midnight Mass. David flatteringly handed him the missalette, and they all seven went to church on foot in the darkness of the snow-sprinkled night. Subsequently, David and Abd saw each other almost weekly. Not infrequently, Mrs. Osgood called Abd by the newly given name "the fourth son." Reciprocally, the young foreign student felt that Mrs. Osgood had a maternal feeling toward him. Three months after that Christmas, Abd took courage during one of his weekly get-togethers with David to ask her, "Where do you get your endurance, your energy, and your love for all of us, Mrs. Osgood?"

Immediately, she drew close to Abd and gave him a tight hug. Smiling and without hesitation, she responded, "From the mighty God, our Father in heaven, our Savior with his unconditional love for mankind." Those words of hers continued to reverberate throughout Abd's entire life.

During the last year of premed study, Abd got to know a few British female students with whom he spent many hours of discussion on Christianity and other religions. They were impressed with his intelligence, his friendliness, and especially his kindness; but Abd was determined to go home and didn't want to get too involved sentimentally. Nevertheless, Abd had experienced an unpleasant story that he couldn't forget for the next several years. The sister of one of these British female students, by the name Alison, met him one summer at the beet-growing farm. They worked side by side and became very friendly to each other. Abd didn't make anything out of this friendship. He thought it was just a transient camaraderie. Alison happened to be an assistant leader of a local Girl Scout chapter. One Wednesday fall afternoon, around 4:30 p.m., as Abd had just finished carrying the heavy English bike up to his six-by-four-foot balcony, the entrance doorbell rang. Abd ran back downstairs and then opened the door. Alison smiled at him. "Would you like to buy a box of chocolate cookies to help the jobless people in town? But you don't have to, if you don't want… I miss you since we left the farm shed on that last working day in August. Do you still remember me?"

Somewhat shocked by Alison's unexpected visit, Abd smiled back and then tried to keep his friend unembarrassed by going over a few things they did together at the farm. They reminded each other of the rare sunny days they had had while thinning the beet seedlings on the field. The conversation gradually extended to other trivial subjects including Alison's sister Julie's whereabouts. Before saying goodbye, Alison timidly gazed at and handed to Abd a pocket-size black-and-white photograph of herself. "Is it all right with you if I come back once in a while to sell you cookies? Here is something as a souvenir of me."

Abd became very touched by Alison's visit and gesture. After climbing back up to his studio apartment, he sat down at his desk, looking for several minutes at the picture of his friend's innocent and gentle face then let go a deep sigh. Actually, Alison lived only about three blocks away from Abd's studio and also on Bayswater Road. However, for the next several months, there had been no sign of Alison. Abd started to wonder why Alison had not come back "to sell cookies" for the second time. Each day, on his way home from school, very often Abd slowed down his bike, looked through the front glass window of Alison's parents' townhouse, but his friend's face was nowhere to be seen. Another summer passed and there was still no sign of Alison, and then came a surprise on a winter day of that same year. The doorbell rang once again sometime after dusk. Abd opened the door and saw a somber and sad face partially covered by a dark-colored shawl. It took several seconds before he could recognize that it was Alison who looked down to the doorsteps, feebly uttering, "I hope you don't mind giving back to me my photograph. I have stopped selling chocolate for over a year now. I am sorry."

Abd went back upstairs, picked up the framed photograph standing on his desk, and then quickly went back to the door. He extended his right arm from which Alison, without looking at Abd, grabbed the emblem of her souvenir and then abruptly walked away with tears running down her cheeks, saying these barely audible words, "Once again I am really sorry. I have to go now."

Then she quickly disappeared in the dark street. Haphazardly, Abd met Alison's sister Julie again at the main Oxford library more than three months later. The sad story finally came to light. Alison's parents had three daughters. The oldest one was married to an assistant professor of chemistry at one of the Oxford colleges. The couple had a happy marriage with two preteen sons. Nine months earlier,

Alison's sister suddenly died of an unknown illness. Shortly after, the widower asked his in-laws whether he could take Alison as his wife, explaining that the proposed arrangement would keep the family bond intact. Alison rejected the idea of marrying her twenty-six-year-older brother-in-law. Furthermore, she was then only seventeen. But for an unknown reason, her parents forced her to accept her brother-in-law's proposition. She bitterly cried at her elaborate wedding ceremony and then secluded herself for months after. Julie also told Abd that Alison was instructed by her parents and her newlywed husband to remove all proof of past connections with male friends. Abd could not forget the sad story for the rest of his life. He could not understand how this forced marriage could happen in a civilized society. Arranged marriage was not uncommon in Afghanistan, but forced marriage was not acceptable among the Afghans practicing Buddhism.

After three long years in England, Abd decided to go into the medical field. He applied and was accepted to enter the three-year premed study program at the University of Oxford. At the end of this period, he passed the final exam with flying colors. Abd's intention had been the same: return home as soon as possible, live near his parents, and set up a joined general medical practice with Zekirullah. Since Afghanistan was under strong overall British cultural influence for many years in the past, all Abd had to do was to take an accelerated four-year course of study that led to MBBS or MBChB (in Latin: *Medicinae Baccalaureus et Chirurgiae Baccalaureus*) enabling him to practice medicine as a medical doctor back home. He chose this path and completed this four-year course without the slightest difficulty. His brother Zekirullah had gone back to Bamyan with a medical doctorate degree over a year ago.

At the end of his ninth year in Oxford, Abd was ready to go home to share the medical practice in general medicine as a country doctor with his brother, when he received a letter from his father describing Zekirullah's first year of joined medical practice with Uncle Faisal and the continuing political as well as military turmoil in the entire country. Abd's father didn't forget to mention that Zekirullah had to work very hard, but because of the country's depressed economy, his annual income was no larger than the financial assistance he had received each year in the past from the Swedish government. Abd read the letter a few times, thought over, and then decided to stay two more years in the UK, waiting for an improvement of the situation at home. He managed to sign a two-year employment contract with one of the main hospitals in Cambridge as a house physician, while preparing his dissertation to be presented before getting the medical doctor (MD) degree, the highest medical certification in the UK. He missed his family, and vice versa; but by staying back in the UK and working as a hospital-based physician, he was able to send home a large part of his earnings. He knew he still had to help with his three younger siblings' education. They kept regular contact with Abd by mail. Aamir wished to become an electronic engineer. Ali mentioned repeatedly in his letters to Abd how badly the Afghan children needed dental care. Nabeela, the youngest in the family, didn't say much in her rare letters to her brother still having education abroad. Instead, occasionally she expressed to the elder Rasulovs her desire of owning a drugstore somewhere in Bamyan Province when she grew up.

Abd finished his research project in infectious diseases, defended his thesis titled "The Formation of the Viral Particle on the Cell Surface," was awarded the MD degree, and graduated magna cum laude.

By this time, Abd had lived eleven years abroad and had not seen his family during that entire period. With his advanced education and a good amount of experience in academic medicine, Abd dreamed of going home and getting a teaching job at Kabul University instead of practicing medicine as a general practitioner. Unfortunately, the political situation in his homeland continued to be precarious. After his ascension to the throne in 1933, King (Shah) Mohammed Zahir's military assistance to the First East Turkistan Republic was defeated by the Chinese Muslim Thirty-Sixth Division in the following year. Despite the growth in Afghan relations with international communities and the admission of Afghanistan to the League of Nations, the country remained as one of the poorest nations in the world. Uncle Faisal finally retired, leaving Zekirullah alone with a large practice. The latter badly needed a partner. Abd was determined to return to his homeland and had sent home a large number of medical textbooks to be used as references in the coming years. Frequently, he reminded himself that his twin brothers Ali and Aamir, in their last year of high school, definitely needed a good education. To fulfill this dream, they must be educated in Western European countries. About that time, the Afghan government was making significant efforts to send young and bright students abroad for education beyond the high school level. Government scholarships for students in the fields of medicine, engineering, agriculture, and management could be obtained if they academically scored well with their bachelor's degree. Both Ali and Aamir received scholarships from Kabul. Abd and Zekirullah continued to financially support their parents and their three younger siblings. The living condition at home had been considerably improved. Since his older brother was not able to save much money after paying his medical office rent, his employees' wages, and utilities expenses related to the medical practice, Abd volunteered to pay for Ali's and Aamir's transportation expenses to the host country and to subsidize their small government scholarships once they started their education in foreign countries.

Then the Rasulov family was abruptly struck by the sudden death during sleep of its head of household. Unexpectedly, Abd's father passed away without warning signs. Abd immediately came home to attend the burial service. Since the deceased was well respected for his integrity, honesty, and compassion, the funeral pro-cession was unusually large and participants were made up of not only local villagers, friends, coworkers, and relatives coming from neighboring provinces, but also provincial dignitaries. Abd saw his father twelve years ago for the last time. He deeply regretted not being able to bring his father to Europe for a visit, although he had seriously entertained this possibility only a couple of months ear-lier. The premature death of Mr. Rasulov placed a deep impact on the entire family. Mrs. Rasulov, bereaved for months by the sudden departure of her husband, felt very lonesome as she would be living alone with Nabeela and Omira. Ali and Aamir were scheduled to leave for France in less than two months. During the subsequent two days after the funeral, while remaining as the solace for the rest of the family, Zekirullah, Faiz, and Abd talked over the family situation and made plans for their mother and sister Nabeela. Despite his lingering but very much recovered adult attention-deficit disorder, Faiz was no longer hyperactive, but still having concentration problems. He was able to assist Zekirullah as the office janitor and medical supply manager. Three months later, before the harsh winter set in, Mrs. Rasulov reluctantly sold the Bamyan house and then moved to a renovated abandoned two-bedroom shed a few blocks away from Zekirullah's office in Tupchi. Faiz, recently resigned from the Tuti Koshteh farm, shared the new home with his mother and sister and happily worked for his older brother as planned. In the meantime, Abd tried to find an academic teaching job in Kabul or be employed as an epidemiologist by the government. In view of the economic downturn, the high unemployment throughout Afghanistan, and the lack of a stable country leadership, all national development programs almost came to a standstill. Frustrated and disillusioned with the search for an employment commensurate with his advanced education coupled with his expertise in a medical field that was practically little known to medical care providers in his homeland, Abd decided to give up the initial hope of becoming a professor in Kabul, the only city with a medical school in the entire country during the postwar period. He discussed with Zekirullah his idea of temporarily living abroad while keeping financial support to his mother and Nabeela. The two brothers agreed, as there were no other options for Abd to make a decent living at home. They felt that Abd's expertise in the field of infectious diseases would be wasted unless he could find an institution where teaching and scientific research were the mainstream activities. No such an institution could be found anywhere in civil war-ravaged Afghanistan at the time. After spending two more weekends with his family, Abd returned to Cambridge.

CHAPTER SIX

Happy Years in Academia and Private Life

A bd arrived to the microbiology lab at Oxford University where he had worked for two years under the supervision of Professor Nottingham, who was his dissertation principal adviser. The famous British Nobel Prize laureate on virology, with his unlit pipe protruding from under the white untrimmed mustache, sitting alone at his glass-covered, care-neglected wooden desk, looked up when the door hinges screeched, as his well-liked student entered. "Good morning, Abd. You are back. You surprise me. How is your mother doing?"

"Yes, sir, I am back, looking for a permanent job this time. In view of the circumstance, she manages. Thank you for asking."

"You return at the right time. I have been negotiating with Professor Hugo Regensberger in Vienna to jointly work on intracytoplasmic RNA [ribonucleic acid] influenza virus encoding. If you are interested in the project after our discussion, I will suggest to the professor that you would be its principal investigator."

The two men spent the rest of the day trying to figure out how the project should be split between the two labs, as each professor was going to use his own government's microbiology grant. After exchanging a few letters and telephone calls between them, the two prominent scientists signed an international scientific agreement of cooperation in research on virus replication in primate cells with Abd as the coordinator. Because the facilities were not the same in the two labs, the first phase had to be carried out in Vienna, and therefore Abd was recommended to station for at least a year in the vicinity of Professor Regensberger's lab. Since foreign scientific investigators were required by the Austrian government to know the German language well enough to communicate, a six-week crash course in this language was offered and the expenses were paid for by the grant. For some unpublicized reason, the courses were given at the German Summer School in Bad Hirschfeld, a small town in southern Bavaria, Germany. Happy for having another opportunity to brush up this language that he already had a solid foundation of, Abd flew to Munich less than a month later and then arrived to the school town on the same day. People of all walks of life and from all over the world gathered at the city townhall that late afternoon where they received the preliminary instructions on lodging, food quarters, and classes sites. From the handout package that contained guidelines written in German, French, and English, Abd learned that the name of the school director was Herr Doktor Hermann Holzburg and that he was assisted by two female teachers: Fräulein Schmidt and Fräulein Herzog. The three teachers intermingled with the crowd. Their personal diverse background and education were briefly outlined in a separate two-page introductory package insert. All three were specialized in German crash courses teaching. Abd reassured himself of a relaxing but productive six-week learning period when he read that the two ladies had been working for several years with German consulates in several foreign countries and that each mastered four to five languages.

Amazingly, Fräulein Schmidt had an impeccable Parisian accent in French, and Fräulein Herzog, a Texan tinge in English. Dr. Holzburg, a six-and-a-half-foot tall, thin, and with a Scandinavian rather than Germanic build, circulated step by step within the jam-packed average-size reception room and its hallway. He stopped frequently to say hello to each of the four dozen foreign visitors. Suddenly he was facing Abd, who was in the middle of a conversation in English with a couple of young students. While shaking hands with each of the three, he addressed in German the following routine sentence to each of them: "Welcome to Bad Hirschfeld. What is your name, and where are you from? My name is Holzburg. I am the director of the summer teaching program."

"My name is Abdulai. And I am from Afghanistan."

Abd recognized the director's German Hochsprache—the standardized version of the language—with the accent from the region of Hannover, the town where his two German friends came from. Dr. Holzburg took out of his blazer side pocket the list of students. He quickly glanced over its entire content and then looked at Abd once again. "You are the only representative of your country. You seem to have acquired the correct German pronunciation. Have you lived in this country?"

"This is my first visit to Germany, but I was befriended with two German students in Oxford, UK."

The introductory reception ended with a joyful crowd's applause. At eight in the morning of the next day, all students were instructed to gather in the large school waiting room adjacent to the director's office. Suddenly the noisy room turned into complete silence. One after another, all three teachers walked to the podium, facing the anxious students waiting for more detailed instructions on what group they would be in. The total number of students was divided into three classes. One was for beginners, the second for those who already had some knowledge in German language, and the third for more advanced students. Abd chose the latter. Fräulein Schmidt was assigned to teach this class made up of people from at least a dozen foreign countries. It was an equal number of males and females. The course began on July 14 morning. The teacher read the

seventeen names on the list she just received from the school's secretary. As expected, each student was requested to introduce himself
in German to classmates. In addition, the students had to give the
answer to five questions listed on the handout questionnaire. These
were their name's spelling, their country of birth, their profession or
specialty schools they were attending, their mother tongue, and the
reason for taking the crash course in German. Frequently the whole
class burst into friendly laughs when mistakes of German pronunciation were made.

There were several well-educated professionals. One of them
was a linguistic professor from Turkey, the second was a car manufac-
ture company CEO from Japan, the third person was an industrialist
from Italy, and half a dozen diplomats from the US and from French-
speaking European countries. The rest of the group was made up of
students still attending community colleges, and they were in the
early twenties. Abd was the only medical doctor among the four
dozen foreigners attending classes. The youngest of all in his class
was an eighteen-year-old female from Karolinska, Sweden. Her name
was Charmina.

The first week of learning went well. Fräulein Schmidt was
very pleased. The persnickety teacher spent her after-school time
in the afternoon answering her students' questions. She was very
friendly and very helpful to them, especially to those who were
eager to learn. Students speaking the same mother tongue tended
to hang out together during the two fifteen-minute breaks of the
day, partially because they were curious about each other's origin and
background and partially because it was still too difficult for them
to converse in German at the early phase of their summer course.
Being the only student from the Middle East and having spent a
good number of years in the UK, Abd frequently intermingled with
the English-speaking group. Charmina, on the other hand, was seen
in either of the two largest ones, i.e., English and French. During
the twice weekly mandatory afternoon outing, Fräulein Schmidt
repeatedly suggested that all students in her class converse in "the
language they came to Bad Hirschfeld to learn." Abd undoubtedly
was her most advanced student. Everybody in his class was quite

serious with the learning process. Answers to questions on written exercises were handed eagerly and quickly to the teacher. Students' attention was totally directed to her when she talked from her desk or wrote on the blackboard. By the end of the second week, the majority of the students in Fräulein Schmidt's class had made significant progress in speaking and writing German. Rather quiet, Charmina made no exception. During class time, and for most part of the day, all eyes were directed to Fräulein Schmidt, but then here and there, Charmina darted an obsequious glance at Abd then quickly looked back at the teacher. Her action increased in frequency in the coming school sessions. At first, Abd didn't pay too much attention to these detoured-from-target glimpses at him. For the next several days, he still thought they were innocent, harmless, inquisitive coup d'oeil coming from a young adult female first time away from home alone. Finally, he got an unexpected answer to his bewildered thoughts on the third Friday afternoon outing.

It was the end of July, but the weather was rather cool and the wind was calm. The advanced class happened to be led by Fräulein Herzog this time. The rest of the students were separated into two clusters escorted by the other teachers. In small clumps of no more than four, teachers and students left the school courtyard, heading toward the Wolkekirchturm hill, two and a quarter kilometers from the school. Fräulein Herzog locked the entrance door and then joined Abd, who was courteously waiting for her at the doorsteps. The two made up the tail end of the school outing crowd. Walking side by side, student and teacher had an intensive conversation in German that was dotted with Abd's occasional English words. Approximately a hundred yards ahead of them was Charmina. She was flanked on her right side by the Japanese professor Yamoshito and on her left side by Charles, a former soldier of the French Foreign Legion. The voices of the two men drowned out that of Charmina, who frequently turned her head around, looking in the direction of Abd. By this time the rear cluster of students was about to turn right onto a narrow grass-islanded dirt road, when a six-wheeler truck, carrying bales of fresh-cut hay, passed them. Within a few seconds, a good number of hikers started to have repeated sneezes with tearing eyes.

Suddenly Fräulein Herzog realized that students under her super-vision were way ahead of her. She shouted, "Professor Yamoshito, please wait for us!" and then ran forward, leaving Abd behind. She joined the Japanese a couple of minutes later.

In the meantime, Charmina slowed down her walk. Occasionally she made a stop, removed her right semi-high-heeled shoe, held it upside down for a second or two, and then inserted it back on her foot. While accelerating his speed to catch up with hikers ahead of him, Abd noted that Charmina had progressively slowed down her walk. Then she made another stop with her full weight on the left leg, right at the moment when Abd caught up with her. Directing his regard to her legs, he asked, "What is the matter with your shoes?"

"I think I have an annoying pebble in my shoe," she thankfully replied.

"Place your hand over my shoulder. I will take your shoe off. Will see what the problem is." Abd removed her right shoe and examined it carefully. He did not find anything that could interfere with her walk but rather had the chance to admire her beautiful legs of playboy models. While still leaning on Abd's shoulder, Charmina's tender gaze met his friendly pair of eyes. "Can I rely on your assis-tance should I have troubles with my shoe again?"

"Of course!" Abd thought to himself that he should not get involved in a casual summer love affair at this time, as he had accepted to be the principal investigator of an important research project in virology to be started in a couple of months. He was fully aware of Charmina's feeling toward him but decided to play safe with his friendly but unintentional response to her question. Meanwhile, the young lady slowed down further her walk while attempting to accost Abd. She pretended that in a hurry she had picked the wrong shoes that caused discomfort and that she was not used to doing day hikes. Abd listened to her patiently and without comments. Eventually the couple was the last to arrive at the isolated regrouping point where Fräulein Herzog was anxiously waiting for them. They were only less than five minutes to the foot of the hill, but Charmina refused to ascend it, giving the excuse of having leg cramps. The teacher had to ask someone among the male students to stay with her, waiting for the whole noisy throng of hikers to descend from the flat summit. Fräulein Herzog looked around. No one seemed to be interested in keeping Charmina company. She turned to Abd, who reluctantly said, "Okay, I will stay with her." On the way back to the school, again the couple was slower than the rest and Charmina was limping.

In the morning of next Monday, classes began as usual at 8:30 a.m. Abd came to the classroom a few minutes earlier, as he had in mind the intention of asking Fräulein Schmidt a couple of questions on German syntax. One after another, the students arrived and sat around the long Formica-surface-finished table. The young Charmina showed up a couple of minutes later, right at the moment when the teacher just finished saying, "We are going to start lesson number 18 this morning."

Charmina pulled an empty chair and then sat down, facing again Abd. All of the seventeen students including Abd attentively followed Fräulein Schmidt chalking examples of complex German sentence construction on the blackboard. Charmina's attention during the entire morning was divided between listening to and watching the teacher's explanations written on the chalkboard. But occasionally she turned her head a few degrees to the left in the direction of Abd and then threw a quick glance at him. The advanced class learning went on as usual that Monday afternoon with many questions from the students on the construction of compound nouns. In the next few class days, the exchanges of tender look between the two sets of eyes were getting progressively intense. Abd's reciprocal affection for Charmina became unquestionable; yet none of the students seemed to be aware of the couple's secret feeling toward each other. Their attention was totally absorbed by Fräulein Schmidt's teaching skill. Suddenly the electric siren announced the end of the afternoon classes at the institute. All the students evacuated the room except Abd. He went to the teacher's desk to ask her a few more questions on what he had missed during the lesson of that day. One can imagine why Dr. Abdulai had failed to sporadically concentrate on his learning during the last few days.

Abd went back to his lodging quarter after school to get his usual short afternoon rest on the couch. He got up, stretched, and then washed himself off, ready to go out for supper. Like the majority of the students from the institute, Abd had become the faithful patron of the most inexpensive but popular restaurant in town after the first three weeks in Bad Hirschfeld. In the large dining room, the students were in queue, waiting their turn to help themselves at the buffet counter. After getting his bowl of lamb stew, a dish of greens, and a couple of flatbreads, Abd sat down at an empty table at the southeast room corner. While his eyes were directed to chapter 19 of the German textbook kept open with his left hand, Abd leisurely enjoyed his favorite dishes. Suddenly, a book similar to his landed on the table across from where he was sitting. He raised his head and was totally surprised to see the red-eyed youngest female student standing alone at the opposite side of the table. "What is bothering you, Charmina? You seem to be hurt and unhappy. How can I help you?"

Charmina pulled a chair and then sat down at the table, facing Abd, who worrisomely inquired further, "Are you going to get something for supper?"

"No, I have not been hungry for the last few days."

Abd insisted, "You must make an effort to get some nourishment to build your physical strength necessary to keep up with the strenuous summer crash course. Three more demanding weeks of intense study are still ahead of us."

With tapering long fingers garnished by meticulously manicured pinkish nails, Charmina discreetly pulled out an embroidered white handkerchief from the right long sleeve of her white silk blouse. She wiped her tearful eyes, remained silent to Abd's suggestion, but realized at the same time that shedding tears could not be caused by just a casual meeting with a classmate. It must be the result of some sort of unusual reciprocal personal feeling. In the meantime, Abd finished his last piece of bread, swallowed the last sip of Coke, and then stood up after grabbing the textbook with his left hand. He walked around the table's end and then stopped behind Charmina, who continued to quietly sob. He placed his hand on her shoulder, saying to her with very affectionate words, "Let me take you to your quarter before dark."

Charmina stood up, sobbed out her grief while following Abd. Side by side the couple left the restaurant and quickly disappeared in the crowd of workers returning from their work at the nearby aluminum can manufacturing warehouse.

In the early part of the following week, Professor Yamoshito, having overheard the rumor that Charmina had won Abd's heart, threw a cold look at him when Abd entered the classroom. "Congratulations for the accomplishment."

Abd tried to dispel the rumor, but he was unsuccessful. Teachers and students in the entire school noted that Charmina and Abd were together downtown during weekends, daily at the restaurant after school, and occasionally in the local movie theater. He walked her back to the girls' dormitory every day before dark. Abd was conscious by now that he was deeply involved sentimentally, but he couldn't help himself to think off and on that it might not be wise to fall in love with a ten-year-younger lady at this early phase of his promising academic career.

The summer crash course was coming to an end. Students said friendly goodbyes to each other after the commencement session on that early cold fall day of the southern Bavaria region. The separation from her summer friend was very hard for Charmina. She bade a tearful farewell while tightly embracing Abd and whispering, "I shall see you again in Vienna." She departed from him with tears running down her blushed cheeks. Abd was somewhat perplexed, realizing suddenly that a casual platonic love during the short summer weeks could lead to a more serious relationship.

This was a Viennese September day of 1952. The steeple clock across the street from the Vienna Hygiene Institute on Grabengasse Street rang out across the northern part of the city. It was a couple of minutes after six in the late afternoon. The cobbled streets were deserted. Abd was again late in leaving the microbiology lab due to the time-consuming go-over of the lab results and the detailed planning for the next day's experiments to be performed jointly with the Oberazrt (head physician) colleague on cellular virus particle's reproduction. The latter rushed out the main gate of the institute and then quickly walked to his rusty Volkswagen parked on the other side of the narrow cobblestone-paved street. Abd slowly descended the huge ten-stepped granite front stairway of the old, but with an imposing look, academic building constructed sometime in the late nineteenth century. Walking along the discolored cement-covered brick wall, he kept his eyes on the uneven worn-out sidewalk while outlining in his head the various steps of the next day's lab experiments. He buttoned his dark-blue blazer and then pulled up its collar to cover his neck exposed to the chilly late October Viennese weather. Heading toward the intersection of Hammerstrasse and Muellerstrasse where he routinely caught the street car to go to his apartment a dozen blocks away, Abd suddenly saw a young lady in a polka-dotted long winter coat slowly walking in his direction. He quickly recognized the same round face he had been discreetly staring at for at least ten weeks this past summer. Yes, the young lady was his Charmina. They were approaching, then they stopped in front of each other. Abd embraced her. Too astonished at first and trembling, he could only utter, "What are you doing here in Vienna? I thought you were joking when you said last summer that you were going to see me again in Vienna."

With tears running down her pale and cold cheeks, Charmina stared at him. "Are you really surprised that I am here?" Taken over by emotion, she paused a few seconds then added, "Wouldn't you be more surprised when I inform you that my father has arranged for me to take one-semester university courses in microbiology, enabling me to become a certified lab technician after an additional year and half of hospital internship?"

The intense feeling for Charmina was rekindled with joy in Abd's heart; and this time the glow had reached the intensity of a real love between a man and a woman. While holding her hands, he asked her this personal question: "Where are you staying while going to school?"

"The school of microbiology itself provides room and board to newly arrived students up to two weeks while they search for six-month or longer rent elsewhere."

"It would be nice if you will be able to find lodging not too far from my apartment."

"I like that idea. Give me your address."

"I will in a moment. Are you in a hurry? Do you have to go back to your dormitory right now?"

"I don't have to be back in my room before ten. The dorm's main gate is locked a few minutes after that."

"Can I have the pleasure to invite you to that restaurant?" Abd pointed his finger to the bistro with the green awning across the street where he had been frequently spending his lunchtime.

Abd offered his left elbow to Charmina. They walked side by side. Occasionally they looked at each other with an affectionate smile, which he rarely saw on her face during the weeks spent in Bad Hirschfeld. By nature, she was a quiet, thoughtful, very reserved, and polite woman with good manners. Abd found out very soon that his friend just received her high school diploma a year ago and was very gifted in painting and pottery. Once inside of the bistro and grill, they sat across the table facing each other. With tender looks, they seemed to privately say to each other that they had to catch up with the time lost since they temporarily bade goodbye last summer. Abd's right arm reached out, across the table, to lovingly touch then instantaneously grab hers. "Glad to see you again. I missed you."

"Wait, I have something for you. I made it myself." She pulled out from her black leather handbag a two-finger-size wrapped packet, handed it to him, and then added, "Please don't open it until you are back in your apartment. It's a surprise."

Abd wrote the address of his apartment on a napkin and then handed it to Charmina. They spent their first intimate moments in the bistro until 9:30 that evening, when Abd decided to walk her back to the dormitory, just a couple of blocks from his lab. At the gate, he said good night to her while depositing his first kiss on her lips. She tenderly reciprocated. "Sweet dreams to you. I will call you sometime in the morning to say hello. If for some reason I will not be able to reach you during your working hours at the lab, is it acceptable that I wait for you at the institute's gate around 5:30 to 6:00?"

"Why don't we say at 5:30, before dusk? I don't want to make you wait in the cold."

"Agreed!"

Abd walked back to the streetcar Bonneville station where he met Charmina a few hours earlier. He could not resist his temptation to open Charmina's gift once he arrived at his studio apartment. It was a thumb-size artistically decorated smooth ceramic candleholder with the letters "CL" at its bottom. The same object was posthumously found a few decades later in his handbag, at his side.

The next day, Charmina went to the university admission office to get the list of rental apartments for students. She circled three possibilities within a few blocks from where Abd was staying. She hopped on the street car, rode no more than three minutes, and then got off at Vösendorf Station. After an additional couple of minutes on foot, she knocked at the door of a two-story townhouse. The owners, a senior couple, were very pleasant to her. They went over the lodging arrangement that had worked out very well in the past with previous students. The only restriction was that the renter was not allowed to have visitors after 9:00 p.m. Charmina signed a six-month contract. On the way out, she saw the wooden crucifix hung high on the inside wall, above the house entrance. She moved in the same afternoon.

Abd's scientific research in collaboration with Professor Regensberger went as expected. He got along well with the Oberarzt, and they worked long hours together in the old but well-equipped lab. Reproducible data on the pathway of the formation of cytoplasmic RNA (ribonucleic acid) virus started to accumulate. In addition to the busy schedule at the lab, Abd managed to attend the weekly combined internal medicine and pediatrics conference with case presentation at the university hospital. This extra activity was very valuable to him, as he was able to keep up with new developments in several aspects of these two medical specialties. He was indeed a very happy young scientist successfully engaged in the molecular level of medical research preparing him for a brilliant academic career.

Charmina and Abd were seeing each other practically every weekday after work and spent time together during weekends, sometimes at the lab when Abd had to perform or to read and record lab results. One Saturday morning Abd came to see his friend at her room. The rare sunny Viennese winter day unexpectedly offered him a pleasant surprise. Quietly on his toes, he climbed upstairs. Her door was kept just a hair open. Lying flat on her back on the platform of the bay window facing the entrance was a well-formed female body tightly wrapped in cream color chiffon. The sunlight shone only on the ample bosom, leaving the rest in a somber shade. As Abd entered the room filled with faint enchanting violin and romantic piano notes of Ludwig van Beethoven's Romance in F Major Op. 50, Charmina stayed silent and motionless. He quietly closed the door behind him while gazing at his female friend's entire body for the first time. Charmina had been waiting for the current ecstatic moment since she arrived in Vienna almost three months ago. Abd slowly tiptoed toward the direction of the window, but then abruptly stopped in the middle of the room, admiring his imaginary earthly Venus for a few seconds. Approaching almost instantaneously the extraordinary beauty, he tenderly looked at her face and then glanced once again at her entire body. Her pair of legs, partially covered by the chiffon, brought back images of models' photographs he had seen in magazines lingering in many doctors' waiting rooms. He indulged himself in the general beauty and purity of a young virgin he had never imagined during his teenaged years until this moment.

He had to utter words expressing his appreciation for her simplicity in reciprocating his sincere and spontaneous affection. "You are truly beautiful, Charmina."

Then, while keeping her eyes closed, she let him slowly and passionately sweep his lips over her tender and smooth skin, from her mouth to her neck, without emitting a single word. Charmina expressed her pleasure with a barely perceptible jolt. "Hold me tight. I am yours, Abd."

Abd helped her to sit up then tightly encircled her upper body part with his two arms. Completely speechless for several minutes, they embraced each other in ecstasy. All of a sudden, the young doctor stepped back, while still holding Charmina's hands that he placed at his lips, detached himself from the voluptuous body. At that precise moment, the Buddhist moral principles Abd had learned from his parents, as well as the Bible's Ten Commandments he had been reading during the last two years, awakened in him. He was afraid of being submerged in prolonged sensual ecstasy. He chose chastity until the day he would legally and morally consummate his marriage. The couple kept each other company everywhere they went, deeply in love, until mid-February when Charmina was about to complete her six-month courses in lab technology. Their love, a little more than platonic, remained truly pure.

A thin coat of snow covered the roofs of buildings and houses in the entire city of Vienna on that early morning of February. Charmina and Abd, in heavy winter coats, were standing on one of the platforms of the Wien Hauptbahnhof (Vienna's main railroad station). They were a dozen feet from an old couple with light suitcases. The train was ready for leaving the Austrian capital city. A shrill loud whistle was followed by the conductor's voice: "Am bord" (on board).

Charmina, with tears in her eyes, pressed herself tightly against Abd. While cheerfully embracing each other, she sadly murmured to him, "I will write you soon. Don't let the Viennese ladies seduce you. I love you."

"Don't worry. Be sure to make the connection in Copenhagen. I love you too."

She climbed up onto the train platform, waved at him, and then entered the second-class compartment that was scheduled to go all the way to the capital of Denmark.

In the next six months, Abd concentrated strictly on his research work, which was progressing well. He and the Oberarzt sat down weekly with Professor Regensberger to go over the results of their experiments during the previous five days. Since the Oberarzt's time was more dedicated to the teaching of medical students and consultation requested by the hospital in-house physicians, Abd was the major investigator and remained so throughout his entire stay in Vienna. After long hours spent at the institute during the workweek as well as weekends, Abd realized how much he missed Charmina, who by now, besides his mother and his sister, had become part of his life. He wrote to her at her parents' address in Karolinska and received an affectionate reply every week. Instead of one year anticipated to be spent in Professor Regensberger's lab, the first phase of the joint project between the two labs was completed just a week beyond the last day of the nine-month mark. Dr. Nottingham, frequently in touch with Abd, realized that the harvest of the research results was ahead of schedule. He wanted Abd to take a couple of weeks off and then return to Oxford to finish up the second phase of the project. Abd thought about bringing his mother, Faiz, and sister Nabeela to Vienna for a visit during his two weeks of paid vacation; but he quickly dropped the idea in view of the enormous expense that he would have to incur. He entertained the thought of making a trip to Karolinska and then trying to see Charmina in strict secrecy; but he knew that wouldn't be appropriate for someone with a religious background like him to carry out such a socially unacceptable trip.

The unexpected news that Abd could hardly imagine arrived in the form of a letter a week prior to the date of his departure from Vienna. Returning late that afternoon from the lab, Abd opened his mailbox located near the apartment building's entrance. To his surprise, it was a pink envelope with a Swedish stamp affixed. At first, he thought it was another weekly letter from Charmina, but quickly he realized that the handwriting of his address was not familiar to him. The content of the envelope was an unscented pink sheet of paper with a printed returned address, identical to that of Charmina, on its left upper corner. The sender was Charmina's mother, who wrote in English:

Dear Dr. Abdulai:

Charmina has been talking about you and your interesting research work since she left Vienna. We too are anxious to meet you in person. We would like to invite you to join us spending a week of winter vacation, sometime in the middle part of the coming December, in Mürren, Swiss Alps. We will provide you with a humble lodging and simple meals that we prepare ourselves after the daily ski runs. Charmina has informed us that you don't ski. Please don't be afraid of this sport. She is an excellent skier and would be delighted to give you a few private lessons. Please reply as soon as possible as we have to make a reservation in advance for a winter cottage large enough to accommodate five persons.

Sincerely,
Inga Larsen

Abd wrote back, accepting the invitation. Joining the Larsen family for vacation was more meaningful to him than taking up skiing at this phase of his life.

Within three weeks, Abd was back in Oxford. He diligently worked on the second phase of the joint research project while spending many hours of his leisure time at home writing an article on the results gathered in the Viennese lab. The manuscript was carefully reviewed by the two professors before submitting for publication in a reputable European scientific periodical, and he was the senior author of the report, which was very well accepted by the international medical circle. He received many letters from medical investigators around the world asking for details on his work. Some of them quickly recognized the important ramification of the discovery made by Abd in the field of molecular biology dealing with virus, proposing to collaborate with him in future related projects. Among these was the invitation to join Prof. Maurice Duvier at the Faculty of Medicine, University of Paris. But Abd had plenty of work to be carried out until the end of the third year in Professor Nottingham's lab.

Despite his preoccupation with getting meaningful results on his research work, the young doctor, whose first publication was frequently cited as reference in half dozen scientific journals, continued to stay regularly in touch with his friend Charmina. The latter had been working as a lab technician in one of the hospitals located in Karolinska for the last nine months. Even though he loved her dearly, occasionally he tried to reassess their relationship. They celebrated his twenty-eighth birthday a few days before she left Vienna, and they were too much in love to be surely objective in the projection of their potential union. Of concern was the fact that she was ten years his junior. He wondered whether she was mature enough to daringly venture in the face of an unknown future when she met him in Bad Hirschfeld. He had discreetly communicated this serious thought to her in one of his early letters written from Oxford; but she promptly dismissed it, contending that he was too cautious with his concern. To a certain extent, she was right in her evaluation of their relationship. First of all, she did not love him because of his physical attractiveness, but rather because of his intelligence and his precision in thought and action that gave him a dignified appearance. Furthermore, both were deeply religious and both believed that their faith was the cornerstone of the family value that governs the union between a man and a woman. In spite of her attempt to reassure him that her love was genuine, he was having that nagging thought that she was too quiet a person, with a possible hidden inferiority complex. Since he was an accomplished intellectual, he dreamed of a female partner who could carry on intelligent discussions of any topics of interest to him, notably scientific discovery, religion, music, and painting, the four most pivotal subjects of his life.

At age sixty-four, Professor Nottingham showed no sign of his pending retirement. Instead, he and Abd got involved in three to four research projects at the same time. They truly enjoyed each other's company in teaching medical students and experimenting in the study of viral propagation. Unfortunately, the unique collaboration between the young scientist and the professor came abruptly to an end. One Sunday morning, while walking to his local Episcopal church, Professor Nottingham was struck by a van. The accident was severe enough to cause his instant demise despite attempts of resuscitation by a surgeon who happened to be in close proximity of the site. Abd was grieving the death of his mentor for many months thereafter. Following the sad event, Abd paid weekly visits to the professor's widow. This lasted until the day he left to move to France.

With a sudden change in the path of his academic career in terms of financial support by grants from Oxford University or from the UK government, Abd had to look as soon as possible for alternatives or options quickly available outside of Professor Nottingham's lab. The long letter Prof. Maurice Duvier wrote to him a few months earlier, outlining in detail the various topics of viral research at the University of Paris, stood out in his memory. After going over the remaining written offers of hiring he received from a half of a dozen foreign university medical schools, he decided to write to Professor Duvier. Abd preferred to stay permanently in Western Europe, but the problem of reciprocity of medical diplomas between France and UK had to be ironed out. Because Abd had achieved the highest medical education in England and was at the time an outstanding scientific investigator and also an active clinician abreast of new medical developments, he was authorized to exercise his profession, like French-born medical doctors do, without further requirements. He settled down in Professor Duvier's microbiology lab within less than a month, and the university gave him the title "visiting guest scientist." Within less than a year, the French Immigration and Naturalization Department granted him the status of a "foreign permanent resident." The only hurdle Abd had to overcome was the language barrier. Up until this time, Abd had not been exposed to French culture, nor had he been in contact with French people. Most of important reviews of international publications in his research field of virology were in English. He knew that French was a beautiful language but difficult to learn. However, he was confident that his knowledge of Latin and his fluency in German would help him master the language of his newly adopted country. He set out to learn French right after he arrived in Paris. Five days a week, Abd stopped at the tobacco corner store, on his way from the metro station to the lab, to pick up his five-cent *Le Monde* newspaper, which he read during lunchtime. At his flat, French stations heard from his pocketsize radio kept his company. He knew by heart and whistled along the French favorite songs "Valentine" sung by Maurice Chevalier and "La Vie en Rose" by Edith Piaf. Within less than six months, Abd's knowledge in French was good enough, enabling him to actively participate in the discussion at the daily morning clinical rounds between the instructor and house staff in training at the university hospital conveniently located across the street from his workplace. Abd's collaboration with Professor Duvier in their research on viral reproduction in cell lines went very well, and by the end of his first year in Paris, two manuscripts on their work were ready to be sent to the French Academy of Sciences for their final critical review and pending publication. He continued to regularly receive love letters from Charmina.

Abd had been keeping in touch with several people he was in close contact throughout the years, from the time he left his high school. John Campbell, one of his classmates at Oxford, who also specialized in infectious diseases, section bacteriology, dropped in for a short visit at his lab. They compared notes on their academic career. John complimented Abd for his astounding academic achievement. Abd was very happy with his professional and private life as well.

In the early part of December of the same year, Abd received a reminder note from the Larsens, in which details of the skiing trip were carefully outlined. Abd arrived in Interlaken Ost by train from Paris on the fifteenth, after a couple of connections. Accompanied by the Larsen family, Abd marveled at the scenic beauty of the train ride to Lauterbrunnen, then from there to Mürren by cable car. In contrast to the fast-paced city of Paris, this car-free Walser mountain village in Bernese Oberland, Switzerland, offered the young doctor a sense of tranquility, calmness, and serenity. At the rented cottage, Abd was assigned to a small double-bed room with private bath and a window facing the gorgeous, breathtaking Eiger, Mönch, and Jungfrau Mountains. At first, he was having some trepidation in conversing with Dr. Larsen, his wife Inga, and their elder daughter Mathilda at the dinner table. But Mrs. Larsen was a perfect host. She managed to break the ice with her many questions on Abd's scientific research work, being herself a microbiologist at the University of Karolinska until her recent early retirement. She also asked him about his living experience in Oxford, London, and Paris, as she was the daughter of a retired deputy Swedish ambassador to half a dozen Western European countries. Probably on purpose, not a single allusion to Abd's background was made at the table. Undoubtedly, Charmina had already informed her parents and sister Mathilda of Abd's personal circumstances and experiences that shaped his life. After asking his wife to move sideways the vase containing a dozen fresh pink roses that obstructed his direct eye contact with Abd, Dr. Larsen, a semiretired dentist, started to discuss the political unrest and successive frequent government replacements in France during the early '50s. He quickly realized that the visitor was a well-educated person, knowledgeable in a wide range of fields. Each day, Abd helped clear the table after their early dinner.

In the afternoon of the second day at the chalet, and after four hours of morning ski runs, Charmina got the okay from her mother to take a walk to town with Abd. She wanted to show him the village she had been familiar with, as well as its winter activities, for many years. Once at the door of the only Catholic church in the whole region, they stopped, looked at each other a few seconds, and then entered the nave. They sat down next to each other on the squeaky rear pew. Abd quietly but reverently said his prayer, while Charmina remained silent, listening to a few old ladies monotonously reciting the Holy Rosary of the Virgin Mary.

The Larsens and Abd packed up and then left the cottage in the early hours of the seventh day. The same porter who transported by cart-horse their luggage to the chalet a few days earlier took them back to Mürren cable car station.

Back in Paris that Sunday, Abd felt as if he was fully accepted into the fabric of a family with a Western culture, and the difference of ethnicity was no longer an issue. He was convinced that a person's physical appearance and upbringing are totally irrelevant if his character, his intelligence, his general knowledge, and especially his professional status are exceptionally remarkable and that the person can happily live anywhere in the world if he knows how to assimilate into a society of which that person has become a part. At times Abd was paradoxical with his thoughts. On one hand, he realized that he was deeply involved in the life of a woman from an educated and religious family, but on the other, he worried that she was not mature enough to be his life's partner. This thinking was further reinforced by the quiet Charmina's personality. Even though he loved her dearly, he still dreamed of meeting another person of the opposite sex who could carry out effortlessly a discussion on any subject or at least on subjects he was interested in. In the final analysis, he preferred to let time dictate the outcome, as he definitely believed in the universal proverb "Man proposes, God disposes."

CHAPTER SEVEN

Life Is Getting More Complicated

Once settled in his Parisian office at University Hospital Necker Enfants Malades, besides having to spend a good deal of time on his scientific investigation and teaching of third-year medical students on microbiology lab experiments, Abd's over-

all activities became more intense. He decided to concentrate his interest on diseases of children through attendance of conferences, rounds, and guest lectures on topics related to pediatrics after having witnessed many severe cases of infants and children admitted to the hospital but who had succumbed shortly to viral and bacterial infections. At the time, poliomyelitis and epiglottitis were among the most common children's illnesses, but there was no vaccine available to prevent them from getting these diseases. In addition to his research pursuit, he volunteered to make himself available for free consultation on infectious diseases to patients suspected to have "contagious" diseases admitted to the emergency room.

Despite his heavy professional schedule, but because of his determination to become a Christian, Abd attended Mass every Sunday.

Being still a catechumen, he could not receive the Eucharist from the priests at the stone Church of Saint-Sulpice in the Luxembourg Quarter of the sixth arrondissement of Paris, just a few blocks from his apartment. For eight long months Abd went through all formal steps toward Catholicism taught by Father Lamans. He started with the rite of reception into the *order of catechumens*, then *the rite of election*, followed by the three chief rituals, known as *Scrutinies* at the local church. Abd solemnly participated in the celebration of the rite of acceptance at the liturgy on the middle of three Sundays of Lent. Then he got the permission from Saint-Sulpice church to take the last step of *initiation* elsewhere. As a matter of fact, Abd's intension to have Mrs. Osgood as his godmother and sponsor was born out of the very first Christmas Eve Mass he attended back a few years earlier in Oxford. In February of the following year, he wrote a note to Mrs. Osgood asking her to arrange with the priest of her church to perform the baptism ceremony. Delighted, this devoted Christian widow, together with her church's deacon, prepared the congregation for the baptism of a converting Buddhist on the Easter vigil. Abd arrived from Paris the Wednesday preceding Easter Sunday. He was joyfully received by an unusually large crowd at the post-baptism reception held in the church fellowship hall.

The early summer was about to take over the spring in Paris. All the benches in Luxembourg Garden were occupied by lovers. Noisy sparrows swooped from their freshly built nests down to the ground, looking for foodstuff crumbs discarded on purpose by park visitors to attract these tiny tamed creatures. Passing by these benches, subconsciously Abd's deep feeling for Charmina abruptly resurged. He wished she would appear miraculously in front of him with her gracious feminine beauty. He envied the lovers that early evening. Abd did not have a good sleep that night and then arrived about half an hour late at work on the next day. He saw on his desk a handwritten note clipped to a flyer: "I want you to attend this important conference." The secretary said to him, "He wants you to go over this announcement and give your thoughts on this international gathering." It was an internal communication between internationally recognized scientific investigators on vaccines against diseases caused by microorganisms. It turned out that Professor Duvier, tied up with the preparation of the annual departmental budget, would not be able to attend the meeting himself and the person most suitable to be his alternate would be Abd. The three-day conference would be held two weeks later at Karolinska Institute. Abd immediately wrote Charmina a short note, announcing his trip. She replied without delay, inviting him to come for dinner at her parents' home one evening during his three-day conference.

On the evening of the second day after his arrival to town, with some trepidation, Abd came to the Larsens' home with a bouquet of pink roses. At the doorsteps, he looked in awe at the massive hinge-decorated antique wooden door. He gently lifted the heavy pewter lion-headed, ring-shaped doorknob and then cautiously let it drop back once. Mrs. Larsen appeared. She greeted him, "Welcome back. Good to see you again, Dr. Abdulai."

Abd handed the bouquet of flowers to her, politely saying, "Thank you for your invitation. I feel very privileged."

Charmina was behind her mother, happy as a lark for seeing her "friend" again. They led him to a large living room lit by a dim antique chandelier light and tastefully decorated with a collection of a dozen Swedish nineteenth-century paintings, each caped with a soft, focusing spotlight. Clean-lined contemporary Danish pieces were accentuated by two reproductions of light-colored upholstered Louis XIV Bergamo chairs, one on each side of the partially shaded double-paneled window. The room was highlighted by a seven-foot Steinway black piano resting on a dark mahogany-colored floor shined, to the point of becoming visually slippery, by the late afternoon sunrays through the side glass door. Greatly impressed by what he saw, the young doctor, who was used to dirt floors and Salvation Army-retrieved type of furniture while still living with his parents in his native land, discreetly took a deep breath in amazement. The contrast was enormous, but Abd held no loathsomeness against the wealthy. He believed in hard work and recompense. Intensive discussion on a variety of subjects was carried out between the two doctors, while Abd's dowsabel was knitting a wool scarf and Mrs. Larsen attentively listened to the two men's conversation while having her eyes motionlessly gazing at the same page of a picture book lying on her lap. At first the dentist still remained somewhat laconic in his expression, but gradually they appeared to enjoy each other's intelligence, general knowledge on scientific subjects, art, literature, music, and especially on worldwide problems the Western civilization was facing. Despite Abd's overwhelming general knowledge, one could not detect any sign of being pedantic or eristic in his conversation. Reading Dr. Larsen's facial expression of contentment at the end of their conversation, Abd deduced that he had surmounted the Larsens' anxiety generated by him since he became Charmina's most affectionate friend. Indeed, the Larsens' fear of a different religious belief and of the possible self-deportation by their daughter through marriage to a poor developing country had dissipated, as Abd intentionally insinuated through carefully selected words that he had chosen to permanently leave Afghanistan to immigrate to a Western European country and that he was recently converted to Catholicism. The only remaining minor obstacle for the Larsens to overcome was how to, agreeably and without local controversial gossip, introduce to their relatives and friends the possibility of having a Middle Eastern man as son-in-law, physically so different from all of them. As a matter of fact, the Larsens resided in the southwest Karolinska suburb among inhabitants believed to be descendants of the Vikings stock. In contrast to Abd's Arabic dark complexion, brown eyes, and curly hair, these Nordic people were tall, blond, with a few of them red, and had blue eyes.

Abd went back to Paris very happy. He continued to exchange love letters weekly with Charmina while conducting daily lab experiments on viral projects.

A couple of months passed. Then without explanation, the correspondence from Charmina started to slow down remarkably. Abd worried but remained patient. One could detect, day after day, a disappointment on his facial expression each time he opened his personal mailbox located in the apartment complex's hallway. One afternoon he unexpectedly received from her a postal package containing a batik painting and this enclosed short note: "You want me to become more mature. So, I have decided to travel to the Far East with 'two of my girlfriends' to visit Professor Yamoshito in Kyoto, Tan Quang and Hon Choi in Taipei, and Kim Park in South Korea. I met these people at Bad Hirschfeld during the crash courses in German. They have invited me and my two classmates to stay at their house during the trip. I am anxious to be exposed to different cultures. You might have met a couple of them. After spending a few months in the Far East, we will be traveling to New Zealand then Australia and will be back in Sweden approximately eighteen months from the start. In order to put to test my love for you, and *vice versa* (?), you are not going to hear from me during my entire trip. Enclosed is a painting I made for your birthday. Sorry! I will not be able to be near you on the occasion. With love, CL."

With his head bent down and held between his two hands, Abd kept reading over and over Charmina's note. He started to imagine all sorts of eventualities that might happen to her during the overseas trip. He was fearful that a nineteen-year-old woman, traveling to unknown territories of foreign countries with two female friends of the same age, might be waiting for all sorts of troubles. He wondered whether he had missed the wonderful opportunity of having for life a gentle and loving companion by indirectly pushing Charmina to take such a drastic measure.

He recalled Charmina's reaction to his realistic fear of the age difference between him and her. This took place in Vienna a few weeks after she started taking courses to become a certified lab technologist. One evening, after a long day of work, while having dinner together at the café across the street from his workplace and familiar to both, Abd suggested that Charmina should get in touch with as many people of her generation as possible in order to be more exposed to realities of life. Charmina, while remaining quiet, attentively listened to his friendly but poignant recommendation, realizing that in his mind she was still immature. Surely his gentle words were taken seriously to heart by the lovely, innocent nineteen-year-old woman who had been very much aware of her friend's concern over their significant age difference. She had told him at least twice that the word *immaturity*, in her simplistic opinion, has only a relative meaning— its level, spanned over a wide spectrum of mental assessment, is made by the more knowledgeable of the two individuals. Nevertheless, the word had been haunting her for days. Depressed, she remained in seclusion in her room for a long weekend, pretending that she was not feeling well. This incident kept recurring in Abd's mind for the rest of that afternoon and subsequent days. Abd spent the rest of the evening admiring the batik painting. He saw in it the expression of freshness, purity mixed with naivety of three young inexperienced female adults extremely vulnerable to the hidden cruelties of this intolerant and nasty world. His heart ached. Kneeling at bedside, he ended the evening with a lengthy prayer for the three traveling ladies and for his family in Bamyan.

Professional success coupled with academic advancement gave Abd the incentive to work harder. He came up with a half dozen new research projects but concentrated mainly on the molecular-level study of chemical receptors and viral attachments at the cell surface. During that period, he often stayed overnight in his office, carrying out complicated experiments. Being alone day after day, Abd developed a bad habit—cigarette smoking, reaching sometimes up to two packs a day. He was convinced that smoking helped him relax and think out new professional ideas and that smoking was less dangerous than drinking.

The image of Charmina continued to haunt him day and night. He admitted to himself that his love for her was immeasurable. Truly he missed her. Realizing, however, that an eighteen-month waiting period is excessively long for a single man of his age of twenty-nine, coupled with the suspended communication imposed by Charmina, and then the absolute uncertainty thereafter, Abd decided to regularly meet new people on Saturday for brunch at the Paris Alliance International Club. His initial intention was to temporarily chisel away from his mind the fear of Charmina facing dangers, waiting for the day of her return. At this meeting place, geared to young people from all over the world, he enjoyed its friendly atmosphere. But it didn't take him too long to pay attention to a young lady from Winterthur, Switzerland. She was a kindergarten teacher who was attending classes in French history and literature at Sorbonne University in Paris. This attractive blond-haired and blue-eyed woman stood out among a dozen females for at least two reasons. Firstly, she tended to be rational in the discussion of a variety of subjects when club members sat down for brunch. She had no difficulty to back up her opinion with published and universally accepted facts that other students, male and female alike, were not familiar with. Secondly, she had an analytical mind that was compatible with Abd's stream of scientific thought. He initiated the one-to-one friendship relation by inviting her to a café grill in the Latin Quarter. They conversed in German "Hochsprach," the standard version of the language, even though she was fluent in French and he could by now write and speak the language with occasional use of borrowed English words. He purposely chose to communicate with her in German for a very simple reason—he wanted to make her feel comfortable when she was in the company of someone who was at ease with the official language she used daily outside of her home. He was hoping that by speaking German, she could translate her relationship with him into that with an imaginative man of her local Swiss region.

One Sunday afternoon, after the brunch at the club, they took a walk along the Seine River, browsing at kiosks of antique books stacked in rows on open shelves leaning against the paint-peeled bricks and mortar waterway wall. She told him that she was hoping to find an old print of the city of Paris as a Christmas present for her parents. Tired from looking at hundreds of these unframed lithographs without finding one that pleased her, he suggested that they get close to the waterfront. Sitting romantically next to each other on a bench a few feet away from the flat-surfaced manmade stone bank, the couple watched the commercial liners, rusty-hulled tramps, and other small vessels passing by at different speeds and often in opposite directions. The heated water surface emitted a dense fog through which everything farther on the opposite riverbank was seen by both as fuzzy undulating objects. Here and there, she mistakenly addressed a few words to him in Zuridütsch (a dialect of her hometown in Canton Zurich) that he could not understand; but they broke out in chocking laughs.

During the next three months, while enjoying each other's companionship at weekly rendezvous at various cafés along the Boulevard de Clignancourt, the kindergarten teacher frequently interested Abd in appreciating French history. Conversely, Abd occasionally explained to her his complicated research work on viruses. They found in each other the intellectualism that frequently associates with highly educated individuals having a postgraduate degree. Abd became gradually interested in her, thinking casually of a long-lasting relationship. However, during these weekend get-togethers, he repeatedly noted that she frequently asked the café grill waitress to bring her, besides the bowl of hot café-au-lait she routinely ordered, a glass of cognac. On one occasion, she consumed up to four glasses of that liquor before she stood up to go home. The observation made brought Abd back to the memories of the violent scenes that took place for years at the home of his drunken neighbor during his childhood in Bamyan. Abd despised any kind of alcohol. One wouldn't have any difficulty to figure out why the relationship between the teacher and Abd abruptly ended that same summer. Abd recovered quickly from the breakup, as his love for Charmina had never left the bottom of his heart.

Winter slowly arrived in Paris. The outdoor air was getting colder at night. Rare snowflakes fell then quickly melted on the parapet of the lab building balcony. The nostalgia for the past ski experience in Mürren last year in company of Charmina invaded all layers of his photographic memory. Alone at his desk after everybody had gone home, often Abd daydreamed. He vividly heard mute words Charmina used to teach him on how to stop and turn and invisibly saw the powdery snow splashing away from the ski each time he placed pressure on one leg. The desire of keeping up with this sport not only helped him relive those pleasant moments of his first visit with the Larsen family but also gave him hope and dreams of feeling that Charmina was closer to him sentimentally, even though she was thousands of miles away, traveling.

He joined a one-week annual ski trip to Chamonix, Mont Blanc, Haute-Savoie, Rhone-Alpes. The tour was organized by the Paris University Alumni Guild. The group of skiers returned to Paris on the latest train of the day. Tired after several skiing days, most of them fell asleep at the repetitive "clunk-clunk" noise of train wheels on tracks. Sitting next to a slender brunette, Abd stayed awake, thinking about his lab experiments for the coming week. Suddenly the young lady, while trying to reposition herself for a nap, inadvertently kicked Abd's right foot. Half asleep, she quickly glanced at him and, with a Nordic accent, apologized. "I am sorry."

"Please be reassured, no harm done."

Abd saw this woman off and on during the past week but, too preoccupied with the image of Charmina when not on the ski slope taking lessons with the instructor Roger, didn't have the opportunity to get acquainted with her even though she seemed to be very much by herself. Now in the train the same person, who happened to be fortuitously sitting next to him, aroused his curiosity. Furthermore, Abd, who believed that etiquette must be part of the interrelation between humans, softly continued, "My name is Abd," while his arm reached out for an introductory handshake.

She jovially smiled. "Maurina, I am delighted."

With occasional loud disturbing snores, the whole group of skiers, taking over almost the entire train compartment, slept through the six-hour train trip. But Maurina and Abd made the exception. Their intense conversation kept them awake all the way to the Gare de Lyon, Paris. They exchanged addresses before Abd stood up and brought down from the overhead racks Maurina's bulky rucksack and her string bag containing her pair of ski boots. They shook hands, saying goodbye.

Three weeks later Abd found in the bulk of official correspondence an odd-size pink envelope with no return address sent to his lab; Maurina invited him to her flat for "a Sunday evening dessert at eight p.m." Abd could barely make out the exact meaning of the letter content in French, the tiny-lettered handwritten note being almost impossible to decipher. On the indicated day and time, Abd arrived on time to an apartment building on Rue Claudet, Paris Quartier Latin. He entered a poorly lit narrow corridor and then found Maurina's surname on one of the multiple occupancy paneled wall-attached mailboxes. He climbed up to the fourth floor on a squeaky old and narrow spiral wooden staircase. With his right fist, he gently knocked at the unit numbered 406.

Maurina, in a dark dress, opened the door. "Glad, you've made it. Thank you for coming."

Handing to her the bottle of Sauvignon Blanc, Abd received a second thank you. Strolling behind his host on a dark floorboard of a short hallway passage, Abd entered a high-ceiling, late nineteenth-century-style plaster molding-ornamented living room. With back facing the chiffon-shaded high and wide windows was a female figure sitting at one end of a brown-leathered love seat. Against the sunlight filtered through the covering, a few semitranslucent hair strands spiked up from her coiffured blond hairdo.

"I want you to meet my roommate, Amelia."

The same female figure, dressed in a light creamy outfit, stood up and then reached out with her right hand, saying at the same time with a typical Scandinavian accent, "Bonjour, monsieur."

"Abdulai Rasulov. Please call me Abd."

"Red or white?" Maurina gazed at the visitor with a smile.

"Either is fine with me."

"Do you have a preference at this time of the day? How about a chilled semidry Pessac-Leognan white of Bordeaux with Camembert and wheat crackers?"

"How did you manage to get it? Pessac-Leognan white is rather very hard to find."

"You seem to be a wine connoisseur."

"Not really. I know a family in Bordeaux, and they love to talk about their wines."

All three sat around a glass-topped table, conversing in French, while savoring the fresh snack and sipping on their glass of the crisp white. Occasionally, and in a very discreet manner, Abd studied Amelia, sweeping his eyes over her entire body at lightning speed. Instantly Charmina's body image reappeared in his mind, but this delightful memory didn't restrain him from getting delicately to know this new acquaintance.

Maurina broke the initial cold atmosphere by reminding Abd about their tiresome night train ride last month. "Have you recovered from the ski trip?"

"Very much so, but it took almost a week before I could climb up to my apartment without having to hold on the staircase railing. You know what I mean, and how about you?"

"It was my third ski trip this winter, so it wasn't too arduous for me."

Amelia cautiously engaged in the conversation, with her smiling eyes often directed to Maurina, as though she was repeatedly looking for an affirmation from her roommate.

Abd mentally registered this observation, which would eventually turn out to be of significance in the coming years. There was no doubt in Abd's mind. Amelia had a typical Germanic clean-looking feature, was pleasant, but rather somewhat reserved and definitely shy. In contrast, Maurina was more outgoing and more talkative. The chat between the three went on until the flickering points of light from the city houses could be seen at a distance in the early evening hours through the narrow coverless side window. Maurina was about to open another bottle precisely at the moment when Abd stood up, ready to leave.

His pleasant visit with the couple had shed some light on who they were and what they were doing in Paris. Maurina was born and lived in Karolinska, and her father was a professor in radiology. Amelia was originally from Stockholm and had been living alone with her mother since the age of fourteen. Recently she found work at Karolinska University Hospitals, where she met Maurina. They became close friends who shared a large apartment facing the bend of the noisy city street cable car and being only a couple of blocks away from their working place. Both were registered nurses and worked in the hospital medical ward. Two months earlier, they decided to take a six-month course in advanced geriatric nursing given at the Hospital Hotel-Dieu de Paris. During the midterm one-week break of the study course, Amelia returned for a visit with her divorced mother in Stockholm, while Maurina had planned to take a trip with her Swedish high school classmate Marie, who was engaged to marry an Italian medical doctor in specialty training at the University Hospital of Strasbourg, France.

Marie suggested that Maurina invite Abd to come along with them for the two-week camping trip to the southern French region of Provence. It was late July in Paris. The temperature reached ninety-five degrees Fahrenheit. French people go on their five-week vacation at this time of the year. The city, as usual, was deserted. Tired from months on end working, Abd also needed a break, so he accepted to share the trip by car with the ladies as their "guardian," so to speak. On their way going south, they made several stops during the day, visiting historic French Revolution artifacts and pre-Roman ruins. They camped along the Rhone River at night. Abd helped the ladies dress the tent and did man's jobs like carrying water from the river or starting the fire for cooking.

All three got along very well, inside as well as outside of Marie's brand-new Volkswagen. They stopped in Nimes on the fifth day and spent the entire week sightseeing the well-preserved Roman Amphitheater, the famous aqueduct Pont du Gard, the Roman temple Maison Carree, and the style-mixed Romanesque-Gothic Cathedral. Side by side, they repeatedly stopped in the middle of the narrow copper-stone-paved, car-forbidden, busy streets of the old part of the town, searching for traces of past cultures while reading information out of the marked pages of Marie's tourism book. Maurina slowly became impressed with the gentlemanliness Abd exhibited. She noted the devotion and reverence Abd expressed from the moment he opened the heavy, squeaky cathedral front entrance door to let her and Marie in, until they descended the worn-out granite steps, leaving the religious monument. Marie continued to read page after page from her book, persevering in the history of Nimes. Occasionally she boasted of her boyfriend's international medical training experience and his manly manner. Meanwhile, Maurina verbally engaged in incessant intense discussions on matters dealing with arts, cultures, religion, and occasionally profession with Abd. She became affectionate to him, and he found her rather interesting to talk to. However, the observation Abd had made on Amelia's repeated rapid glances at Maurina during his past visit to apartment no. 406, rue Claudet, alerted him and prevented him from getting "burned" by a decent-looking, passably intelligent but somewhat domineering lady.

One Sunday afternoon of the same month of August, Maurina came alone to Abd's apartment. She gently knocked at the door of Abd's apartment without advance notice. Abd got up from his couch, still half asleep, running to the door. "Bonjour, Maurina. Good to see you. Please come in."

"Would you like to take a walk in the park Foret de Senart? It is beautiful outside."

"Sure." Abd took a couple of seconds to reply.

They descended onto the almost deserted street and then took the metro to the entry of the park. The clean and calm air of the silent forest was occasionally awakened by a short breath of the northwest face-caressing breeze. Strolling side by side with their heads bent and their eyes sweeping the dirt path tramped hard by generations of promenaders, both were absorbed into their intensive conversations, paying no attention to their surroundings. Occasionally Maurina darted a sinless glance at the face of the young and handsome doctor. A relaxing stillness stretched out over the entire region, as though Paris was in the middle of a resting siesta. Suddenly a red-faced man with an unbuttoned dirt-spotted white shirt jumped out from behind a thick shrub to a few feet in front of the couple, waving an opened switchblade at them. His repugnant alcohol-smelling breath polluted the clean air. His violent intension could be readily detected in his bloodshot eyes. He kept steadily advancing toward Maurina. Abd immediately stretched out his left arm, signaling her to stop walking, and then quickly moved his body forward, placing his back against her chest, keeping his eyes fixed on the approaching perpetrator while rolling his Leica camera shoulder strap around his right wrist, ready in position to defend her at any cost.

Just at this fleeting moment appeared a six-foot-tall bearded and muscular jogger with one dumbbell in each hand. He stopped and stood next to Abd, staring at the perpetrator, facing him. "What's the matter?"

The latter quickly turned around and then took off, running as fast as he could. Maurina and Abd thanked the athlete and then walked back to town, frightened and shaken by the incident. Subsequently, each time she saw Abd, Maurina praised him for his courage and self-sacrifice in order to protect someone else in imminent danger.

Even though Abd found Maurina interesting to talk to, he realized, after running into her a few more times at Paris Alliance International Club, that there was no chemistry between them. Moreover, he found her a little too assertive for his taste. In the meantime, Abd's attention had been directing progressively toward Amelia. He saw her twice at the hospital cafeteria at lunchtime without the presence of Maurina, feeling somewhat uneasy. However, during a casual conversation, Abd learned that Amelia's roommate had been writing back and forth to a college classmate of her brother presently in banking internship in Montreal, Canada. During the subsequent few weeks, Amelia and Abd saw each other during the weekend either at the club or at one of many cafés along the busy Boulevard de Clignancourt.

They fell in love quickly despite Amelia's revelation of her turmoil-laden childhood and her ongoing difficult relationship within a year with two successive doctors doing their postdoctoral fellowship at the hospital's fifty-bed medical ward. As a matter of fact, Amelia dated first with an internist. He was a decade and a half older than her and still lived at home with his mother. She confided to Abd that this bald and tall man was too settled in his advanced-age bachelordom. Too often he brought into their conversation the image of his "wonderful" mother, and this irritated her. Amelia's relationship with this nettlesome individual lasted only four months. She broke up with her second boyfriend and was still suffering from his abrupt rejection a few weeks before she met Abd for the first time. Abd happened to know this man. He was Abd's classmate at the University of Oxford. This Briton was a studious student who had to struggle unfortunately with his back problem for at least a good part of his years in medical school. The story goes like this. After he graduated from Oxford, this young doctor had undergone two major surgical operations on his back afflicted with a congenital lower lumbar vertebrae disease called *spondylolisthesis*. Miraculously, he recovered very well from the ailment and ended up a year later at Karolinska University Hospitals for his specialty training in psychology, where he met Amelia. This man was quite polite and courteous in his manner. His intelligent conversations on a variety of subjects beside medical topics impressed Amelia from the first day when he invited her for supper at a nearby restaurant then walked her home, a couple blocks from the hospital complex. This charming young and handsome doctor's preference for the rendezvous place was at the movie theater fifteen minutes' walking distance from Amelia's flat. Strangely, he instructed her on several occasions, and each time, while she was still at her medical ward nursing desk, to arrive about ten minutes before the show and to sit in the middle of the back row with her handbag occupying the very next seat. As soon as all the ceiling lights were turned off and noisy ads began, he came in and sat next to her. At the end of the session, they kissed goodbye, not knowing what had been all about on the screen during the entire show. She left the theater by the south entrance, and he exited it on the north side. While still actively dating him, one evening in the company of Maurina at one of the three upper-scale Thai restaurants in the city, Amelia fortuitously saw this same man walking in with a smiling flirting brunette. Subsequently she had no further movie theater rendezvous with him. She realized and Maurina agreed that he was a womanizing doctor.

Paris was entering rapidly into the fall season mood. The windows of shops along the Champs-Élysées Boulevard were decorated with colorful stone maple leaves, assorted gourds, and signs reading "Late Summer Sale." With her left arm around Abd's torso and her head resting on his right shoulder, Amelia was strolling along half a dozen ladies' clothing boutiques, window shopping in company of her new friend. "I am a city girl who can appreciate these beautiful and elegant winter coats." She pointed her finger to an artfully window-displayed dark-blue cashmere coat, smiling. The words *city girl*, for some reason, resonated in Abd's mind for a long time; and yet Abd was not quite sure at the time why she had to use them in his company.

In less than three weeks, Amelia and Maurina would be finishing their course in nursing and returning to Sweden. Due to his workload, Abd saw Amelia only a couple more times after work at her apartment and each time in the presence of Maurina. He didn't spend enough time alone with Amelia to know her better before she left Paris. Why Abd, a man with ample life experiences, succumbed so quickly to Amelia's charm remains to be elaborated in the subsequent chapters. He wrote and recorded his feeling about that determining period of his life in extensive details; all of this was later, posthumously, found in the inside pocket of his memoir book.

CHAPTER EIGHT

Looming Difficult Lifetime Decisions That Surely Shaped Up His Unhappiness

I t was early September. Paris was wet and cold with a misty rain. Staring at the dusk-faint stars appearing occasionally from behind thick low clouds hovering over the city seventeenth ward, Abd regularly puffed at his cigarette clumsily held

between two fingers. While concentrating his thoughts on how to clearly present the research results on his manuscript to be submitted the following week for review by the French Academy of Sciences, he was suddenly awakened by a noisy commotion. A dozen neighbor offices' employees were bending forward to help the mailman pick up scattered mail spreading all over several steps of the staircase leading to the concrete floor below. Apparently, the two-wheeled post office cart hit a railing corner post, spilling almost its entire contents. Abd participated in the gathering of the spill and then quietly went back to his desk, resuming his work on the manuscript. Half an hour later, the same mailman handed to him the mail of the day. Among a few official envelopes addressed to Prof. Dr. Duvier, there was a Swedish-stamped bluish one addressed to "Docteur Abdulai Rasulov," with the lab address in cursive handwriting. Before inserting the letter opener to open the envelope, Abd was bewildered, wondering who might be the sender. But instantly he realized that the sender had to be Amelia, as she had never come to his apartment and that she had only met him a few times at the hospital cafeteria and on rendezvous with him at the cafés on Boulevard de Clignancourt. With a facial expression of apprehension reflected in his dark-brown eyes, Abd glanced first at the bottom of the enclosed cheerful and friendly note. The diminutive "Melie" ending the short letter confirmed Abd's suspicion. During the entire afternoon of that day, he was distracted by the disputatious thoughts about his private life. He couldn't concentrate on the proofread of the last paragraph of the manuscript. So he decided to go home earlier than usual, a few minutes after 5:00 p.m. After squeezing himself into the tightly packed Paris subway, comparable to the sardines laid in the can, Abd's mind was wandering between the image of two women, paying no attention to the exchanges of angry shouts between tired and exhausted commuters.

After quickly swallowing a few spoons of yogurt, Abd stretched out on his couch, going over once again Amelia's note. He abruptly got up, went to his desk, and pulled out from the bottom of the drawer the laminated infographic sheet he found in a Paris bookstore last November. For some reason, Abd had been for years very fond of graphology. He spent a good thirty minutes analyzing Amelia's handwritten single letters, syllables, and words, using the laminated printed sheet of graphologist's interpretation. He suspected that Amelia's personality was the amalgam of distinguishable character traits of a person who was people-oriented, outgoing, attention-loving, uncomplicated, but somewhat naive and behaviorally dependent and submissive. Abd placed Amelia's delicately perfumed note on his chest after reading it at least three times, vaguely staring into the emptiness of the space below the room ceiling, as though he was dreaming. Not able to rid himself of the conflicting images of Charmina and Amelia from his thoughts, restlessly Abd got up, grabbed his thick fall coat, and then descended into the poorly lit narrow street leading to the Seine River. He sat down on an empty metal bench chained to a concrete block, facing the waterway. He started to reason with himself. He was a man of principle. His decision was based on principle rather than expediency. Here are a couple of examples. In the lab, quantitative test results differing of less than one standard deviation were not good enough for him and therefore not acceptable for publication. He was very meticulous with everything he did. To arrive at an accurate diagnosis of the disease affecting his patient, Abd started to take a detailed history of past illnesses, the medical family history, and the present illness. Then a thorough physical examination followed. These steps provided him with information that must match well with the patient's lab results before he entertained the accuracy of his diagnosis. These personal characteristics made Abd occasionally at odds with his colleagues' opinions as well as with his choice of life mate. Often, he asked himself whether these characteristics on top of his strong religious faith and his intellectualism could make his life more complicated in the eyes of an individual of average intelligence.

Charmina had not been heard from for over a year, but he didn't want to bother calling or writing to her parents for an undefined reason to himself. Possibly he was afraid to learn of the news he didn't want to hear. But the image of a gentle, quiet, soft-spoken young female with a physical beauty kept haunting him. However, the thought of having to wait for an unknown timeline until the return of Charmina on one hand and his yearning for having a wife and a couple of above-average intelligent children at his age of thirty-one on the other made him extremely ambivalent. He was facing a real dilemma—the choice between a physical beauty with an average intelligence or a much more perspicacious mind but with a less attractive appearance. He flew twice to Stockholm to visit with Amelia during the next three months. He took the latest flight out on Friday afternoon to hop the earliest flight back to Paris on Monday morning. Intentionally, Abd made several attempts to dig into her background while dining at the restaurant or at her apartment she was sharing with Maurina. Amelia didn't seem to volunteer much information on this aspect, which somewhat bewildered him; but Abd fairly fast succumbed to her intelligence, her general knowledge, and her devotion to the nursing profession. He tried to convince himself that Amelia had all qualities to make her a perfect wife and an exceptional mother.

During the two weekend visits, and once back to the hotel after spending time with Amelia, Abd continued to give serious thoughts about the unique relationship he had with Charmina in Bad Hirschfeld then in Vienna. He dreamed of the delightful moments he spent with her alone or in the presence of her parents. The memories of his very first steps on the wooden skis in the company of Charmina and of their visit to the old Wengen Catholic church kept coming back every time he tried to close his eyes to sleep. Undoubtedly, Abd must have gone through a terrible time for at least three months, dividing his love between two ladies, each having her own merits. "I wish I had a dual heart," Abd wrote in bold characters on the header of page 189 of his memoir notebook found posthumously.

After much self-debate for days and perhaps weeks on the choice of the right life mate, Abd decided to concentrate on getting to know more about Amelia's past through frequent exchanges of letters with her and occasional long-distance phone calls on weekends. Delicately but deliberately, he repeatedly tried to learn more about her childhood. Eventually she revealed to him her most difficult years of her life. Right after the WWII had ended, her father, Wilhelm, deserted Amelia's mother and her and then moved from Orleans to the outskirt of Bordeaux, France, where he was hired as a desk clerk at an internationally known winery. Amelia's mother worked as an interpreter for the German occupation army in France during the war. Half German and half Swedish, she was very fluent in both German and English. Once the war was over and the German army surrendered to the Allied forces, she was jailed by the American troops, for unclear reasons to Amelia, then only eleven years old. Amelia was brought back to Sweden to live with a paternal aunt who was, apparently, very insensitive to her need of love and affection the little and thin blond girl badly deserved after her parents' divorce and permanent separation. "Amelia still sobbed bitterly when she recounted her preteen years," Abd wrote and underlined this sentence at the bottom of page 183 of his memoir notebook. Abd became deeply moved by subsequent sad details of Amelia's youth. She related to him the few long years of infantile regression with embarrassing psychosomatic symptoms.

The last of two weekend rendezvous with her at Stockholm King's Garden in the fall of that year was not at all joyful. With her head resting on Abd's shoulder and his right arm circling her upper torso, both remained side by side for hours on a deserted bench hidden behind a hedge, peering at the city Lutheran church's copper-covered steeple without uttering a single word. Episodes of silence lasting for several minutes were occasionally interrupted by Amelia's sobs. At the Stockholm airport departure gate, Amelia had a hard time to let her date pass his check-in point. In the airplane going back to Paris, Abd couldn't fall asleep as usual. His mind was preoccupied over and over by the same question: Should he marry her, or should he continue to wait for sign of Charmina?

Back in his lab, Abd tried to hide his dilemma by being very quiet for days on end; but Professor Duvier and lab personnel were fully aware of the doctor's unusual state of mind. To keep his personal matters as private as possible, Abd decided to take ten days out of his four-week annual vacation after he had a short meeting with his boss.

During the subsequent years of marriage difficulty, Abd frequently asked himself whether the period preceding the engagement was too short, not enough time to know Amelia, and whether his pity for her was mistakenly taken as a real love. He realized that this mistake had cost him a happy conjugal life that he had been wishing for from the early years of medical school. As a matter of fact, he had been dreaming of starting a family with a loving wife and a couple of bright children after completing his fellowship in internal medicine in the UK. This natural and old-fashioned thinking of being the sole breadwinner in a small but happy family in which the equally important role of the mother who looks after the children when they still live at home resonated in his mind ever since.

This dream was further reinforced on a summer Saturday when Abd was traveling by motorbike with Dr. Kuchenthaler, an assistant in microbiology at the Vienna Hygiene Institute on Grabengasse Street. Both were about the same age and were still single. They became good friends a couple of weeks after Abd arrived in this gorgeous cosmopolitan city in October 1952. On that day, just a fortnight before Charmina was spotted in the late afternoon in front of the institute, they drove to Amstetten, a small but quaint town west to Vienna, to visit the family of Dr. Kuchenthaler's brother. Abd was pleasantly received by the young couple whose three-year-old daughter was adorable and the centerpiece of an interesting conversation on childrearing in many parts of the world. The memory of that afternoon's visit induced Abd to yearn for such a delightful small family with no more than a couple of healthy, bright, and loving children. But his indulgence in daydreams of an exemplary family nucleus interspersed with his worry about the possibility that the Western noncommunist society might be influenced by the decree of the Soviet Russia Council of People's Commissars issued on December 18, 1917, enabling women of the proletarian class to easily divorce their husband with an uncouth behavior by mutual agreement.[1] This thought came to his mind when he realized that the difference of culture between him and a European woman is real, even though both have the same religious and the same moral values.

The phase extending from infancy to preteen years, despite repeated bouts of childhood diseases then scholastic setback, has proven to be a model of family harmony that had deeply influenced Abd's thinking during his entire adulthood. The mutual respect and love, based on the Buddhist principles, between his parents was unsurpassed. His subsequent exposure to the Osgoods' solid Christian foundation further reinforced his belief in the unsolicited, peaceful deity influence on mankind.

Winter had returned to Paris earlier than usual that year. White flakes of snow cemented to the scattered frozen orange-red maple leaves on both sides of Luxembourg Garden walkways. The secretary and lab personnel came to work in the morning heavily bundled up. For weeks, Abd had been feeling lonely in his apartment after long working hours in his lab. Here and there he received letters from members of his family, but there was no sign of Charmina. He continued to regularly attend Sunday masses. Then on December 5 arrived from Winterthur a card from the German Swiss lady he met at the Paris Alliance International Club announcing her wedding to a recently installed principal of her neighboring town high school. A vague feeling of being "rejected" haunted him day after day. The lack of concentration gradually affected his research work. Lab experiments had not been too successful, and recorded results were meaningless or at best scientifically contradicting. It was the first time in his life that Abd felt depressed. He continued to cherish Charmina's memory. Alone in his apartment, Abd frequently stared at the candleholder standing on his work desk, which she gave him when she was taking courses in Vienna, dreaming of her gentleness, of her beautiful body with all the charm and attractiveness of youth; but she was not around to give him moral support and to enliven him.

In the summer of that year Abd received from his mother a letter insinuating that he should start to think about having a family himself, as traditionally Afghan men get married before twenty. At this crossroads, Abd had to make a serious decision that would permanently affect his life. He opted to reject the idea of waiting for Charmina.

The gusty northwest wind and torrential rain flapped forcefully the large glass windowpanes of his apartment that evening. The telephone connection with Stockholm was interrupted at least three times while he was talking to Amelia. Due to the noisy outdoor deluge interfering with the reception of telephone signals, Abd wasn't sure that Amelia had gotten the message that he was coming to see her in the next few days. He arrived six days later to Amelia's apartment. Maurina was out that evening with her boyfriend who had just returned from Montreal, Canada. Amelia was not able to hide her emotion when quietly Abd slid the engagement ring onto her left hand. The wedding date was set for June 18. Abd discussed with his fiancée about the invitation list of her relatives and friends. Both agreed that the wedding formality should be kept as simple as possible. On the side of his family, only Ali would be attending. Aamir, studying engineering in Germany, frequently in disagreement with Abd over unimportant family issues, had no interest in witnessing his brother's marriage ceremony. When Abd asked Amelia how to make an announcement of their engagement, she became quite embarrassed; and then she wept on his shoulder: "My mother doesn't want me to marry a non-Swedish man." Abd was not surprised at all, as he had found his future mother-in-law rather cold and somewhat domineering over her daughter when he met her for the first time three weeks earlier at her country home located on the west bank of Lake Malaren. A few days after returning to Paris, he wrote a very nice note to Amelia's mother, Margaret. Nobody but his mother and his siblings knew that he was engaged.

It was 4:05 p.m. Abd was sitting in front of the Zeiss microscope examining the monolayer tissue culture tubes under low-power lenses. Suddenly Dr. Duvier's secretary hurriedly came to Abd's room, stepped to his desk, leaning to his ear. "A lady with a Nordic accent wishes to talk to you. I will transfer the call to your extension if you wish to take it."

"Thank you, please switch it to my extension."

Abd got up quickly, walked to the door, closed it behind him, walked back to his desk, and then picked up the combined transmitter-receiver handset from a rotary-dialed black desk phone. He listened to the female voice for less than a minute without uttering a single word, and then with his regard cautiously sweeping across the glass wall panel, he discretely gave his home phone number to the person at the other end. "After 5:30."

Hurriedly, Abd left the workplace earlier that afternoon. The metro train was not quite crowded at that time. He got off at Gare Saint-Denis and ran to its spacious public waiting room already crowded with commuters. Upon his appearance at the main entrance, Charmina darted across the room to stop right in front of him while his eyes were still sweeping the rows of benches facing the two ticket counters. She tightly embraced him. The memory of the wonderful time she had with him in Vienna, then subsequently in Wengen, lit up her eyes for a fleeting moment; but then tears started instantly running down her cheeks, as though her expression of persisting love for him was not enthusiastically reciprocated. Walking side by side with his right arm circling her waist, they silently strolled back to the metro platform, heading for Abd's apartment at 29 rue Gregoire de Tour, arrondissement 11, Paris. She stopped a few times to dry her tears with the embroidered handkerchief he gave her on her twentieth birthday. Feeling guilty, he hesitantly asked her, "Where have you been during the last eighteen months, and why didn't you try to get in touch with me?"

"Likewise, why didn't you contact my parents if you had truly been thinking of me? Remember, I had explained to you that you wouldn't hear from me during my overseas trip, as I always believe that a long silence between two persons who love each other and want to become lifelong partners is the real test that both have to pass. I returned from my trip over two months ago and have been working at the Lille University Hospital's main lab. My parents and I have been trying to find your whereabouts for months through phone calls to several universities in France and letters to persons my mother knew during the later years of my grandfather's diplomatic career. We made several attempts, but it was in vain."

She admitted to him that her seven-by-five-centimeter green-covered address notebook somehow disappeared while she was in Seoul; and unfortunately, she could neither remember the name of the professor who had offered him an academic job somewhere in France nor the name of the institution Abd was associated with. Then she proceeded to say, "Last Sunday night, the word *virology* suddenly popped up in my mind and woke me up, vaguely bringing back the memory of your research work in the field of microbiology at Karolinska Medical School, and that you were returning to permanently live and work in France once your cooperative research project there was completed. The next morning, I telephoned the Paris School of Medicine, Section of Medical Research. With some luck, my call was transferred to your lab, and I was told that you were to return from your vacation on Tuesday."

While glancing occasionally at Abd's face, Charmina chronologically recounted all experiences she had lived through during her long but interesting world tour in the company of her three school classmates. She related to Abd that she had managed to visit all Bad Hirschfeld friends who had invited them except Dr. Yamoshito, who was on honeymoon with his newlywed second wife when the four European ladies arrived in town. Just by watching Abd's facial expression, she realized that he was not listening and appeared to be disengaged. This observation further brought tears to her eyes.

From the moment when Abd picked Charmina up until they got off the metro, Abd indeed was quiet most of the time. He felt guilty and embarrassed for having changed his heart. He didn't know how to reveal the truth to Charmina without causing her pain and disappointment. Facing Charmina across the table at the nearby café for supper, before they walked to Abd's apartment, he finally took the courage to say to her, "Charmina, you are going to hate me from now on. I am deeply sorry for taking a wrong turn at the most important crossroads of my life. The long silence during your long eighteen-month travel on one hand and the realization of the big difference of age between us on the other had eventually convinced me that it might not be wise for you and me to become partners for life. Then slowly I started to imagine that likely you had found a much younger and handsome lad and wanted to unilaterally sever your relationship with me. The turn I took at that very first crossroad of my life had led me to a new sentimental and emotional territory, but while facing you now, my heart is aching, simply because I cannot lie to myself: I still love you. I know, you think that I am a liar. I accept whatever you think about me without reticence. Can you forgive me?"

"Abd, please stop. I now know for sure the truth. There is no need to elaborate further. Honestly, I was convinced that you had wanted me to become more mature if I could take a several-month trip 'to see the world,' so to speak." Charmina sobbed; then she got up from the table and walked away from it, hiding her tearful eyes. Abd took a deep sigh, gazing at her familiar faintly curly long brown hair tuffs that partially hid the bra's back straps outlined through the same chiffon she wore two years ago.

That same night, Abd tossed and turned in his sleeping bag on the carpeted floor of his flat while Charmina silently sobbed all night long lying on the apartment's only double bed, not able to close her eyes. He tried to comfort her by saying repeatedly, "I am truly very sorry," while handing to her the tissue box.

The next morning, she quietly got out of bed before dawn when the Latin Quarter was still in a deep sleep. She returned from the bathroom with her hair presentably combed, but her face was puffy with swollen, inflamed eyelids. He handed to her a cup of coffee he hastily prepared. She shook her head, refusing to drink, while she austerely looked in his eyes, sniffling. "Why don't you want to admit to me that you are dating another girl?"

"Truly I am not dating anybody."

"So why are you so strange and cold to me?"

"As I alluded to last night, I was patiently waiting to receive at least a few words from you six months after your departure from Sweden, then many more months had passed and I still had no idea where you had been while traveling. After long working hours at the lab, I reluctantly came home, in this too quiet apartment, afraid to be lonely, longing for you. I stared for hours on end at the very first symbol of our reciprocal feeling: your handmade candle holder on that table next to where you are standing and alternatively at the framed batik you made for me almost two years ago. This was—and still remains so—the sole consolation I had while you were hundreds of thousands of kilometers away." Abd hesitated to continue further. Charmina noted his somber facial expression as he gazed at a fixed area on the wooden floor.

"Go on!" Charmina insisted.

"Eight months ago, the nurse who had regularly brought blood specimens to our lab for analysis while I was working at Karolinska University Hospital, to my surprise, dropped in to pay me a visit at the lab. Her name is Amelia. She was visiting her cousin who took a semester of French literature at Sorbonne. As a courtesy, I took her out for lunch. At the time, I thought it was just a casual visit from someone I happened to know professionally and didn't make anything out of that visit. Three days later, coincidentally I heard someone calling my name as I was taking a shortcut passage through the Luxemburg Garden. I looked up. Here she was, just about four to five meters away, facing me. Then we started to exchange letters, and I made two visits to Karolinska to visit her family."

"So, I presume you are engaged."

"Yes!"

Not uttering another word, Charmina put on her London fog beige coat, gave Abd a weak handshake, and then walked to the door. Abd quickly grabbed his blazer hung near the entrance and ran after her. They walked to the metro entrance in silence, boarded the half-empty car, and then sat down next to each other. Charmina, with her eyes half closed and a sad facial expression, let Abd gently squeeze her left hand all the way to Gare Saint-Denis, where she caught the direct train to Lille. They bid a somber farewell on the train platform. That was the last time they saw each other; but their reciprocal friendly feeling remained for many years after she got married and lived in a faraway land with "plenty of orange fruits."

Abd's wedding to Amelia took place in a small Anglican chapel located just a few miles in the southwest suburb of Karolinska, less than three months after his very first visit. Ali came early to privately congratulate his brother. A meager attendance was noted. Amelia's mother, whom Abd had met only once, came with her boyfriend, a wealthy Swedish industrialist whose wife was placed in a luxury nursing home for advanced Alzheimer's disease. Mrs. Osgood and her son David of Oxford, as well as former classmate John Campbell, were present at the solemn church service. There was no fanfare at the wedding ceremony. After the brief reception under a tent in the chapel garden, the attendees dispersed into various directions. Amelia and Abd got into a rented Volkswagen heading for their honeymoon in Bergen, Germany.

The life with a new wife started out peacefully and reasonably harmonious just like most newlywed young couples did. They rented a two-bedroom apartment not far from the previous studio at rue Gregoir de Tour. Amelia found a nursing job in a clinic owned by a private corporation, and Abd continued to exercise his profession as a pediatrician-internist in-house physician while assuming the medical student teaching and virology research at the same time. He was fully absorbed in his academic career. Often, he returned to the lab in the middle of the night to read and record the result of his research experiments. Dr. Duvier was very pleased with their joint publications in reputable medical periodicals. Amelia didn't seem to mind about Abd's long working hours at the hospital. When being alone at home, she occupied herself with letter writing or knitting while listening to classical music on the radio. They couldn't afford to have a black-and-white television set. Being also in the medical field, Amelia tolerated fairly well the busy professional life of her husband as a doctor. She was herself a very dedicated nurse. Often, after spending extra unpaid time with patients at the clinic, she came home late from work. Neither one of the couple seemed to object to the lack of free time for intimacy.

Then an official letter came one Wednesday afternoon from the teaching University of Saint Mathieu Hospital located in the north-east section of the French capital. This news arrived two days after the couple's first wedding anniversary. Abd was offered the position of assistant professor with a much better salary that would be hard for him to turn down. Constrained by budget limitations, Professor Duvier was not able to match the newly proposed salary. Abd took the offer, but because his professional as well as personal relationship with the latter had been impeccable, both decided to maintain the same research cooperation in virology between the two university hospitals. Amelia and her husband moved to Le Pré-Saint-Gervais where they had found a two-bedroom apartment overlooking a quiet little city park. They had just only a few pieces of furniture—a used couch they bought from the former renter, a card table with folding legs given to them by the nearby church as dining table, and two wine-bottle-shipping cases they retrieved from the local open market as seats. The couple willingly accepted this temporary Bohemian way of life. After their second wedding anniversary, they agreed on start-ing a family. Emal was born at term with curly reddish hair eleven months later. He sat alone without support at five months and made his first step alone at eleven months outside of the apartment and under the neighbors' friendly watching eyes.

At the new institution, Abd remained very active academically. He assumed once again the same teaching responsibility and medical consultant role while continuing with research interest in the isolation and growing of viruses affecting human's respiratory system. Amelia worked at the same hospital as an instructor in nursing. The only moment the couple managed to spend some free time together was on Sunday afternoon. Three and a half years later, another son was born from the couple. This one was slightly smaller than his brother. As soon as his head emerged from the womb, he opened his eyes and looked around, smiling to the delivering obstetrician. They named him Yasir. Mother and son were discharged from the hospital on the second day uneventfully. Abd took a week off from work to help Amelia in caring for the two boys. He sensed that God had finally given him a dreamed family nucleus he was hoping for. The next three years were very productive for Abd academically. He was made the director of the university hospital microbiology department. The French Academy of Sciences recruited Abd as "scientific critic" to evaluate annual university grant applications for research on microorganisms causing human diseases, as he had become one of the youngest authoritative investigators in virology at the time. His reputation within the academic medical circle made him a regular guest lecturer in many European and North American medical schools. Abd was at the peak of his medical research career, and he was very proud of his accomplishment. At the end of his third year at the University of Saint Mathieu Hospital, Abd was promoted to the level of associate professor and received a tenure-track with a salary guaranteed for life.

Emal and Yasir, now respectively three years and four months old, were growing and disease-free except for the occasional common cold in winter. Amelia and Abd decided that the children should be totally looked after and cared for by their mother 24-7 and not by a hired helper. Daycare centers were then practically nonexistent. On sunny days Amelia took the boys to the park for a one-hour walk. She stopped occasionally to talk to neighbors strolling crisscross park alleys. Amelia seemed to have taken the role of wife and mother with pride and dignity. Except for out-of-town trips for medical meetings or as a guest lecturer, Abd managed to find time for intimacy with his wife. The family life was harmonious and his academic career proficient during the next two and half years, but it was about to change.

Abd came home one Friday evening later than usual as he had to read and record the results of a couple of research experiments before the weekend. He called his wife to let her know that he would be late coming home. He opened and then quietly entered the apartment door at around eleven that evening. He hastily swallowed the dish of food Amelia kept for him after she prepared the boys for bedtime, then he took a shower and then tiptoed to the queen-size bed, where Amelia was in the third stage of her deep REM sleep. The unusual outcome of one experiment kept Abd awake for at least another hour. Then he was awakened by the commotion that took place outside around six in the morning. He opened the window looking over the park and saw a large crowd listening to a man shouting on a bull-horn. It turned out to be the beginning of the social unrest created by the public demand for better living conditions, i.e., higher salary but reduced work hours and longer annual vacation. The French government could not come up with a solution to quickly fix the weak postwar economy. The Socialist Party and the Russian-influenced Communist Party represented by blue-collar workers and university students took to the streets in several French cities protesting against the government. As a result of the general population mistrust, the French government changed its prime minister and its cabinet members two to three times a year during that period. Frequent clashes between police and demonstrators took place in many French cities but especially in the French capital. The labor union kept public city transportation, made up of buses and subways, standstill for days.[2,3] The economy of France was experiencing a rapid decline due to repeated lengthy strikes. For over a week, Abd had to walk home from his office at the end of the day, taking detours to avoid rampageous destruction of stores by looters, burning cars, flying Molotov cocktails, flaming tires, and furniture as barricades. Schools were closed for days, and universities were opened but unattended. A good number of Frenchmen feared a second national revolution. It was not exactly the kind of political atmosphere in which Amelia and Abd wish to bring up the two boys. They had to find another country or perhaps another region somewhere in the southwest of France where Emal could go to kindergarten peacefully the next year. Patiently, the couple started to pay a great deal of attention to daily events reported on the French national radio station and in the *Le Monde* newspaper. Abd could easily get a job in Sweden, and that alternative would make Amelia very happy; but this idea was quickly discarded because Abd didn't want to start learning another language, adopt another culture, and integrate into a society much less cosmopolitan at the time. They decided to wait it out for a few more months, up to a year, to see whether a more stable government more acceptable to the population would be installed.

Summer came. People went to the countryside on vacation. The political unrest was temporarily on hold in many cities, but especially in the capital. Abd and his family of four also prepared to take a holiday trip by car to the region "des Pyrenees" in the southwest part of the country. They had never been there. Tenting in public camp-grounds was very popular for the French middle-class folks. A tent to sleep six campers was brought home by Abd one afternoon from an army surplus store. He opened its huge green bag and showed it to Amelia. Emal was all excited seeing the "movable home," as he coined it. The next Friday the whole family was on the road. Amelia wanted to make a detour to the Upper and Lower Normandy regions, as they were entertaining the idea of a possible move away from Paris. Abd agreed, and they decided to drive through Caen, Rennes, Nantes, La Rochelle, Bordeaux, Biarritz, and Bayonne, as neither husband nor wife had visited the French Basque region. They made several stops along the way, searching for camping grounds near streams or rivers. It took almost three quarters of an hour every day for the couple to dress the tent. The three-year-old Emal ran around at the camp-ing site, carrying light tools to assist his parents while Yasir, barely nine months, was kept in his foldable carriage covered by an insect net and topped by an umbrella to keep his tender skin from being burned by the blistering sun of Southern France. Abd helped Amelia feed the baby while his wife prepared dinner on a public charcoal grill. After dinner, Abd played ball or read children storybooks with

Emal. Quite often, he went fishing with his son, trying to teach the boy how to hook worms and catch, if lucky enough, a few native brook trout.

Abd's family arrived on day 11 to a little town named Foxeline in Midi-Pyrenees. As they drove into town, a huge banner hung over the main and its only street with an inscription in bold letters, "Our town is recruiting medical doctors," attracted the attention of Abd and Amelia. Curious about the real meaning of the sign, they stopped by at the mayor's office and got the following information.

The entire town had a core population of four thousand, but it could swell up to an additional 15 percent with winter sports vacationers. The town inhabitants depended on the paper industry all year round for living. There was a twenty-five-bed neatly kept hospital, and it was run by only three aging general practitioners (GPs). The townspeople had been trying for years to recruit younger GPs, a general surgeon, a pediatrician, and an internist, but so far, they were still unsuccessful. The town clerk related to Abd that there had been many cases of meningitis in children and rheumatic fever in young adults during the last five years. The outcome of these affected patients had been rather poor. "We need specialists in diseases of children as well as in that of adults," she said. Then she added, "Major surgery cases have to be sent to Toulouse, almost two hours by car from here." Abd and his family drove up to the hospital located at the highest point of the town, hoping to talk to the management or hopefully to one of the GPs. After a quick walk through the combined medical-surgical floor, they were led to the obstetric section and the adjacent newborn nursery. From there Amelia and Abd were amazingly impressed by the panoramic view of the region with the rolling-hill evergreen in the forefront and the pointed peaks of the Pyrenees in the background.

The head of the household seemed to thoroughly enjoy the leisurely time with his wife and two boys; but for the first time, he was conscious of a difference in personality between Amelia and himself. Her careless good humor and clumsy ways to do things markedly contrasted with his fastidious thought and conscientiousness in judgment. This dissimilarity eventually and to a certain degree affected the couple's married life. The relaxing vacation trip to the region des Pyrenees was quickly replaced by the worrisome effect of the political turmoil resurgence in Paris during the next several months. Abd and Amelia, while worrying about their future, were trying to go about their personal life with two fast-growing children. Despite the country's political strife, Abd continued to shine in scientific research and teaching. Up to that point, he had already written nine impressive papers in microbiology, and all of them were published in international reputable medical periodicals. He tried to ignore what was going on outside of the hospital and to concentrate on his work at his lab. Then one day the following incident became the straw that broke the camel's back, forcing Abd and Amelia to make a drastic decision.

Abd returned to the lab from his week-long lecturing trip on that Monday morning. He was surprised to see a stranger sitting at his senior technician's desk. It was a red-haired, bearded man in his early forties. The man slowly got up upon Abd's entry through the door:

"I am a floating lab technician working for a placement service company. My name is Dominique. I am assigned to come here to temporarily replace your technician. I have been working for the last nine years with half a dozen investigators in the field of microbiology."

"Thank you for accepting to come and for your willingness to work in this lab. I will fill you in with our current project of research after I have the chance to find out what was going on while I was away last week."

Abd walked to his office, closed the door, and dialed the hospital administrator's number. The latter informed him that his senior technician, Annette, had to undergo an emergency surgical operation this past Tuesday and she was currently on convalescence leave for at least six weeks. They went over her sudden illness, her complicated surgery performed by the chief of gastroenterology service, and a couple of unanticipated complications during the immediate postop period. Behind the closed door, Abd heard his personal secretary, Jeanne, talking with the man. He called her in and instructed her to get in touch with the company the man was working for and to do a quick verification of his employment. He also wanted her to show Dominique all the lab amenities, including the empty desk at the end of the staff room that he could use to write research data. Abd insisted that she clearly explain to this newcomer that everyone in the lab strictly adhered to the working hours and to the time for breaks during the workweek. The secretary was very well aware of her boss's neatness, meticulousness, and sharpness in thinking. She knew that her job was to convey to Dominique right off the bat these qualities, hoping that he would be able to adjust himself quickly to the lab's working atmosphere. Abd spent the rest of the morning with the temporary technician, going over the three experiments scheduled to be performed during that week. He wanted to intentionally read the test results himself, constantly keeping in mind that competition among researchers was fierce and project or data stealing was not uncommon in academia.

The first week went as anticipated, as the chief of the lab wanted to give some time for Dominique to adjust to the new working environment. The hospital administrator forwarded a memo from the placement service company to Abd that read, "Your newly hired lab technician was a former soldier of the French Foreign Legion. He fought in the Dien Bien Phu battle against the Vietcong and left his regiment after the five-year contract ran out in June 1954. He has passed the 'functional capacity' test a few years back, fairly bright, but at times contemptuous. At the moment, our company doesn't have another microbiology lab technician. Please keep our company informed of his performance on a regular basis." Dominique, assigned work during the next three weeks, was acceptable except for a few trivial mistakes resulting in repeated testing that caused a slow-down in research progress; but Abd realized that he was only a temporary substitute for Annette, who was in her fourth week of convalescence. The lack of her reliable daily participation in many research tasks under Abd's instruction was profoundly felt for weeks. Abd was keeping in touch with her husband weekly. He was more concerned about her slow recovery than the effect of her absence on his research work.

One Friday afternoon around six o'clock, Abd decided to leave his office for home. All electronic equipment in the lab was turned off, and an unusual quietness started that October weekend. He grabbed his winter coat, put it on, and locked his office door. He noted that the light was still on in the next room. About the same time, Jeanne opened her office door and appeared face-to-face with her boss. "I am still here, waiting to talk to you. You were on the phone, and I did not want to disturb your conversation."

"What is it all about?"

"About Dominique! He tends to take too many breaks when you are not around. He gets out on the balcony and smokes. I repeatedly remind him that, as a general rule for all of us employees in your research department, we are allowed to have only one break in the midmorning and another one in mid-afternoon besides the forty-five-minute lunch period."

"How did he respond to your reminder?"

"'Leave me alone,' he said. 'I have worked in a half dozen research labs, and I know how to conduct myself.'"

"Thanks for keeping me informed. I will have a talk with him Monday. It has been a long week for all of us. Go home and have a restful weekend with your family. See you Monday. Go ahead. I will make sure that the main entrance door is locked."

Abd was always thoughtful and considerate in dealing with everybody around him. But in dealing with a temporary employee, he had to double his effort and figure out a peaceful way to make sure that his academic activities would not be adversely affected by the lazy Dominique until Annette returned to work. Despite a few gentle direct talks with Dominique, the latter failed to improve his working relation with Abd. He came in to work sometimes one hour later than scheduled, and often he started to look at his wristwatch at three o'clock in the afternoon and then left the lab before other staff members, leaving his workplace in shambles.

The incidents that took place on his last day of temporary employment gave Abd bitter food to swallow. Dominique was sitting at his desk when Abd came to the lab to find out how the assigned experiment was performed by the tech on that day. "Have you detected so far any sign of viral activity in tissue culture tubes #NCI-29 and #NCI-30? You were supposed to look at the tubes every morning, starting four days ago. I want to see what you have been writing daily in the logbook about what you have observed under the Zeiss low power [microscope]."

"Sorry, sir. I inadvertently dropped both tubes while carrying them from the incubator to the microscope."

"Why didn't you let me know right away when this happened so that we could restart the same experiment without losing the whole week? Have you carefully disinfected the area contaminated by the content of the tubes?"

"I don't know why. I am tired of being told day after day how to carry out the same type of experiment and how to take precautions when working with viruses. I have plenty of experience in performing microbiological experiments. You know that."

"Dominique, you are hired to do the experiments I design. I don't want to hear arguments."

"Doc, you should go back to where you came from and take up arms to fight against your belligerent warlords. I fought against these bandits with a couple of friends in the same regiment, and in the end, the barbarous thugs managed to cowardly kill both. France has plenty of doctors. She doesn't need foreigners like you." Dominique became excessively angry, grabbed his coat, and walked out.

Abd was very humiliated by Dominique's attitude, and the above incidents suddenly instilled a new unanticipated thought in his mind. He asked himself if the encounter with Dominique represent an isolated trivial incident or the general feeling of the French people against immigrants as the country was going through a dangerous phase of political upheaval with a down-turned economy?

Annette called Abd's office five days after the departure of Dominique asking Jeanne to let her talk to her boss. Abd greeted his most trustworthy lab technician on the phone, "Nice to hear your voice, Annette. I am late in calling you this week. As you can guess, we have been very busy this past week, as the lab is short one person. How are you doing?"

"Thank you for asking, I think I am fully recovered. I saw my internist this morning on follow-up. She told me I could go back to work and she will send you a note about my health status. I am anxious to resume my duty, starting this coming Monday if you still want to keep me."

"Annette, you know everyone here wants to see you rejoining us soon, but first, we all want to be sure that you are well."

"Doctor, I feel that I am ready to perform any test you want me to carry out this coming week. Please design a couple of them. I will go over each of them, get detailed instruction from you Monday morning. If you are scheduled to go out of town on a lecturing trip Monday, I can come in already this Saturday to see you. My husband will not be on call this weekend, and he can look after the kids for me."

"No, I am not going anywhere until three weeks from today. Monday morning at the usual morning conference time will be fine. Have a restful weekend."

Abd hung up, walked over to Jeanne's office, and handed to her three French francs. "Annette will return Monday. Please get something for lunch to welcome her back. Thanks."

During the next two months, the work in the lab was going on as scheduled. Important research data accumulated at a rapid rate. Everybody was happy, and Abd was about to start writing another article on the effect of interferon on the growth of viruses. But the harmony and the productivity in the lab suddenly experienced a "jolt" due to the change of the hospital personnel at the upper level.

The hospital governing board had decided to create a new position of medical director to oversee all lab investigators. These scientific researchers soon would have to report weekly to the director of their professional activities. The reason for this change was kept secret among board members. Even though being one of the most prominent medical investigators and medical professors in Paris at the time, Abd had not been consulted before the governing board announced the drastic change. Within less than a week, a special meeting of all upper-level hospital personnel took place one afternoon at the main conference room. A clean-cut young doctor with a distinctive accent from French Brittany was introduced by the president of the board to the crowd. The newcomer took the podium, outlining his function. At the end of his speech, he asked that the chief of each hospital research lab call his secretary to set up a one-to-one meeting with him within the next thirty days. Many questions about the role of the new director were raised during the gathering. Whispering among attendees during the session and their louder comments in the corridor, at the completion of the meeting, indicating a general dissatisfaction, was the highlight of that afternoon. On the next day, Abd went to see the hospital administrator to get some preliminary information on this man's background and education. It turned out that the new doctor was the son of the newly installed dean of Nancy College of Medicine, very powerful politically within the French medical circle. The father, apparently, wanted his son to start climbing the Parisian academic medical ladder, which was the most prestigious but also the most competitive in Europe during the immediate post-WWII period. The newly appointed medical director just finished his "clinical" pathology residency last July, had no experience in any particular field of medical research, but had recently taken a two-week course in electron microscopy technique at the University of Ontario in Canada. In one of his letters to the president of the board prior to his installation as medical director, he expressed his interest in cancer research and admitted that he still needed to find someone in Paris who was willing to teach him the technique of tissue culture, which was the cornerstone in cancer cells studies.

A week later, Abd met with him in his office. The one-hour meeting was rather professional, but Abd was noncommittal on any of the suggestions made on administrative-related discipline in research. He also expressed to the director his independence when the latter carefully proposed a bilateral cooperation in joint research projects. When Abd stood up ready to leave, he heard the director say, "Per hospital governing board, you are supposed to meet with me every month."

With his brilliant scientific mind, Abd walked out of that office with two thoughts in mind—academia politics and/or French discrimination against foreign immigrants of different ethnicity and race. Up until that time, he had thought promotion, especially in academic medicine, was based strictly on performance in teaching and achievement in research, not on favoritism and cronyism. But he was wrong and naive. The idea of having to report monthly to a new boss who was by far inferior academically to a well-established scientist like himself was totally unacceptable. This new *modus vivendi* between the hospital governing board and its management was an insult to Abd because he was overnight stripped of his research autonomy, and it was the straw that broke the camel's back.

During that weekend, husband and wife talked over the next move they had to make in order to permanently settle down in another region of France where the boys could peacefully go to school and grow up in an environment tainted as little as possible with political unrest. They realized that this was a decision that could not be made lightly. Abd, with a precise and rational mind of a scientist, came up with pros and cons on the relocation of the entire family. On a sheet of paper, he listed on one column all reasons for which they should make the move; and on a second column, all reasons suggesting that the displacement might have serious consequences. Abd and Amelia took several days and lost a lot of sleep, carefully going over each and every one of these items listed on these two columns. But most importantly, a few anticipated and crucial issues eventually had to be dealt with. Among those were the following ones: the elimination of Abd's growing scientific prominence, the loss of financial security guaranteed by his academic tenure, the dealing with many unknowns that the whole family would have to face in a remote part of the country where the indigenous people might have a mentality totally different from that of large cities' dwellers, the lack of a good educational system, and last but not least, the deprivation of many cultural forms that Paris was offering.

In the end, the decision of relocation to a small French town prevailed by the following aspects of mental analysis. With his advanced knowledge in the field of medicine, Abd convinced himself that he should be able to provide specialized care to small-town people. He was fully aware of a drastic decrease in income during the next several years, but the yearning of pleasing God through hard work with the low middle class prevailed. In addition, the welfare of his two sons was of the utmost importance to him. Even though the pre-high school phase might not be most desirable in rural areas where the education was mainly geared to the formation of millworkers, Amelia would have the time and devotion to look after the boys' earlier years of learning. With her bachelor's degree, she would be more than adequate to help them with their homework.

Abd feared that Amelia would be too isolated from the big cities where she grew up and successfully exercised her nursing profession. To counter his anxiety, she repeatedly reassured Abd that she would try to blamelessly continue her role of a wife and a mother and would unconditionally support her husband's final decision. In the later part of his life, Abd expressed his regret on one hand for not having consulted with people dear to him like Mrs. Osgood or David Campbell, but on the other, he was convinced that God had guided him in his decision-making to relocate his family in the rural economically deprived area where his double specialty in medicine could be of an enormous help to the locals.

Abd gave his notice of resignation from the University Saint Mathieu Hospital, and within a month's time, the whole family was settled in the town Foxeline in the Midi-Pyrenees. Parents and children fairly quickly adapted themselves to small-town living, enjoying the fresh air and the characteristic slow-pace attitude of the local people. He was the only doctor specialized in both nonsurgical specialty and a subspecialty in the whole county where people lived in small hamlets scattered in narrow valleys. At that time, in France, physicians trained in the subspecialty of infectious diseases were hard to find in private practice, and practically all of them remained in academia with two main responsibilities: research and teaching. But very soon Abd and Amelia realized that in order to make enough for a living and save enough for the boys to pursue future advanced education, the newly relocated doctor in this rural area needed to see at least between twenty to twenty-five patients a day and to get regular patient referrals plus medical consultation requests from the other four well-established colleagues. Since the four-thousand population of Foxeline obviously could not provide the sufficient financial income to permanently keep another doctor, let alone a super specialist like Abd, the only solution husband and wife could come up with was to reach out for potential additional patients from neighboring towns. The closest town named Lazerat, with a population of over twelve thousand and an aged thirty-five-bed hospital, was forty-five minutes' driving distance from Foxeline. A few weeks after arrival to the area, Abd drove to Lazerat to determine whether he could set up a combined private practice covering the two small towns. He thoroughly appreciated the beautiful landscape along the hilly and curvy country roads. The arid, dry terrain on which stood occasional abandoned crumbled farmhouses on both sides of the passage was reminiscent of the scenery that he was familiar with in the Bamyan province, and this experience brought back the frequent nostalgia for his homeland he left almost thirteen years earlier. But Abd didn't have to convince himself that at this point of his life he had no other choice but shoulder the heavy load of responsibility for looking after the welfare of his family. He knew, as a head of the household, he must carry out his duty with love that was the cornerstone of an intact and happy family that he had experienced from birth until he left home for further education abroad.

CHAPTER NINE

Unanticipated Problems of Various Natures After Leaving the Big City

Unseasonal stormy summer weather continued to batter Carbonne and the surrounding villages of Midi-Pyrenees for over twenty-four hours, and the accompanying flashfloods caused severe damage to livestock in the entire region. Foxeline made no exception.  Surging waters flooded the floor of the late Dr. Beaumont's house that Abd and Amelia rented upon arrival to the area three weeks earlier. Confined to the house's upper floor, Emal and Yasir became cranky, even though Dad, house-bound, was spending time trying to entertain them. The family was lucky enough to have brought to their upstairs bedrooms five cans of sardines and two bags of crackers before the water level reached the first-floor windowsill. Somehow a garden snake managed to get into the house, swimming toward the tightly closed main door when Emal, quite frightened, saw it through the staircase opening and yelled, "Snake, snake." The floodwater crested that same evening, and the reptile was found on the muddy floor, upside down and motionless, a few feet from the west window. While the boys were kept in bed upstairs, Amelia and Abd moved the thick coat of mud to the outside with newly purchased aluminum shovels and then thoroughly washed the entire undamaged wood floor with an outdoor faucet-attached water hose. They became exhausted and finally went to bed after midnight. That was the very first hardship experienced by Abd's family after their relocation to the countryside.

The next few months were uneventful on all fronts. Amelia drove Emal to and from his kindergarten school five days a week by car in the company of Yasir, securely belted in his bucket seat behind his brother.

Abd used the eight-year-old two-door Citroën to go back and forth between Hospital Regional Charles Duquette in Foxeline and Hopital de Lazerat. Since the workload was still small, he was permitted to see his private patients at these two hospitals. Shortly after his arrival into town, local newspapers had made repeated announcements about the new doctor, his training, and especially his expertise in handling all nonsurgical diseases of children and adults, as well as infectious diseases of all ages. Patients came from distances as far as fifty kilometers to see him. Local doctors turned over to him their patients affected by all kinds of meningitis and encephalitis for his special care. The word spread quickly that Abd was not only a doctor with a large body of knowledge and experience but also with compassion. But his reputation could not go on without incident.

One evening a well-to-do lady in her late fifties living in town brought her six-year-old grandson to the emergency department at the Regional Hospital Charles Duquette. The child had a high fever but otherwise did not appear to be very sick according to the on-call general practitioner, or GP for short. The doctor sent him home with a few tablets of antibiotics and aspirin for fever control after checking him over. The same lady brought the boy back in the late hours of the next morning because of persisting elevated fever and two episodes of vomiting. The ED charge nurse called in another on-call GP to reevaluate the medical condition of the patient who became rather toxic in appearance. Abd happened to be at the hospital making rounds on the ward. The GP called him on the phone and asked him to give his opinion on the boy's illness, knowing that very likely the latter was having some sort of serious infectious disease, as he still remembered the consecutive deaths within a month of three children in the county with meningitis last year. Abd agreed to see the child if his caretaker signed a request form. The GP feared that this could be another case of the same lethal disease. He turned to the grandmother and told her that an immediate hospitalization was necessary in view of the child's serious medical condition. He recommended her to let Abd take over the diagnosis of the disease and the complicated treatment course from here on. She murmured to the doctor's ear, "I don't want a foreign doctor."

While still in the ED and in the presence of the orderly, the doctor worrisomely looked at her. "I want you to think it over. The boy is very sick, and I don't have the training or the experience to take care of him. We are lucky to have Dr. Rasulov in town, and he is right now in the house. This man has the expertise in treating not only all patients with serious infections, but he is also a specialist in children's diseases."

The GP was finishing up his ED note on the boy when a code red was heard on the hospital loudspeakers followed immediately by the ringing of the ED desk telephone. The head nurse called out to the doctor still sitting at the desk behind her, "Doctor, the child just wheeled to the ward is having a seizure. They want you there as quickly as possible."

There was a commotion throughout the entire two hospital floors. The doctor and the boy's grandmother rushed to the boy's bed. They found Abd in the middle of trying to insert a tongue blade between the child' s clenching jaws while having an aide hold the oxygen mask to the patient's nose. At the same time and under his watch, Abd ordered one of the nurses to give IV Pentothal, an anticonvulsant drug, slow push. Within less than three minutes, the seizure abated and the boy was resting comfortably with the lady and the GP at his side. Abd wrote the medical notes on the events, stood up, ready to talk to his medical colleague about what to do next, when the lady stepped forward and looked at Abd. "Doctor, may I ask you to immediately assume the care of my grandson, if you don't mind? Your colleague had recommended earlier that I should ask you to take over the care of Adrian, as you are the expert in handling difficult cases of infectious diseases and you are also a pediatrician."

"With pleasure, madame. Please have the nurse give you the authorization form and carefully read it and sign it if you agree with the hospital policy on patient transfer to a different doctor. After that, I need to go over with you the boy's current illness and the proposed treatment schedule. I want you to know that a spinal tap to get the fluid from his spine is mandatory in order for me to establish with certainty the final diagnosis and the proper course of treatment."

"The spinal tap must be very painful!"

"I usually minimize the pain by slightly sedating the patient with medicine by mouth or by IV and by local anesthetics before I perform the tap. I have carried out this procedure hundreds of times, so please don't worry. Subsequently, when you want to call me for any question about your grandson's condition, please feel free to do so. I will stay in touch with the nurse throughout the night after I finish examining him, ordering a few urgent lab tests and performing the tap. Then I will start the treatment without delay."

The lady appeared to be very reassured. She shook the GP's hand. "Thank you for your suggestion. Sorry for my initial narrowmindedness."

The final diagnosis of the boy's disease was bacterial meningitis and sepsis. He was fully recovered a week later. A photo of Abd at the boy's side and on the hospital ward with words of praise appeared on the front page of local newspapers a few days later. This incident ironically boosted Abd's reputation further, and within less than a year, his medical practice flourished without having to resort to any type of advertisement. The word of mouth did it instead. As the in-and out-patient number increased, Abd had to work long hours covering the two offices and both hospitals. Because the area was economically depressed, a good percentage of his patients were either on public assistance or had no medical insurance at all. As a result, Abd's annual income was way below average for a nonsurgical specialist when it was compared to that of his colleagues in Toulouse or in other larger cities of the Southwest France region.

During the next few years after relocating to Foxeline and while Emal and Yasir were still toddlers, Abd managed to spend at least one hour a day with them during the weekdays despite his extremely busy working schedule. He got out of bed at around six in the morning, at about the same time as his two boys did. After joining his family for a quick breakfast, he got on the road heading for either or both hospitals. After the morning rounds to see inpatients, he started his office hours. He stopped for lunch at around noon and then tried to take a catnap while lying on one of the examining tables. Not infrequently the quick rest was interrupted by calls from the hospital EDs or hospital wards. He resumed his office hours until around five thirty to six in the afternoon and then returned to make the evening rounds at Hospital de Lazerat. Driving back to Foxeline, Abd stopped by his temporary-rented house and then had his supper with his family, which was faithfully preceded by a reverent prayer. Before rushing out to see a few more patients at his Foxeline office, he helped Amelia give baths to the boys, dressed them up for the night, and then all four silently knelt at their bedside for another prayer of gratitude to God. The evening office hours usually lasted only one to two hours. But if he had inpatients at the hospital, he willingly made rounds before heading home. During the week, Abd never came home until ten to eleven in the evening if he was lucky for not having to go back to the ED of either of the two hospitals. Being the only specialist in nonsurgical medicine, Abd could not have the luxury of cross-coverage to get a few days off. No matter how busy he was, Abd managed to spend as much time as possible with his two boys.

Over the next several years, in winter, Abd made an arrangement with one of the five GPs in Lazerat to take all his calls during the weekend when he sneaked out to do a couple of hours of skiing with his family on the slopes of Ax-les-Charmes resort. In the summer, the same GP was always willing to provide Abd with a few hours of daytime relief so that all three, father and sons, could spend a few hours together doing brook trout fishing or mountain peak hiking. However, occasionally Abd's beeper went off while away from the hospitals trying to get some time off in the company of the boys. These beeping calls came from either of the two hospital EDs staffed by well-trained nurses 24-7. They urgently needed his expertise. In those instances, Abd and his family had to immediately drive back to the hospital, and the leisure time abruptly ended. Except for skiing, Amelia was not eager to accompany her husband and the boys in other types of activities, although she became suddenly interested in ice fishing introduced six years later by a new "friend of the family." This will be a story to be told in the next few paragraphs; but for now, the following story will highlight the natural bonding between a loving father and his two sons.

August was the vacation month for inhabitants of the Midi-Pyrenees region. Foxeline aluminum can factory was shut down, and the town was almost deserted. The number of patients seen in Abd's office during the week was drastically reduced to about ten a day. The school still remained closed for summer vacation on that last Friday of the month. Abd decided to take the boys for a day of brook trout fishing trip on the next day. Once again, he relied on his GP colleague in Lazerat to answer all in-coming patient's calls to his practice on that Saturday and, if necessary, to have the very sick and complicated cases transported by ambulance to the University Hospital of Toulouse.

At five in the morning, the whole family was already up. After a substantial breakfast, the boys got on the road with their father, heading toward the brooks at the foothills a half hour away from Foxeline. Wearing sneakers, they waded in the shallow brook water running over a bed of large slippery stones. The eight-year-old Emal got his first native trout within less than fifteen minutes. With one hand holding his three-and-half-year-old younger son's wrist, trying to keep the boy from falling in the cold water, Abd paid very little attention to his fishing line. Instead, he tried to coach Yasir how to look for the spots where the boy would have a good chance to catch his first fish while keeping his eyes on every step his son made. He wanted to make sure that his son wouldn't hurt himself by his own line's hook. The joy of fishing in the company of his two sons was suddenly interrupted. Yasir, too eager to compete with his brother, freed himself from his dad's hand, ran toward a fish, and tumbled off an algae-coated glistening rock. Wet and cold, he sobbed and shed tears. His dad picked him up, removed his drenched clothing, wrapped him up with a dry towel, and carried him on his back, walking downstream back to their car parked at least a kilometer away. Can one imagine how frustrating it could be, when father with his son on his back, tried to free the fishing lines repeatedly entangled in the bushes while walking on a narrow stream running between steep banks with dead branches and twigs overhead and mosquitoes everywhere? Without losing sight of his older son, Abd whistled to him to signal an abrupt change of fishing activity. All three finally reached the car after half an hour of struggling with the undesirable slippery waterway. The party had their packed lunch in the car and then resumed fishing for a couple more hours in another wider, deeper, and more rapid beck.

In the end, Emal had caught seven fish, but Yasir's fish stringer carried only three. Frowningly, Yasir lamented, "I have never caught as many fish as Emal does." These words had a special implication, as the reader will recognize it in the next remaining chapters.

As the practice was getting busier, Abd became overworked and gradually developed insomnia caused by frequent urgent consultations from the two EDs afterhours. Not uncommonly, Abd came home from the hospital at two to three o'clock in the morning after having to accept the transfer of inpatients from another doctor who did not want to get out of bed and go to the hospital after midnight. A large majority of these forced-transfer patients were on public assistance or had no medical insurance. The federal government paid hardly anything to doctors who cared for patients on welfare assistance. As a result, Abd worked no less than eighteen hours a day for months on end, but the income during the first two years was barely enough to support his family. On top of the financial setback, Abd had to have a roof over the head of his family members, somewhere between the towns Foxeline and Lazerat. To come up with enough money for the down payment, he had to dig into his meager saving. Additionally, a local branch of Banque de Lyon let him borrow money for a mortgage, but unfortunately with a steep interest rate;

and finally, his mother-in-law pitched in an additional 2 percent of the house value.

Chronic fatigue quickly settled in with constant back and neck pain, which was eventually diagnosed as *fibromyalgia/myofascitis* by a professor in neurology at Toulouse University Hospital. But it seemed that something else must have triggered Abd's depression with symptoms of hot flashes, relentless sweating, and significant weight loss for three months. He became more and more irritable with Amelia, who tended to be disorganized and forgetful in many of her daily household activities; but he managed to remain cheerful with his children and to enjoy the company of his two dogs.

Abd came home one Sunday afternoon from the hospital, exhausted but happy for having correctly diagnosed and successfully treated a five-year-old girl living in a foster home who developed urinary tract infection and sepsis.[5] He stretched out on the couch, reading medical newsletters and periodicals that he had not gotten to for over a week. Lali, an extremely intelligent but domineering female crossbreed between a German shepherd and a golden retriever, was on the floor, a few feet away, looking at her master for quite a while but got no attention from him. Then suddenly she growled at the four-year-old pure-bred Belgian shepherd, Seppo, lying not far from her.

Abd took his eyes off the reading material he was holding in his hands. "What's the matter, Lali? You want to go for a walk?" Lali wagged her long tail and then made two soft brief sounds while tenderly gazing at Abd for a few seconds. She repeated the same cycle three times until Abd leaned forward and gently stroked her shiny dorsal fur. Then she rolled over on her back, peacefully closing her eyes, joining her master for a short Sunday afternoon nap.

Her keen sense of detecting and differentiating noises was remarkable. She never failed to wait at the entrance when Abd came home. As he entered the house, she gently rubbed his pants with her head, wagged her tail, and then slowly walked in the direction of the living room while perusing him with her warmhearted look. When he stopped to hang his coat, she stood still next to him and then resumed her guiding role until she reached the couch where she flattened herself on the floor with her head facing the cushions, waiting for Abd to sit down for a few minutes' rest. Routinely Abd followed her, so to speak, wordless instruction. This unique relationship between Lali and her master instilled in him a sense of energy restoration and peace. But Abd's life in the countryside continued to be plagued by one worry after another.

Frightened by their own living experience, Yasir and Emal quietly told their father one Saturday at bedtime the following story. On two occasions and within a period of a month, the car driven by Amelia, in the company of the two sons, ran out of gas while traveling through a dense forest on a deserted three-kilometer country road. At the first incident, the boys reported that a strange bearded old man stopped his truck when he saw Amelia and while leaning on the car's hood, waved at occasional passing motor vehicles. The man refused to accept cash after he poured some gas into the tank to get its engine started again. Four weeks later, when a similar incident took place, all three had to walk to the next gas station and have the owner's wife drive them back to the disabled car with a full five-gallon gas can. These two episodes caused a great deal of concern for Abd. He worried that his young wife and their two children might one day be harmed by an unknown criminal on that stretch of deserted tall-tree-canopied roadway.

On the next day, at around midafternoon, Abd brought up this serious matter for discussion with Amelia. The two of them were alone in the living room. The boys were in their room, taking a Sunday afternoon nap or reading. Calmly, Abd started to explain to Amelia that she should look at the gas gauge each time she got in her car and that she should never let the gas level go down below one-quarter in the tank. He related to her the murder incident on that stretch of the road a few years back, before Abd's family moved to the area. For years, this violent crime remained the centerpiece of many locals' gossip during their daily shopping trips at the town supermarket. Amelia did not want to take Abd's advice seriously by saying to him that she was "a grown-up"—the word she used fairly frequently—individual who did not need to hear banal warnings and that she should be able to handle each unexpected situation appropriately. Her lack of imagination concerning such a danger irritated Abd further. The difference of personality between husband and wife started to take a toll on their relationship. Pessimistic thoughts on their marriage started to haunt him day and night. There were no better days in sight. Rather, a serious health problem was about to happen to Abd.

The phone on his night table rang. It was 5:15 a.m. Routinely Abd got out of bed every morning around this time. He picked up the handset. The night nurse at Foxeline Hospital nursery called to let him know that a full-term female had been born during the night, and her mother had requested that he be the baby's pediatrician. He had difficulty sitting up in bed. He felt as if his feet were not in contact with the mattress. Swinging his body to the left, he tried to stand up at the bedside. He fell and his left elbow hit hard the carpeted bedroom floor. He couldn't pull himself up. He had no strength in his two legs, but otherwise, had no other symptoms. Amelia rushed to his side and, together with Emal, managed to pull him back to his feet. Dressed up quickly, the nine-year-old Emal and his mother, with some difficulty, dragged the patient to the car. Yasir ran ahead of them to open the car door. Without delay, they drove to Toulouse. At the university hospital, extensive lab testing, spinal tap, and muscle biopsy revealed that Abd had *thyrotoxic periodic paralysis* (a toxic condition due to hyperactivity of the thyroid gland), which was quickly treated and the recovery was uneventful; but Abd had to stay on the antithyroid drug Propylthiouracil for the next two years. Abd resumed his professional activities without delay.

The intimate time spent with his wife had become only occasional and finally limited to an unaffectionate hug when he went to bed, exhausted from uninterrupted patient contact all day long. But no matter how tired he was at the end of the day, he never neglected to go over the boys' homework, alone or jointly with Amelia. Gradually, as the children passed their childhood, they seemed to have lost the routine daily bedside saying of grace. Rather, they spent time reading before falling asleep. Abd missed those earlier years when he was still able to, so to speak, indoctrinate his boys to keep Christianity alive and well at least within his family. Lack of adequate income despite long hours of hard work, chronic fatigue and insomnia, fibromyalgia pain causing depression and distress all together did not appear to haunt him enough. Additional problems were about to arise within his family nucleus.

Over the next several months, the intimacy between Amelia and Abd came to an end. Amelia stayed late at night almost every day of the week after the boys and her husband went to bed. Before their wedding, she had reassured Abd that, unlike the majority of her colleagues, she didn't care for watching TV, but she rather preferred to devour good books. This preference and enjoyment of reading had soon gone by the board. Now, on a daily basis, she isolated herself in the family room as soon as she finished cleaning up the kitchen after dinner. She spent hours watching soap operas until one or two o'clock in the morning. This pastime was then frequently mentioned in many European and American newspapers as "the late-night movie syndrome" that usually preceded a divorce.

During the day, after driving Yasir to school, she made the habit of visiting a few "new ladies" in town. The majority of these women came from the shoreline beach resort Biarritz, the neighbor historic city Bayonne, or the famous wine city. They either followed their husbands who were transiently relocated at the local ski resort or long-term employed by the aluminum can factory. Some of them came from Austria, Germany, or the Netherlands. Amelia, being Swedish, fit in very well with this group of females whose husbands were well paid and therefore they didn't have to work. Soon they formed clubs of all sorts of activities, but gossiping became the menu du jour. They eventually reached out to local working wives who were teachers, hospital clerks, private music teachers, owners of utility stores, and others and started to spread the British "Women's Liberation Movement" (WLM) of the early '60s, then still at its embryonic stage. A rumor circulated among locals that some members of the clubs had tried to brainwash them, hoping to infuse their thinking with a sense of new independence from their male partners in all family matters. This sabotaging wave of the traditional family value was met with some success. As a result, the rate of divorce in the Midi-Pyrenees region at that time was growing at an alarming speed. Amelia was not spared by the influence of the movement. At the dinner table, Abd regularly heard from Amelia slogans reflecting the revolutionary direction in which the movement was attempting to sway these hardworking local wives from their belief in the Bible's Ten Commandments. Emal, by now twelve years old and having a solid Christian education, often had serious arguments with his mother when she took sides with the social media in endorsing the movement. Feeling powerless in confronting her teenaged son who had his own opinions and ideas, Amelia repeatedly blamed her husband for not trying to use the paternal authority to control the youth. Abd, on the other hand, maintained that he would not set new rules to defend her as long as the boy remained respectful to his parents during exchanges of opinions between family members on any topic. Instead, he strongly believed that giving personal but rational opinions is a good mental exercise.

Obviously, Amelia was deeply influenced by the movement's hardcore members, and this social aberration had a very negative effect on the marital relationship between the spouses. Sensing that a family breakup was imminent, Abd called and talked to Mrs. Osgood about his marriage difficulty. She advised him to seek psychotherapy. Reluctantly, Amelia agreed to go with her husband to get counseling.

At the very first visit with the psychiatrist, whose office was in Toulouse, Amelia showed no interest in working at improving the verbal communication between Abd and her. She also insinuated that the era of husband's dominance was over and that women must have the right to file for divorce, using "irreconcilable difference" as "the cause" regardless of the circumstance. Since the marriage counseling didn't get anywhere, Abd anticipated that sooner or later one of the spouses or both would eventually resort to other means in order to cope with frequent discords that most of the time ended in shouting or using profane language. It appeared as if both Amelia and Abd were entering into a critical phase during which listening to each other was out of question. Their behavior was absolutely antagonistic, and observers would have thought that they were living in totally different worlds. Arguments between the spouses were getting more frequent and louder, especially when the boys were not around.

A very sad event occurred on one Sunday afternoon after lunch. The boys were playing in the courtyard with the two dogs, Lali and Seppo. Amelia and Abd were reading the Sunday newspaper in the family room. A loud argument suddenly broke out between them over the traditional role of a husband in a Christian family. Amelia brought up the subject of Abd's "paternal authority" and insisted that he should use it to subdue Emal's "rebellious" behavior toward her that, she believed, had disparaged her maternal command. She contended that Yasir, three and half years younger than his brother, had started to behave the same way, ignoring her after-school rules.

Abruptly, Amelia got up, angry and defiant, and ran to the direction of the kitchen. "You are a draffish father, a phony individual."

Immediately, Abd ran after Amelia and pinned her against the kitchen corner. He then pointed his finger to her face. "Don't you ever dare say those words again!"

Amelia forcefully pushed him back, but unfortunately, her right fist landed a blow to his mouth. Blood dripped down to his white Sunday shirt from his cut lower lip.

Hearing the commotion, the boys happened to be at the door, coming from outside. Not knowing what was going on, they worrisomely sat their father down on the kitchen bench. Immediately, Yasir brought to his dad a dry wash towel, and Emal applied pressure on the wound with it. Amelia quickly left the scene and was slowly walking upstairs, mumbling, "I am sorry, but I had to react, as you have been verbally challenging me all the time. I didn't mean to hit you."

Exasperated, Abd kept quiet while firmly holding and pressing the boys' bodies to his sides with his trembling hands. The distraught Abd witnessed his children's eyes filled with tears. He reassured them that it was just a "trivial accident." Of course, neither Yasir nor Emal could believe in their dad's comforting explanation. It wasn't difficult for them to figure out the whole truth: Mom and Dad just had their first physical encounter. They stayed quiet downstairs while hearing Amelia sobbing in the master bedroom. Abd turned to the boys, saying, "Please, go to see Mom. She surely needs your attention."

Both boys followed their father's suggestion, and finally calm returned to the house. Amelia, with her puffy eyelids, came down to the kitchen to assist Abd with dinner cooking. Neither of the two talked. An atmosphere of silent sadness reigned at the dining table that evening. Not a word was heard during this Sunday meal. All four left the table around eight o'clock. While Amelia cleaned up the table then washed the dishes, Abd prepared the boys for an early Sunday night sleep. Another school day started early the next morning. He gently closed their bedroom door after he reverently said, as usual, a bedtime prayer with them. The uncomfortable silence in the entire house was occasionally interrupted by the sleeping dogs' deep sighs.

Abd went to his study room, gathered unread medical materials of the week, hurriedly placed them in his briefcase together with the in-place clean underwear, walked down to his old Citroën, and drove away in the darkness of the night. He decided to be alone for a few days in his Lazerat office after hospital rounds and office hours. He used his patient-examining table as a sleeping bed for the next three nights. All sorts of negative thoughts haunted him that Sunday night. He tossed and turned on the improvised bed but could not fall asleep. The nearby church's bell ended its hourly toll at the stroke of midnight. Abd was back on his feet, pensively pacing the corridor adjacent to patient examining rooms. But the idea of doing harm to himself, being a devoted Catholic, never came to his mind.

After doing their homework, Yasir and Emal were at the dinner table without their father on the next day, a Monday, but they thought he must be detained at the hospital for an urgent consultation and didn't make anything out of his absence. So they went to bed after asking Amelia to say the daily routine "Good night" to their father on their behalf. On the next day, Tuesday, they had their breakfast without their father and then took the bus to school. Around four thirty in the afternoon, one after the other, the boys got off the school bus almost simultaneously. They ran up to their house on the hill. They shared a snack in the kitchen after a brief wash-off and then went to their room to do their homework. Amelia was in the kitchen preparing dinner. Yasir kept the door of the boys' room wide-open today so that they could hear their dad's Citroën entering the garage. The clock in the living room just had struck six, and their father was still not home for supper. Both boys started to wonder why Abd had not been in touch with either of the family members for almost two days. Worried but calm, Emal looked at his brother's somber face. "It's possible that Dad is tied up with emergencies two days in a row at the hospital."

"If so, why hasn't he called home as usual to let us know?" Yasir replied.

Amelia called out for the children to come down for supper. She knew Abd was not coming home for dinner. Earlier that afternoon, before the boys came home from school, she had left a message at the Lazerat Hospital for Abd to call back, but she hadn't heard from him. At the table, both boys kept looking at their mother, hoping to hear her comment about their father's absence. Finally, she admitted to her children that for quite a while there had been many marital differences culminating in the showdown on Sunday.

Emal abruptly interrupted his mother's lecturing comment. "As long as you continue to bring home slogans coming from the 'ladies' [he was intentionally referring to members of WLM], there will be more friction between you and Dad."

"Here we go again. Are you trying to teach me about the necessary male dominance in the household instead of female equality? You would be better keeping quiet!"

Emal and Yasir speechlessly got up from the table and went upstairs. Emal closed the door behind them. Yasir picked up the phone handset and dialed Abd's office in Lazerat. The phone was ringing for several minutes, but there was no answer. Nervously he hung up and then proceeded to call the Lazerat Hospital's evening receptionist. He trembled at the phone but managed to leave a message with a lady at the other end. "Please get in touch with Dr. Rasulov and request him to call home as soon as possible. Thank you."

Five to ten minutes later, Abd returned his son's call. Amelia was downstairs, letting the dogs out for the evening. Yasir answered the phone, crying. "Dad, please come home. We know why you have not been home for three days. Emal and I miss you very much. Please come home."

Emal asked Yasir to hand to him the handset. "How is your lip? Still swollen? Please come home. Things are going to be okay. Mom has promised us to be more understanding with you from now on. I miss you terribly, Dad."

Abd also terribly missed his two sons. He came home before dinner, tired and exhausted for not having enough rest and sleep for over three days. Emal and Yasir, after greeting him at the garage connecting door, accompanied their father to his study room. He slumped in the upholstered couch with a somber look on his face. His unbearable back pain because of the fibromyalgia had returned, but he tried to hide his suffering from the boys, who sat tightly close to their father's torso. Father and sons remained silent for quite a while until they heard the ringing of the two finger-size porcelain service handbell, announcing dinnertime. At the dinner table, one could practically hear nothing but the discreet food chewing sound coming from the boys' mouth. The spouses barely looked at each other during the entire evening. After dinner, as usual, Abd prepared the boys for bedtime. Neither the father nor the sons had a peaceful sleep that Tuesday night. Thoughts of parental discord kept returning to the boys' mind until the early hours of Wednesday morning. In silence, they left the house in the freezing morning to catch the school bus.

Amelia got a call on the twenty-sixth of December from one of those "new ladies" whose husband worked in the Foxeline aluminum can factory office. They got married a couple of months after he met her during his vacation five years earlier with a few friends in Innsbruck, Austria. Amelia and Abd were invited to join a dozen of the so-called "emancipated" nonlocal ladies and their husbands for a New Year celebration. Amelia accepted without reservation. In order not to show the townspeople of their marriage difficulty, Abd reluctantly agreed to attend the event.

On the evening of the thirty-first of December, the blond-haired Amelia, dressed in attire of festivity that made her stand out, arrived with Abd to the host's house up on the Foxeline hill near the hospital. A large and noisy crowd was already in full swing with a variety of alcoholic beverages. Abd was the only invited doctor. He was quickly introduced by the male host to each one of the "new ladies" and their spouses and two bachelors. One of these two singles happened to live down the road from Abd's house. They called him Antoine. Alcohol odor and cigarette smoke filled the entire house. Loud laughs could be heard a street block away. Amelia was in the process of emptying her second glass of whiskey. The male host of the house offered to Abd a glass of red Bordeaux, but he quickly replied, "I am on duty. Please just a little to keep your company. Thank you." As a non-drinker and nonsmoker, Abd could barely tolerate this environment but consciously held the half-filled glass of wine to his mouth each time anyone in the crowd looked at or talked to him. Eventually he managed to sneak into the bathroom and emptied the glass contents.

Suddenly the beeper vibrated at his waist in three short consec-utive bursts. Abd knew that the call must be from Lazerat Hospital. Quickly he asked the female host the permission of pulling the kitchen counter telephone extension cord through the back-entrance door so that he could talk without being disturbed by the noisy crowd. It was just a question on a patient's medication by the evening nurse. Abd did not have to leave the gathering.

When he got back inside with the crowd, he noted that his bachelor neighbor had his hand on Amelia's left shoulder with a flirt-ing look while being in the process of pouring another drink to her empty glass. Amelia reciprocated his attention to her with forced loud laughing spells. Abd was keeping his eyes on his estranged wife while responding to everyone who spoke to him. One after another, three of the "new ladies" attempted to engage a conversation with Amelia; but they were unable to sway her away from the man. Amelia's behav-ior shocked many partygoers that night. At this point, Abd realized that Amelia had drunk much more than she should have. Amelia's head was squarely rested on the man's shoulder. Her speech was get-ting slurred on several occasions, and she uttered almost incompre-hensible words and sentences.

With a great effort, she eventually arrived to say, "I am a city girl."

Then Abd, while talking to the CFO of the local ski resort, overheard the man saying to Amelia, "Would you like to fix me a breakfast some day?"

She looked straight into his eyes, saying, "With pleasure, any morning of the week, but not before seven." Indeed, Abd left home for hospital rounds, every morning, no later than six thirty.

Abruptly, Abd approached the bachelor. "May I take her home? I think it's getting late." The man reluctantly stepped aside, not responding to Abd's request.

Amelia disdainfully looked at Abd. "I am not ready to go home yet. Why do you want to deprive me of the fun I am having?"

Quietly Abd leaned to her ear. "I have to take you home right now. You are drunk. It's embarrassing. Have you noticed that everybody is watching you?" Abd grabbed her left arm by the elbow and guided her to the door.

She was so drunk to the point of continuing to utter over and over, "I don't want to go. Let me be alone." Not being able to walk without stumbling, she had to be pushed by her waist in the direction of the parked car. Finally, Abd managed to push her into the fully reclined passenger front seat and lay her flat on her back without incident.

Two weeks had passed during which Amelia remained rather quiet, and Abd was hoping that she had learned a bitter lesson from the New Year's Eve party. Then a predictable event took place. Abd was late in getting on the road that Friday morning due to four successive phone calls from both hospitals that he had to respond to. After the stroke of seven, the town church carillon almost drowned out the sound of the Rasulovs' residence doorbell. Emal just finished his breakfast, ready to walk a block or so to the school bus stop. Their mom was still in the powder room, dressing up Yasir. Abd, with his outer coat on, rushed to the door, wondering who was at the door at that early time of the day. He opened the door. There stood the bachelor, Antoine, who evidently was very embarrassed. He didn't expect to see Abd still at home after seven in the morning on a weekday.

Sternly, Abd looked at the dissolute man facing him. "Good morning, Antoine. Please come in. I am about to leave. Amelia is waiting to have breakfast with you."

Embarrassed, Antoine glanced at his wristwatch, not saying a word, turned around and ran out toward the gate, crossed the dirt road, then quickly disappeared behind the bushes lining the collateral side road leading to his house.

That same evening, after the boys went to bed, Abd told Amelia, "I have noted that you have been drinking too much lately. Don't make a fool of yourself in public. Your behavior at the last December party was not acceptable, neither to me nor to the boys. Watch your language after a couple of drinks, before your speech starts to get slurred."

To this remark, Amelia defiantly replied, "Don't try to lecture me. I am an adult that has borne two intelligent children. I don't need advice from anyone. Mind your own business."

With that kind of response, one would expect that the marital discord had already evolved into a crescendo pattern, culminating in occasional loud arguments. The gentle, soft-spoken Amelia had become a contemptuous and absolute uncooperative spouse.

But this marriage difficulty was not caused solely by one spouse or the other. His way of responding to Amelia's behavior was to be desired too. Verbally neither husband nor wife was kind to each other. Every time Amelia said or did something irrational, Abd said, "stupid," "don't be stupid," or "it's a stupidity." He did not mean to belittle Amelia at all, because he knew without any doubt that she was a very intelligent woman; rather, he meant to give her his opinion that what she had said or done was out of line. Unfortunately, Amelia took Abd's words and expression as insults to her, for, in her mother tongue, they could mean and convey the sense of being "idiot" or having a substandard IQ. This misunderstanding stemmed from the fact that they spoke French at home, a language neither of them had truly mastered. Later on, specifically during the immediate post-divorce period, Abd deeply regretted, thinking that his conduct *vis-à-vis* Amelia had been perhaps also inexcusable in the eyes of the public.

It had become obvious to Abd that the family value that he lived for had been gradually replaced by an artificial arrangement to coexist between two individuals of the opposite sex who had totally different aspirations for life. The successive events during the last few years, and especially since the year-end party of last December, had convinced Abd that the cornerstone of his family unit had been shattered, and it would take a miracle to repair the damage.

A sense of hopelessness started to haunt him. He was not able to rid unpleasant thoughts from his mind each time he lay down to rest. Insomnia was getting worse, and fibromyalgia pain aggravated him further. Abd became more depressed. On several occasions, shortly after the divorce, he conveyed this feeling of failure to his two sons, undoubtedly as a form of *mea culpa*. But in retrospect, one wonders whether Abd's behavior was under the influence of his poor physical health or simply a hidden mental derangement resulting from years of suffering of fibromyalgia pain and of thyrotoxicosis's jittery nervousness, irritability, palpitation, weight loss, and insomnia. This last symptom started sometime during his preteen years, suggesting that his thyroid illness could have initiated early in life. The excessive workload at his office and at the two hospitals after Abd left his academic career undoubtedly had adversely affected his overall health. Despite physical and mental suffering, Abd refused to take the prescribed medications. He was a stubborn individual. Drugs and alcohol had no part in his life. He contended that the cavemen didn't have these "poisons" and yet they did fine with their steady procreation generation after generation.

Given the enormous difficulty with his marriage at that point, the reminiscent memories of the last ten or fifteen years resurged in his consciousness. Abd regretted not having taken advantage of the unique opportunities presented to him in the past that could have changed the course of his life. There were at least two such main opportunities. The first one was the love for life Charmina had for him. He vividly remembered that Saturday morning in Vienna when he rose to his tiptoes to kiss her as she angelically lay immobile at the bay window in her white chiffon. The second was the offer made by the French government to install him as medical officer in the air force with the rank of lieutenant colonel two years after he moved to Foxeline area. But for fear of displacing his two sons' schooling every two to three years while in active duty, he hesitantly turned down the offer.

The marriage difficulty got worse by the day as Amelia's visit with the in-town members of the Women Liberation Movement took place on every workday of the week. Abd could not reason anymore with her. She contradicted every idea or opinion he presented to her. Liberated women's suggestions and recommendations were only the right ones. She strongly objected to the boys' responses to her statements during dinnertime. She was unable to keep Emal quiet. Most of the time he gave his opinion, which contradicted hers. At these tense moments, Amelia insisted, again and again, that his father must use the paternal authority to quiet down the son. Abd refused to intervene. She got up from the table angry. The scene repeated itself two to three times a week until Emal went to boarding school away from home. The children sensed that their mother was trying to unfairly exert her "contaminated" influence on them. Abd frequently noted a deep sadness in the eyes of Yasir and a somber facial expression on Emal each time he came home from his boarding school. Their school performance was affected, as their year-end report cards had showed. But problems affecting the marriage had not stopped coming.

"Yasir and Emal, the ice is rather thick today, but be patient, with my new ice auger, I will drill a hole for each of you and for your dad. I'd rather see you sitting next to him so that he could help you with the baits. I will be helping your mom. We should scatter out a little so that the smelts would come in schools," said Jean-Marie loudly.

The boys yelled back as hard as they could, but very likely Jean-Marie couldn't hear them as he was now several yards away from Abd and his two sons and he was in the middle of drilling the fifth hole immediately adjacent to his for Amelia. The strong, gusty northwest wind noisily swept over the icy lake, and swirling clouds of fine snowflakes made Abd's and the boys' observation of Amelia's fishing activity rather difficult. However, from a distance the trio had occasionally observed Jean-Marie's hands over Amelia's face, trying to put back in place her long blond hair strands tossed into the air each time the freezing February gust whipped at her heavy navy-blue winter coat. Abd found that Jean-Marie's intentional closeness to Amelia was strange, but he did not want to make anything serious out of it. After all, the boys were very friendly to this man and had been calling him "Uncle Jean" for the last year and half. Jean-Marie was a handyman recommended to the Rasulov family by one of the locals who recently joined the WLM, to do minor home repairs that Abd neither had the time nor the capability to tackle. He was a few years senior to Abd and appeared, at first, rather reserved but very friendly to the whole family. He didn't have much education and could only brag about his expertise in fishing and hunting that made him a real buddy to the boys.

In the next two freezing winter months, when ponds and lakes were solidly frozen, "Uncle Jean" managed to allure the Rasulovs to go ice fishing with him almost every Sunday. On several occasions, Abd had to let Amelia and the boys go without him because of the workload at the hospitals. Oftentimes he had to come to his office in Lazerat to see patients even on Sunday afternoon after hospital rounds and attending Mass in the morning. At the end of these fishing trip days, Jean-Marie came back and cooked the fish they caught during the day in the presence of Amelia. After dinner, the boys quickly took their shower and then went to bed. Likewise, Abd had to do the same. He must struggle with his constant fibromyalgia pain while trying to get some sleep, in order to prepare himself for a busy week. Long after the children and their father were in bed, Jean-Marie still sat on the kitchen bench talking to Amelia until the early morning hours of the next day. This scene took place almost without exception every Sunday after the day fishing trip. Abd gradually realized that this married man should be given a warning that *ménage à trois* (French for "household of three") was against his religious belief and harmful to the upbringing of his two young children.

One Sunday evening in February, after spending the whole afternoon and most part of the evening at the Foxeline Hospital with a life-threatening case of infantile bowel intussusception requiring urgent surgery, Abd came home around eleven thirty. Jean-Marie's truck was parked in the driveway. Dirty dishes were still on the table in the kitchen, and Amelia was sitting on the other side of the table facing Jean-Marie. Emal and Yasir were not there, undoubtedly in bed sleeping.

"Hey, Doc," Jean-Marie, noticeably embarrassed, looked at the doctor and uttered those words.

"It's time for you to say good night, don't you think so, 'Uncle Jean'?" sternly Abd responded.

Abd rubbed the dogs' head, as usual, each time he came home; and then he opened the side door to let them go out one last time for the night. He went upstairs, tiptoed to the boys' room, pulled up the blankets to fully cover their torso, and gently deposited a kiss on their foreheads before walking to his study room. He couldn't fall asleep, having pessimistic thoughts about his deteriorating relationship with Amelia. He came up with a couple of possible solutions. One of them was to get counseling.

Suddenly he heard the rumbling engine of a truck. He looked down to the courtyard through his foggy window. The same parked truck he saw earlier on the driveway was slowly heading toward the property entrance. He looked at the clock above the door. It was 1:47 a.m.

The next morning, right after Yasir and Emal left for school, Abd came downstairs, ready to go to work. Amelia was walking to the kitchen. Abd stopped in front of her. "We need to see a counselor, and I am sure you know the reason."

"You are jealous. Jean-Marie is not only a friend of the family, but also someone the boys can relate well with. You have been neglecting not only your wife but also your two children. All of what you know is the patients and the hospitals."

"Working long hours is, at least for now, not by choice but rather by necessity. If you want to live in your own home and not in a rented apartment, I have to work more hours than my colleagues in the big cities do. We are living in a poverty-stricken region. Many patients, except those on public assistance, are not able to pay expenses on drugs, let alone the office visit fee. You knew before we got married that I am not a banker who works from nine to five but instead a doctor whose working hours are longer and unpredictable, and you repeatedly had insisted that, being a nurse, you wouldn't have any problem sharing the busy life of a doctor. So, what makes you change your mind? I know for sure why you have been behaving differently than when we first created our union. Yes, I have not been very pleasant and cheerful with you at times since we left the big cities. I am sorry, but I have no control over my illnesses that you are well aware of, and the pain and suffering aren't, intentionally, made known to you and the children. I also want to apologize to you for having initiated an argument that ended up with a wound on my lower lip last year. We will never succeed in resolving our differences by ourselves. Amelia, if you want to save our marriage, I would propose that we see an out-of-town counselor."

"Let me think about it for a few days," Amelia defiantly replied and then walked away from him.

Walking to the garage, Abd took a deep sigh; and then left for Lazerat Hospital. While at the wheel, he promised himself not to say anything to the boys about his suspicion of a "special" relationship, rather than just a pure friendship as she had claimed, between their mother and Jean-Marie. He also said to himself, "I have so far fulfilled my duty as husband and father by being present practically every day of the week for dinner with my family and by participating in the daily physical, emotional, and religious care for the children. I work hard to provide them with healthy food and warm clothing plus a nonleaking roof over their heads. What else could I do to make Amelia happy, as long as she is under heavy influence from WLM? I am sure God knows my good intention."

Abd was unable to catch up with lack of sleep during the entire week. He tried to figure out other alternatives in case Amelia refused to seek counseling. He asked himself whether a temporary consensual separation or an out-of-province professional relocation could overcome his marriage difficulty, bringing back his lifelong dream of a happy family with a loving wife and two well-behaved children living in harmony. But Amelia would never accept to go back to stay with her mother in Stockholm for a while for the following reasons.

Her mother was a very domineering person who continued to hold grudges against her daughter for her union with a Middle Eastern man. Additionally, asking Amelia to leave Foxeline area, even just for a few months, was like depriving her food and water during that period. Core members of WLM and Jean-Marie constituted at the time the joy of her life. Relocation of Abd's medical practice wouldn't be practical either, as he had become attached to his patients who needed his specialized service. He would feel as a coward—especially to God—if he decided to leave this medically deprived area. Abd mulled over other alternatives night after night, but eventually he realized that his life had come to a dead end.

Abd's feelings of sadness, hopelessness, and loneliness bothered him quite a bit; but suicidal thoughts never came to his mind, thanks to his religious devotion. His irritable behavior, caused by agonizing pain and relentless insomnia, seemed to be directed to his wife only—for which he deeply and life-long regretted—but not to the others. Ironically, the Rasulov family was regarded at the time by the region's inhabitants as an exemplary one, as they saw the doctor and his wife attending Mass every Sunday with two well-behaved, bright sons who were not only very good students but also loved the outdoor sports like skiing and fishing. He managed during his entire twelve years of medical practice in the Foxeline area to hide his suffering from his two young sons, his office staff, and people he was in contact with at the two hospitals.

The lack of a straight night's sleep, coupled with long working hours, aggravated the symptoms of his fibromyalgia/myofascitis syndrome resulting possibly from a neck injury sustained during his childhood. This disease started to cause left shoulder and back pain at the beginning of his premed education years. Despite the debilitating constant pain, Abd managed successfully to go through four years of medical school, three years of residency in internal medicine, and three years of fellowship training in infectious diseases without resorting to painkiller medication. During the postwar years, not much was known about *fibromyalgia/myofascitis* syndrome, two diseases with overlapping symptoms; but Abd seemed to be able to live with his chronic illness, during his pre- and postdoctoral periods, by playing tennis and track-and-field noncompetitive moderately fast running, sports that are highly recommended nowadays to patients suffering of these diseases. But Abd's difficulty in falling asleep after hours of reading remained annoying throughout his life. He attributed this abnormal experience to some sort of lack of coordination between "alerting areas" and "sleep-promoting areas" of his brain.[4] But he learned how to overcome this inconvenience by waking up in the early hours of the morning, then doing the necessary reading of medical literature before going to work.

Like the previous four years, Abd reluctantly accompanied Amelia, Emal, and Yasir for another trip that summer to Sweden to visit Amelia's retired mother, who lived in an upscale Stockholm suburb with her boyfriend in a sumptuous house looking over the Södermalm waterway. Abd kept totally quiet during the ten-day visit, hoping that Amelia could take the initiative to reveal her marriage difficulty and ask her mother for suggestions on how to find a practical solution to the problem. Unfortunately, Amelia, terribly afraid of her mother's authoritarian attitude, didn't dare say anything about her feeling for Jean-Marie and the strong influence of WLM on her life since her family moved to Foxeline. Because the relationship between mother and son-in-law was at best cold and correct, Abd didn't want to say anything either. So, the ten-day forced vacation brought home no hope for improvement in the relationship between spouses.

But despair didn't seem to be enough for the head of the Rasulov household. A week after returning from the trip overseas, a fortuitous discovery confirmed Abd's suspicion about the "special" relationship between Amelia and Jean-Marie. That was around two o'clock in the morning. Abd had a nightmare that woke him up less than an hour after he managed to doze off on his study room couch. He went downstairs to get a drink of warm water, hoping it would help him to get back to sleep. He was quite shocked to see the white envelope with handwritten letters "JM" which was partially inserted into Amelia's half-zipped brown leather handbag left on her kitchen secretary desk. Having in general a tendency to be sloppy, undoubtedly Amelia had forgotten to securely hide her secret by keeping the envelope totally out of sight. Without hesitation, Abd opened the unsealed envelope and found a note Amelia wrote to Jean-Marie reminding him not to forget bringing her the "nerve balls" next time they "would meet at the designated site," and the note ended with "My deep feeling for you" and signed "A." Abd asked himself why a medical doctor's wife had to resort to an uneducated layman for getting drugs for "nerves" instead of legally asking for a prescription from one of her husband's medical colleagues to calm her nerves. In Abd's mind, after reading the note, there was no doubt anymore: Amelia was using very likely illicit drugs in addition to her abuse of 80-plus proof alcoholic beverages, as many empty bottles of bourbon whiskey were found by Emal and Yasir scattered and hidden at the bottom of several first-floor cupboards a few months later; and now she was found to have an intimate relationship with her so-called "friend of the family." Quietly, he walked downstairs to the boys' plain and simple woodworking table, and with his Leica II, took a photo of Amelia's note under a bright spotlight. But Abd hadn't given up hope for a solution to their marital discord at this point yet.

During the next few weeks, Abd tried to convince Amelia on counseling. At first, she resisted to the idea, but eventually she yielded to Abd's reasoning that emphasized mostly on the deleterious psychological effect on the boys' life should the marriage end up in a bitter divorce. On two consecutive Friday afternoons, they drove to Toulouse to see a well-respected university hospital-affiliated psychologist. Right from the beginning, Amelia showed her unwillingness to seriously participate in her psychoanalysis, while Abd insisted on his inexcusable behavior toward his wife. At the end of the second visit, the counselor gave up, saying that there had been imbalance with regard to personal background input, and therefore there was nothing else he could do to help. At the exit door, he shook Abd's hand and then that of Amelia. "Please come back to see me if you decide to be candid about the early years of your life."

Abd's sense of hopelessness became insurmountable, especially when one afternoon he unexpectedly received a Western Union telegram at his office notifying him of Mrs. Osgood's sudden death. He finished his office hours on that day, dashed to the hospitals for evening routine rounds, and then drove home. He called his GP friend/colleague to take incoming calls for him that night. After hugging his two sons, he closed his study room door and sat down on his couch with his head between the hands, mourning his second mother's death. He skipped dinner that evening. Yasir knocked at the door. Abd didn't respond. Barely audible noises were heard in the bathroom and footsteps in the corridor. Abd got up from his couch and lumbered toward the children's room. Emal and Yasir were reading in bed. In unison, all three muttered a brief daily prayer. Then quietly Abd said the daily "Good night" to the boys. Before he closed their door behind him, he deposited a fatherly kiss on each forehead and then slowly lumbered back to his room. The face of Mrs. Osgood reappeared in his mind. It brought back memories of the years she took him under her wing as his second mother, especially of the walk in the dark freezing night he had with her entire family to attend midnight Mass several years past. He swallowed his tears…

During the next year and a half, Jean-Marie was seen at home two to three times a week when the children returned from school. Abd had not come up with a solution to the deepening of his marriage difficulty. Yet arguments between spouses were becoming more frequent. The boys' awareness of their parents' struggle was apparent. Emal, now thirteen, was definitely affected by the conflict between his parents. One could read on his face a serious concern over the pending disintegration of the "model" family unit so much praised by everybody the Rasulovs had been in contact with shortly after they moved to the area. Yasir frequently had nightmares for the last several months. He woke up at night during the non-REM phase of his sleep with loud screams followed by constant tossing and turning in bed until the early hours of the day. Emal seemed to be able to partially mask his worrisome thoughts by spending more time after school with classmates. He managed to grapple with the unavoidable reality and arrived to do passably well in his first year of boarding school. However, at the end of the second-year trimester, the school supervisor, Einucle, sent a note to Abd saying that Emal's lack of interest in learning was a worrisome sign and asked whether he would be permitted to see the school counselor. During the holiday recesses spent at home, Emal consistently exhibited an emotional body language that his somber facial expression didn't betray: he worried about an inevitable breakup of his parents' marriage. Yasir was not much luckier either. His male teacher, a very committed person to his teaching and also a dedicated soccer coach, was very well liked by the third and fourth graders and their parents. Very worried about the negative effect of the deliberately concealed marriage difficulty on his son's education, Abd went one late afternoon to see this teacher at school after soccer practice. The latter hesitantly reported that the boy had been showing lack of concentration in class. This was indeed confirmed by his poor third-grade report card at midterm. Notably, this same outstanding teacher was "cleverly promoted" as assistant principal the following fall at another smaller elementary school twenty-five miles away by the district school board made up almost entirely of WLM active members. They brought in, at the chagrin of the third and fourth graders, a newly joined WLM young female teacher to replace him. Consequently, there were no more soccer games during afternoon physical exercise sessions. The WLM association was actively recruiting new members, not only in the Foxeline area but also in several neighboring towns. Its members capitalized on brainwashed women who were looking for the so-called "personal independence," and they encouraged—according to a disillusioned faction that eventually left the movement—divorce by introducing the notion that under the local district law, the assets of a couple are "equally split" at the final separation, regardless of the difference of education, training, and earning capacity of either spouse. Many local general lawyers became overnight divorce "specialists." It was, for a while, an upside-down local society.

The civil war in Afghanistan between warlords intensified. Daily basic human rights violations were countless across this nation deeply in turmoil. Abd initiated the idea of bringing his mother Elaha and his eighteen-year-old sister Nabeela to France as refugees. After serious discussions with his elder brothers Zekirullah and Ali and informing Aamir, who was still studying in Switzerland, Abd helped his mother and his sister prepare the necessary papers for immigration to France. In addition, Abd, with Amelia's consent, agreed to send monthly financial assistance to supplement his mother's only source of income, French financial aid to Afghanistan refugees. But in order to fulfil her sister's earlier desire to become a pharmacist, Abd committed himself to put her through four years of study in Reims, a region of Champagne-Ardenne. At home, in Tupchi, Dr. Zekirullah's earnings were barely enough to support his own family of five. But after he started working for the government, he was able to send occasionally some money to improve his mother and sister's diet. Ali, struggling with his mentally ill wife, was dirt poor. Aamir, still a student, took odd jobs to be self-supporting and managed to pay his school tuition but evidently was not able to financially help his mother and sister. In the final analysis, Abd was the only person who could assist the Rasulov matriarch and his youngest sister on a regular basis and over a period of twelve years. The reader shouldn't be surprised to be told that Amelia had a heart of gold; during the years of difficult marriage, and despite her active involvement in the WLM, she never forgot to send a monthly bank check to her mother-in-law. Abd continued to bring up this admirable attribute to his children each time he referred back to the wretched predivorce years.

Following a period of nine months' waiting, Nabeela and the elder female Rasulov immigrated to France and chose the city of Reims as their home. A year later, by traditional Afghan arrangement, Nabeela married the son of her father's classmate, and all three lived under the same roof while she attended the local pharmacy school. Since French was not taught as a second language in Afghan schools at the time, Nabeela had difficulty in following lectures on chemistry and physics during her first year. But with the help of her husband, who was also studying pharmacy, she managed to pass all her year-end exams. Life went on peacefully in that household for the next two years.

Then, one day Ali called Grandma Elaha from Vienna, where he was employed by the Austrian government, asking whether Grandma would take charge of her twelve-year-old grandson for a while, as the boy was having a hard time coping with his mother's unrelenting obscure mental illness. The poor Ali had to work double jobs to earn enough money to defray meal and board expenses for his son living away from home under the supervision of his own grandmother. Not too long after the boy came to live with his aunt Nabeela, difficulty of human interaction developed between the two. This had been an insurmountable problem for Elaha. On one hand, she dearly loved her occasionally misbehaved grandson; and on the other, she wanted to remain on good terms with her daughter, who continued to struggle with the language.

In addition, Nabeela was overwhelmed by compulsory pharmaceutical subjects that constituted the base of her professional formation. She gradually became irritable, not only with her nephew but also with her own mother and even with her husband. This led her to insomnia, anorexia, periodic vomiting, and eventually weight loss. The whole situation became critically unbearable for everybody in that household. To find a solution to the problem, Elaha sent a note to her son Abd and discreetly mentioned the crisis. Abd wrote back advising her to talk with Ali, suggesting him to take his son back and then send the boy, now fifteen, to a boarding school. He urged her to think about cohabitation with one of her sons living outside of Afghanistan and let her daughter Nabeela and her husband alone. After bringing up the issue with every one of her children, Grandma Elaha decided to move in with Aamir and his second Afghan wife in Aix-en-Provence, French Riviera. She knew that Abd's marriage was not stable and that Amelia wouldn't be able to communicate with her in Afghan anyway. On the other hand, the climate in Cote d'Azur, nice warm all year-round, would suit her very well, and there were a large number of refugees from Afghanistan living in Marseille and surrounding cities and towns. Among them were a few of her relatives with whom she kept contact on a regular basis.

At this crossroad and weighed down by many uncertainties, Abd continued to pray that God would lead his way and bestow on him a lasting peace that he desperately deserved. He kept praying, but so far luck was not on his side.

It was only five thirty in the afternoon of a late fall day, yet there was complete darkness outside. His office staff just left. A phone call came in. The neighbor who sold the piece of land on which Abd built his house was on the phone. "Can you stop by my house on the way home this evening? I have something important to tell you."

"What is it, Paul?"

"Too long to explain to you. Wait until you get here."

"Okay, thanks."

Paul was a transportation department supervisor. He had taken Abd out for fishing a couple of times. They helped each other cut Christmas trees on several acres of land owned by Paul's family every winter since Abd came to town, and they had become good friends. As a matter of fact, the Rasulovs were invited to attend Paul's daughter's wedding reception two years earlier. Every so often, when he had a few free minutes, the doctor stopped by Paul's house to say hello on his way home or to Foxeline Hospital.

On that evening, Abd arrived to Paul's home around six thirty after making a few calls responding to his patient's questions that his secretary received earlier that afternoon. He opened the squeaky outer steel-framed glass door at the same time when Paul appeared to greet his friend at the front entrance. "Hello, Abd. How are you? Please sit down near the fireplace. Blanche is out shopping this evening with her mom. So I am alone, and I want to share this news with you alone too, as I have known you long enough and want to absolutely respect your privacy. What I am about to tell you has at first greatly flummoxed me, but then I started to realize that all is possible these days in our region currently, as you undoubtedly know, under steady incoming waves of assault on our traditional family values." Paul austerely directed his regard to Abd. "Last Friday around midmorning, one of my crew members while driving to his camp saw from his truck a thin, light blond lady of average height, wearing glasses, walking out of Jean-Marie's hunting cabin. A few seconds after, he noted that a much older man was rushing out of the same shed and then quickly joined the lady. He was very familiar with Jean-Marie's physique and therefore recognized without any doubt that it was indeed him. Since he saw Amelia only a few times while working on the roads, he could not be 100 percent sure that the lady was your wife, but his description of the lady's appearance made me think that was indeed Amelia. You might not be aware of people's scrutiny when educated professionals settle into small towns like Foxeline or Lazerat. You happen to be one of them. Reportedly, she was seen a few times by locals alone with Jean-Marie, eating lunch at a neighbor town's food stand. Have you been told by anyone else about similar observations? I hate to be the first to inform you of this possibility."

Discreetly Abd replied, "Thanks for keeping me informed of what you have heard about gossip turned into fact from people in town. I'll see you and Blanche sometime next week."

Abd drove home, saddened by the story he had heard from his friend Paul. He ate the dinner Amelia saved for him in a hurry, took a quick shower, and then went to his room after spending a few minutes with Yasir at his bedside. Emal was back in boarding school after his fall break last week. While having trouble with falling asleep, Abd devised a plan to determine once and for all whether Amelia was having indeed an affair with "Uncle Jean." He got out of bed and made the phone call asking his friend GP colleague to cover for him for a few hours the next morning. On the next day, he acted as if he was about to drive to Lazerat after having his breakfast. He left the house just a few minutes before Amelia drove Yasir to school in her sedan Peugeot. After driving a few miles in the direction of Lazerat Hospital, Abd turned around and proceeded to drive to the elementary school at which Yasir was supposed to be dropped off. He carefully stayed out of Amelia's sight while snooping from the steering wheel of his rusty Citroën. Once he saw her car leaving the school, he took a side road and drove to Jean-Marie's home. This man's truck, usually parked on the dirt road in front of the house, wasn't there. Abd turned around at a cul-de-sac half a block farther and then drove home, wondering whether this vehicle was at his house. Sure enough, it was once again parked on the narrow paved courtyard, blocking the garage entrance. The doctor left his car a couple of hundred yards away, walked up the long driveway, and quietly entered the house. Lali and Seppo were at the door, wagging their tails at their master. There stood Amelia next to "Uncle Jean" in the living room.

Looking at the couple, Abd casually said, "I've forgotten my briefcase with my beeper in it and have to come back."

Not waiting for a response from either of the two facing him, Abd rushed to his study room, grabbed his briefcase, and hurried to the door. Obviously, it was an excuse cleverly made up by the doctor to minimize his wife's suspicion that he was spying on her. In reality, the briefcase was empty and the beeper was intentionally left in his Citroën. On his way going to Lazerat, Abd tried in his mind to put all pieces of the puzzle together. There wasn't any more a shred of doubt in Abd's mind; what he had witnessed that morning had clearly substantiated the story Paul told him the week before. His wife was having indeed an affair with another man in addition to her alcoholism, her use of illicit drugs, and her cult for personal independence through WLM, which drove her to a complete denial of traditional family values. It had become quite clear to Abd that he and his wife were living in two different worlds for quite a while, but how he had to deal with all these dilemmas remained a serious struggle for an overworked doctor with all sorts of physical and emotional problems himself. For days, he kept saying to himself, "I wish Mother Osgood was still around to assist me in times of distress like this." Abd was fully aware that his biological mother, Elaha, now living in Aix-en-Provence, wouldn't be able to help him, as she had not been exposed to the Western culture. At this juncture of his life, he had to make a decision for himself, and it wasn't an easy one—the divorce.

CHAPTER TEN

The Beginning of a Lifelong Disappointment

The word *divorce* is a dirty one for a practicing Catholic like Abd. But when facing an impending breakup of a family unit, the ensuing ramifications became bitter pills for him to swallow. In his mind, divorce was condemnable not only by his  God but also by his conscience; it was comparable to committing a crime. He considered divorce was equated with cowardice and definitely shameful. Being raised in a Buddhist environment and subsequently assimilated to Catholicism, Abd was convinced that divorce was absolutely antagonistic to his religious belief. For weeks on end, he struggled with the search for a solution enabling his two sons to keep daily contact with both parents while the latter lived separately. This was his utmost concern. Secondly, he worried about the disastrous emotional effect of divorce on the children, especially on the nine-year-old Yasir. He had no one around to guide the youngsters living through the post-divorce years until they left home and were on their own. The very first task and also the most difficult one Abd had to accomplish was how to explain to his two sons that he had tried to keep the family unit intact but failed; and therefore, the only solution left was the divorce with shared custody.

Abd had known for years that Amelia was the sole beneficiary of a very large asset worth at least a few million dollars left behind by her mother's recent death, but he was not swayed by wealth or prestige. In order not to further emotionally disturb Emal's and Yasir's school performance, Abd waited until the end of the school year to reveal to his children his decision of separation. On that first Saturday morning of July, when Amelia was out visiting with Mrs. Heireteid, a hardcore member of the WLM, Abd took the boys for a ride. They drove to Lake of the Clouds high up in the foothills of the Pyrenees Mountains. After wiping off the dust on a paint-peeled bench, quietly Abd sat down on it with the boys on his sides. In silence, they faced the tranquil blue water of the lake in the forefront and high majestic peaks in the background. Somberly, Abd looked in the distance while gently squeezing his two sons with his trembling arms. "I am very sorry for having to make this painful announcement to you. The legal union between your mother and me, as husband and wife, is going to be dissolved under the rule of District Esset law, and she and I will live separately. I am very much aware of the hardship resulting from this permanent and inevitable separation on all four of us. I ask for your understanding and forgiveness for my failure of keeping our family unit intact."

Yasir broke down, turned his body away from his dad, and while tightly holding the back of the bench with two hands, greatly distressed, began to weep softly. Emal, sitting on the other side of Abd, had tears welling in both of his red eyes. "Dad, your decision of a separation is not new to me. I knew all along that you and Mom had been having problems. I had confided my concern to Mr. Einucle at school. He has been fatherly, preparing me for this eventuality for months since Jean-Marie started to pay a great deal of attention to Mom. I got the impression that you know a lot more than I do about this 'unusual' friendship between them, but you don't want to share with us. Dad, I am thirteen and old enough to share with you your concern and worry. I have noted that your facial expression has been the true indicative of your physical and emotional suffering. I have been worrying a great deal about your health since you had the attack of paralysis due to a disease of your thyroid gland. In order to find out whether you have other illnesses besides your toxic thyroid, I took the liberty to search for additional ailments by looking at your personal medical file hidden behind the alphabetically well lined up medical periodicals on the bookshelf of your study room. After begging Mrs. Stanlag, your senior and most trusted secretary, twice on the phone, she finally gave in and confirmed the names of all diseases I read to her from your file. She could not lie to me. I am the culprit. So please do not scold her. I also learned from her the reasons why you didn't want to say anything to us about your suffering. You are afraid that our anxiety and concern over your health and your marital difficulty could severely affect our performance in school. We appreciate your unselfishness, but please look after your health. Dad, imagine for a moment, if you become ill and cannot work, who will take care of us?"

Abd reached out with his left arm and pulled Yasir back toward him. Then he directed his somber regard to the boys, one after another. "Here is my plan. I will try as soon as possible to find a two-bedroom house within a radius of two to three kilometers from the house where we live in now. This arrangement will enable you two to comfortably stay with me or with your mother. The only difference will be that you don't have both parents at the same time at the dinner table anymore once the separation is officially finalized." Abd purposely left out the word *divorce* for reasons mentioned earlier in this chapter. He drove the boys back home that late afternoon then left for rounds at the hospitals.

Since the children were baptized at a Lutheran church in Stockholm, the next day Abd decided to see the pastor of a local church of the same denomination after the Sunday service. Emal asked to accompany his father. They were hoping to hear some guiding advice from this young man of God. Consciously, Abd tried very hard not to put blame on Amelia for the marriage breakup, but rather to incriminate himself for having underestimated the delicate relationship between spouses, especially when dealing with two individuals having different characters and personalities. Father and son were disappointed; the pastor didn't say much of anything except these words at the church exit door. "It sounds like watching a soap opera. I can't believe everything you say and therefore I cannot be of any help to you."

As usual, Abd signed out to his GP colleague that following Monday morning before he left town. In order to keep the pending divorce strictly confidential, Abd drove to Carbonne, a town approximately fifty-nine kilometers away from Foxeline, and officially filed the divorce papers at a law firm office.

During the next three weeks, Abd diligently searched for someone who could pick Yasir up at school on certain days of the week, then go over his homework until Abd could bring his son home after office hours. Alternatively, Yasir could stay for dinner with that person in case his father was tied up with an emergency and late in coming home. One religiously devoted young couple whose baby daughter was Abd's patient and whose home in Tarte Hollow, a tiny hamlet in the neck of the woods but near the local elementary school, offered to help. Unfortunately, they had only a small truck that the husband needed to go to work with. For Yasir to take the bus, then to walk half a kilometer on an isolated dirt road to get to the hamlet was not too practical. Paul, his neighbor friend, who knew the area very well, was unable to find a house in the vicinity of Foxeline for Abd to rent. Building a second house near the existing one was out of question; no bank would be willing to offer a mortgage loan to a divorced doctor whose income was below average. Besides, Abd's small savings was not enough for the down payment. Therefore, the ideal arrangement to have the two boys see both parents several times a week was not realizable. The next best arrangement was for Abd to permanently relocate his practice in a larger city where he could easily find a home for rent no more than a couple of hours away from Foxeline. With this *modus vivendi*, the children would be able, per court order, to see their mother every two weeks instead of every day of the week. But Abd had to think over about leaving a busy and well-established medical practice in a small town to start all over again elsewhere.

Two weeks after Abd had filed the divorce petition, a county sheriff came to his office and asked "to see the doctor alone." Abd was served a court order notifying him that Amelia had filed a legal divorce from him. This came as a complete surprise, as Abd had already filed the divorce petition. From being a plaintiff, he had become a defendant because his lawyer had failed to initiate the divorce papers in a timely manner. A few days later, Abd received in the mail a notice from a local lawyer, notifying him that the District Esset Divorce court had appointed him to serve as "the guardian *ad litem* for the children." The latter requested that Abd make an appointment to see him in the presence of Emal and Yasir. The events that took place during the last month suddenly brought Abd to the realization that the divorce was indeed real and pending. At this juncture, he had no other choices but to find out from the children with whom they wanted to live once the separation was finalized. He anticipated an unbearable emotional pain for all four members of a shattered family unit from which he would have to pick up the broken pieces, to save what was salvageable and move on.

Emal gave his answer without hesitation when Abd discreetly mentioned the possibility of a relocation. "I want to go and live with you where you will start a new medical practice."

With Yasir, it was harder for his father to know exactly whether he wanted to stay in Foxeline and live with Amelia or to join his father and his brother. After school, he locked himself day after day in his own room, grieving during the next several months. At the end of the day, he came down to the dining table just for a few bites and then excused himself to return to his room. To the sadness created by his parents' pending divorce was added another serious blow related to his schooling.

Mrs. Heireteid, the laugh-before-talk teacher and a hardcore WLM member, had a son named Wehtham, who was of Yasir's age. They were in the same fourth-grade class at the Foxeline Elementary School. Wehtham had always been the top-notch student in every subject from kindergarten on, but he disliked gym and therefore was somewhat chubby like his mother. He believed soccer was for the intellectually underachievers. Not a single classmate liked him because he had the tendency to show off. On the contrary, Yasir excelled in this game but was not as good a student as Wehtham. Since Amelia was unofficially a new member of the local WLM chapter, she became a close friend of Mrs. Heireteid. As already mentioned above, Amelia's Peugeot ran out of gas twice on her way to visit Mrs. Heireteid. The following scenario took place the year preceding the divorce.

One morning, at the shriek of the school siren announcing the beginning of the school day, Wehtham ran fast to his classroom with his leather school bag mistakenly left unzipped. Suddenly, his shoes got caught in a cement floor crack. He tumbled and fell flat on his abdomen. The entire contents of the bag were thrown out of it by the impact and scattered on the floor. His tallest and strongest classmate, Pierre, happened to be behind him. The latter helped to pick up one item after another. Among these was a book entitled *Teaching Guide for Schoolteachers: Grade One through Five.* Wehtham thanked Pierre, and both quietly accessed the classroom.

At the end of the afternoon classes and once outside of the school building, Pierre leaned toward Wehtham and whispered in his ear, "Now we know for sure that you have been having the privilege of knowing in advance, before you go to school, the answers to the teacher's questions every day. Too bad, you had forgotten to hide the book from all of us this time. You should have left it in a secure place at home before going to school. From now on, all your classmates should stop wondering why you have been the first to raise your hand, offering always the right answer to each and every question the teacher had asked. How did you manage to get the book and from whom? Why has the rest of the class been kept away from having access to it?"

Wehtham, humiliated, walked away fast, giving no answer to Pierre. The incident was quickly made known to the entire class by Pierre. Within a few days, Yasir told his father the whole story. Not wanting to show his discontentment to his son and without consulting with Amelia, Abd decided to go and see the elementary school's principal. The latter, a lady in the late forties, as already previously mentioned, was brought in from Rennes to replace a male school headteacher the year before by the newly elected school board, made up almost entirely of active members of WLM. Politely but firmly, Abd demanded to borrow the *Teaching Guide for Schoolteachers* book, citing that as a French citizen and a taxpayer supporting the public school system, he had the right to inquire about any issue related to the teaching of children. The principal steadfastly refused to answer why the book was made available only to the schoolteachers' children but not to the rest of the class, even after Abd had pointed out that her policy was unequivocally unfair to taxpaying parents. To Yasir's chagrin, Abd came home emptyhanded and profoundly frustrated. He conveyed his thought of getting the same book for teachers through the Minister of Education's office, but Amelia disagreed. She gave the excuse that she didn't want to create the precedent, but in reality, she didn't want to rock the boat because of the arrival of the new female teachers who were known to be die-hard members of the WLM movement like herself. Instead, she attributed Yasir's lack of brilliance in school as being solely due to the fact that "he doesn't have Emal's intelligence and musical gift." Yasir, afflicted by the mounting differences between his parents, the removal of his male role-model soccer-coaching teacher, the declining performance in school, and perhaps other concerns, became very quiet. He showed signs and symptoms of depression. Indeed, he woke up at night with nightmares two to three times a week. His sunken cheeks, his dark-circled eyes, his frequent complaints of unexplained "pain all over" or stomachache, and his irritable response to his mother's trivial questions denoted a serious emotional childhood problem. In addition, Yasir became very self-critical and had low-esteem. He lamented for being born less intelligent than his brother and having no great natural ability. His social withdrawal was getting worse, to the point that he refused to go out for a game of basketball or soccer with his friends after school. He preferred to stay by himself in his room as long as he could. Abd became extremely concerned over the personality change Yasir was going through. He purposely increased the frequency of his being alone with his son. Not uncommonly, they sat next to each other in the children's room, looking out to the mountain peaks without uttering a single word to each other. But Yasir's body language was clearly indicative of Abd's main fear: even though Yasir understood the reasons for which his father had decided to terminate the union with his mother, the thought of having to separate from one of the parents had become a heavy burden haunting him day and night.

After a couple of telephone consultations with one of his colleague pediatric psychiatrists in Toulouse, Abd knew how to handle the situation, not only very professionally, but also extremely fatherly. He learned from the latter how to choose the right words and sentences each time he was talking with his son alone. Minutes of silence while looking to each other meant a lot to them. Abd felt somewhat reassured each time Yasir gave him a tight hug at the children's room door, saying, "See you tomorrow, Dad. I love you."

Worries and concerns about the pending divorce didn't seem to harass Abd enough. Within the next five weeks, he was plagued by another close-call event. Already suffering from the inevitable parental disunity, Yasir repeatedly missed soccer practices, complaining of being tired. He seemed to have little appetite at dinnertime. He looked pale and depressed. At first, Abd attributed these observed facts as expressions of a mental depression related to the painful family circumstances. Then Yasir woke up one morning with a low-grade fever and sore throat. Abd laid him down on his bed and gave him a complete examination. His pharynx was red hot with cauliflower-like white specks on his enlarged and inflamed tonsils. Large lymph glands were readily palpable around his neck and under his armpits. His liver was somewhat enlarged. Abd took him to Hospital of Lazerat to have the necessary lab tests performed. By the end of the same day, the in-house hospital pathologist called him to nervously report that Yasir had acute lymphocytic leukemia (ALL), a disease fairly common among young children, and their five-year survival rate was only 2 percent at the time. Since Abd wanted to be sure of the accuracy of diagnosis made by the local pathologist and knowing that the unknown-cause ALL and the disease called infectious mononucleosis (IM) caused mostly by Epstein-Barr but rarely by other viruses have overlapping symptoms and physical findings on examination, he took his son's blood smear to Toulouse University Hospital the next day to see the chairman of the hematology and oncology section for a second opinion. It turned out that the blood cells of IM were mistakenly interpreted as that of ALL. It was a relief for Abd. That evening he skipped dinner and went to the empty dimly lit church to thank God. Yasir recovered fully within two months.

Like the majority of individuals who contemplate divorce, Abd was very concerned about its effect on his children. For several weeks before he filed for a legal and permanent separation from Amelia, and while trying to keep his decision strictly in secrecy vis-à-vis his office staff and people in the Foxeline and Lazerat area, Abd dwelled on writings by reputable psychologists on the adverse outcome of spousal disunity. He realized that he was about to land in an uncharted territory. In order to help his two young sons emerge from this perturbing time strong, confident, and resolute in character, he must successfully navigate through a series of difficult situations. In his memoire notebook, Abd systematically jotted down on four pages the "most appropriate ways to deal with Amelia and the boys" during the pre- and post-divorce. He seemed to give a great deal of importance to his children's potential list of "wants" by making sure that he was actively involved in their personal life through direct communications, avoiding arguments with their mother, especially on matters related to them, reassuring them that both of their parents equally loved them and both were part of their life, and most importantly, restoring confidence to convince them that they could count on their parents to help them when they faced problems. Abd repeatedly assured the boys that they had done nothing wrong and therefore they shouldn't feel guilty. He understood from consulting with the head of Toulouse University Department of Psychiatry that he should encourage his two sons to talk in order to share their feelings of sadness and loss and not to dismiss them. Instead, he should inspire trust by showing that he had recognized and always wanted to hear their worry and concerns. He knew that most children have a remarkable ability not only to learn how to cope with their parents' separation, but also to heal when given the genuine support and love they needed. He wanted to let the boys know that whatever they said to him was acceptable. He had learned from his childhood while still living at home that physical closeness as expressed by pats on the shoulder, hugs, or simply compassionate eye-to-eye contact could convey to a child a real love.

As far as having to reveal to his children the reason for divorce, Abd didn't have much to say because they had on their own discovered that their mother had committed three most common social blunders, namely, adultery, an out-of-control bad habit of drinking alcohol, and drug usage. This unusual circumstance unequivocally spared Abd from having to go into detail explaining to his sons why it was no longer possible for him and their mother to live under the same roof. Emal, just turned fourteen, so determined to go with his father after the divorce, posed no great deal of concern for Abd, at least at this juncture. However, the ambiguity in discerning what was going through in Yasir's mind at that point was difficult to overcome. At the age of ten and a half, this child's natural attachment to his biological mother remained undeniable to him on one hand; on the other hand, he was old enough to grasp what was wrong with her behavior. Therefore, Abd doubtlessly recognized that his younger son was in the middle of a tug-of-war but having trouble to put an end to this game and join either the winning side or its opposition.

But Abd found solace in only one article among many writings on child psychology made available to him through correspondence with Toulouse University: children are in general objective and pure in discerning between right and wrong; but as they grow up, their thoughts and actions tend to be tainted by adults' selfishness and corruption. Emal's behavior had drastically changed since the trip with his dad to the Lake of the Clouds. Each time he came home from the private boarding school, instead of teasing as he had done in the past, he tried to gently talk to his brother about the inevitable negative effect of divorce on both of them; but at the same time, he took pains to cultivate in his brother's mind the notion of having to accelerate the growing-up process to quickly reach a state of self-sufficiency and independence that he had learned from Mr. Einucle. Yet, no one could ignore or fail to recognize the sadness on Emal's face as well as in the sounds of his impromptu piano pieces he played on the secondhand six-and-a-half-foot Steinway clavier his parents bought for him a few years earlier. The same anguish could be felt when one listened to excerpts of music written for French horn, here and there, in the evening during his vacation and long weekend breaks. Even though he only stayed home just a few days during the two school semesters, he continued to have arguments with Amelia, not only at the dinner table but also when they watched the local channel that strongly endorsed the WLM on a black-and-white TV. It was not uncommon to see the mother stand up and walk away from her son, angry for losing an argument in relation to the "modern" role of Frenchwomen in the society. In those instances, when Abd happened to be present with the children in the living room, he quietly and discreetly shook his head, signaling to his son a reminder: "Be kind to your mother, as you won't be able to see her every day after the separation."

The anticipated day scheduled to see the guardian *ad litem* lawyer on a Saturday had arrived. The counsel was alone in his small-town office. He asked the boys to stay in the waiting room, well equipped with picture books, sport magazines, and scientific publications, while he interviewed their father alone. Facing the lawyer across the table, Abd told him the reasons leading to his decision to file for divorce. In his *mea culpa*, he revealed to the latter that he was having more than one medical condition that could have made a change in his personality. He named them all and insisted that he must be the principal culprit causing the family breakup. The lawyer emotionlessly listened to Abd's story.

An hour later, the counsel opened his office door to let Abd out and to bring the boys in. With a smile on his face, he reassured them, "As you already know, through your dad's counselor, I am requested by the court judge to look after your welfare before, during, and after the separation until you both reach adulthood. In other words, I am assigned to represent the best interests of you two."

Among many questions, two important and relevant ones were raised by the counsel.

"I want you to tell me whether the following observations and witnesses by both or either one of you two were true. First, you have fortuitously found many hidden empty bottles of whiskey in the house and have reported this discovery to your father, whom you know is not an alcohol beverage drinker? Second, Jean-Marie's relationship with your mother is certainly not that of a true 'friend of the family' as your mother had claimed? Anything else you want to tell me?"

Emal and Yasir, almost in unison, replied to the counsel, "All of that is true and accurate."

Next, the counsel brought back Abd into the room and asked the boys to let him have a conversation alone with their father. He closed the door behind the children and asked them to stay in the waiting room separated from his office by the receptionist's chamber. In the absence of the children, he gave a brief enunciation. "I am very sorry for your suffering, the kind currently caused by proponents of a drastic change of the conventional family structure, whereby equality of rights between spouses is not enough. This new movement [he meant the WLM] has so far induced and encouraged separation and divorce at a rate never seen before in this calm and rustic southwest region of our country. Now that I have heard from you and your children your personal story independently, I want to close this visit by having all three of you together for a few minutes."

The counsel called Emal and Yasir back into the office. Yasir clung to his father's side. As soon as they sat down facing the lawyer across his desk, Emal looked at his father. "Do you have with you the copy of the letter she wrote to Jean-Marie, asking him not to forget bringing her the 'nerve balls' at their next rendezvous?"

At this indirect request from his son, Abd pulled out from his vest's inner pocket the photograph of the letter Emal was referring to—and already mentioned earlier in a previous chapter—and then handed it over to the counsel.

The lawyer turned to Yasir. "Your brother has decided to follow your dad everywhere he goes. How about you? Do you have the same desire or rather wish to stay with your mom and continue to go to school in Foxeline? You don't have to give me an answer today. You may call me to give an answer within the next two months, as I will have to write a tentative report to the court. Being still a minor, less than thirteen years old, you are going to be under my supervision and my guidance that will lead you through this rocky phase of your life. I want you to think it over, and if you have doubts or concerns on your final decision, please call me and talk to me. I will keep our conversation confidential. I am here to help you and your brother. Please don't hesitate to get in touch with me. Just say to my receptionist, 'Please let the attorney know that Yasir has called.' Okay?"

Led by his father and his brother to the car, this child, just turned ten years old, sobbed all the way home on that afternoon. Abd, saddened by the unavoidable legal separation, kept his emotion to himself. He realized how much suffering his two sons were going through, let alone the ordeal he was facing and would have to endure. So a few words of encouragement and reassurance here and there from him, in addition to the increased frequency of personal contact he had with them, meant a lot to the boys. They knew with certainty that their father would never desert them for a better new life elsewhere. They were fully aware that their father was trying very hard to pick up the broken pieces to unselfishly spare what was left from a broken family unit and move on. They were also very concerned of his physical and emotional sufferings.

The following Monday and by the end of the day's office hours, when the staff had left, Abd got a call from the attorney *ad litem* father and sons saw two days earlier.

The lawyer asked whether Abd could talk to him for a few minutes. "As you know, in order for me to be helpful to you and especially to your two boys, I need to know more about the 'nerve balls' your wife mentioned in her letter to Jean-Marie. I am wondering why she had to go through a layperson with so little education to get the drug(s). If these were for the treatment to calm her nervous condition caused by her feeling of guilt, why couldn't she get them through the legal pathway, i.e., through one of your colleagues in town? I am asking myself whether these 'nerve balls' represent in reality illicit drugs so commonly used by outsiders moving recently to the area. In my report to the court, I have to list unequivocally the reasons for the divorce. Based on the interview I had with you and your two sons, the main three justifications for filing of a legal termination of the union between you and your wife are adultery, alcoholism, and 'very likely' use of illicit drug(s). Do you have anything else you want me to include in my report to the court?"

"Thank you for getting back to me on the subject of divorce. I think I should leave out my suspicion that my wife is under the destructive influence of the WLM, because, despite the keen observation made by me and my sons on this strong possibility, we still have no concrete proof of it. As far as the 'nerve balls' are concerned, I think you are having the same suspicion as I do. I have hesitated initially to mention this issue in front of the boys until Emal brought it up himself. My concern was that by openly talking of illicit drugs, I could unwillingly but inadvertently seed in their mind the wrong idea of resorting to these for the cure of all malaises, including suffering caused by the dissolution of their parents' union."

"I fully understand and appreciate your prudent forethought to minimize the risk of unintentionally introducing illicit drugs to innocent children like your two sons. In view of the fact that you are a well-respected doctor in the area, I am not at all surprised that you had refrained from bringing up this matter yourself during your visit with me. But because of the required thoroughness with my report, I have to ask you how Emal had come to know of your wife's handwritten letter to the so-called 'friend of the family'?"

"The boys had been watching every move I make, especially after they had repeatedly observed the unusual relationship between the latter and Amelia during and after each Sunday ice fishing trip. On that particular night, when I accidentally discovered her letter and decided to take a photograph of it, I thought I was alone and nobody was around—I assumed that Amelia and the boys were sleeping—to know what I was about to do with the letter. To my big surprise, Emal quietly appeared behind me when I aimed my camera to the content of the letter."

"Based on the conversation I had with all three of you and letters of support from your housemaid and your patients you had submitted to the court through your lawyer, I have decided to recommend to the court judge that you should have the custody of your two boys. Here is how I have come to this decision. Emal had steadfastly, from the beginning of the cross-questioning, rejected the idea of living with your wife after the divorce, citing that she had deserted him and his brother by having an affair with an unworthy 'friend of the family.' The poor Yasir, just turned ten, had some difficulty to realize suddenly that the imminent breakup of his family unit was real and inevitable. But before the visit with me, he had spent many days mulling over the root cause of the rift between his parents, but in spite of his suffering, he conveyed to me in the end his desire to follow his brother and his father to start a new life, away from having to witness day after day the newly created relationship between his mother and a man whom he had thought a real 'friend' but turned out to be a home wrecker destroying his parents' marital union. He accused Jean-Marie—referred to as 'friend of the family' during the entire conversation I had with him—for having the malicious intention of interfering with his parents' marital relationship. Dr. Rasulov, your case is not as complicated as many others I have had during the last eight years since I was selected by the court as attorney *ad litem.*"

Life became more difficult for Abd during the next nine months of waiting for the final day in court. Not being able to find a lodging facility somewhere between Lazerat and Foxeline and someone in the same area to care for Yasir after school due to financial constraint, the only choice left was to move his practice out of town, to another larger city not too far from Foxeline. Abd's intention was to make sure that the boys would be able to see their mother at least once every two weeks after the divorce. The name Naguda suddenly came to his mind. Abd met this radiologist during a one-day medical conference held in Toulouse last year. He called this doctor, and they talked on the phone for at least half an hour. Dr. Naguda reassured Abd that he would be undoubtedly welcome by the entire medical circle in Odinard, a city located within no more than a two-hour drive from Foxeline, with a population of fifty-five thousand.

The next most important issues that needed to be resolved before moving to Odinard were the finding of a roof over the head for Abd and his two sons and the setting up of an office for medical practice. Abd had less than 160,000 French francs, or 40,000 US dollars, and all invested in a pension account. He and Amelia had very little cash since they moved to Foxeline almost twelve years ago. Abd's earnings were barely enough for a family of four to frugally live on. Taking money out of the pension investment was absolutely discouraged by his financial adviser. Abd lost a couple of night's sleep trying to figure out where he could get enough cash for the down payment of a small house and for the rental of an office for his medical practice in Odinard. He decided to place a call to this city's Chamber of Commerce.

The president of this institution was more than willing to be the go-between the local commerce bank and Abd. "Your reputation has been known to us here in Odinard for quite some time. The people of our city and of its surroundings would be delighted at the prospect of receiving the specialized care from a doctor with your advanced training and experience. I will do my best to support your application for a bank loan adequate to cover all expenses incurred right after you move to town. In case this approach fails, I will resort to other alternatives. You can count on our business to help you. So, please go ahead and send your application for the membership of medical staff at our hospital as soon as possible. I will intervene on your behalf in dealing with the bank once your application for hospital privileges is approved. Please, call me if you have more questions about our city. We are here to help professional newcomers."

Abd happily thanked the man and then went back to his office that same evening to punctiliously make the two applications in question. Abd's membership on the Odinard General Hospital medical staff as a newcomer with two specialties was announced two weeks later in the local daily newspaper. The bank loan was approved a few days later. As a result, the worry about possible insurmountable issues related to the relocation in a different city was at least partially abated, but the realization of the soon-to-be single parenthood considerably frightened him.

After several months of negotiations between Amelia's and Abd's attorneys, Abd's lawyer informed him that a tentative agreement had been reached with regard to the spouses' estate: the pension investment under Abd's name would stay with him. To compensate for this and because "the future potential earning of a doctor is several times greater than that of a certified registered nurse," as agreed upon by the lawyers on both sides, 80 percent of the proceeds from the sale of the property and the meager bank savings would go to Amelia. However, Amelia continued to insist on having sole custody of the boys, instead of letting them decide for themselves on this matter, the last recourse was to have a trial in the local divorce court.

Finally, the day in court to finalize the divorce had arrived. Abd received a notice from the clerk of Esset District Court to appear at the courthouse, room no. 207 at 2:00 p.m. on a Friday in late November. The court ordered that the two children must spend an hour with the attorney *ad litem* before the arrival of the judge and that they could accompany either of the spouses on that day. Abd assumed that Amelia had received the same notice and that Emal and Yasir had the last opportunity talking to their guardian lawyer before the judge pronounced the parental right to the custody of the children.

Emal and his brother, accompanied by their father, climbed up to the second floor of the courthouse at five minutes to one on that windy and cold afternoon, somewhat frightened and bewildered. There stood the attorney *ad litem*, waiting to have one last conversation with the boys before the trial session started. Abd was requested to wait in room 207 while the lawyer spent a few moments with the children in a secluded room at the end of the hallway. Entering the spacious room, Abd immediately recognized the presence of two hardcore WLM members sitting in the back row next to a few ladies Abd had never seen before, Mrs. Heireteid and Mrs. Lambert. The latter, recently divorced, lived across the street from the Rasulovs' property. Abd sat down on one of the benches reserved for contenders and their family members. For a moment, he felt as if he would have to represent himself as the *pro se* litigant, being alone without supporting witnesses. The strange thought that he might end up with only a visiting right instead of full custody of his two sons, the only remaining intact elements of his broken family, suddenly invaded his preoccupied mind while he was reviewing his notes on reasons for his decision on a legal and permanent separation from his wife. Suddenly he heard the noise generated by people entering the court-room no. 207. He looked up at the clock hung behind the judge's desk. The long hand was on number 10, and the short one, slightly left to number 2 on the dial. One by one the lawyers sat down on their designated seats side by side with their paralegals.

By this time Emal and Yasir, accompanied by the guardian *ad litem*, arrived. Emal was allowed to sit next to his father, but Yasir was kept on a separated seat at the site of the guardian. The second lawyer Abd hired to replace the one in Carbonne with whom he had initially filed the divorce papers walked in about the same time. He sat down on a chair immediately adjacent to Abd. Finally, the court judge appeared at the door facing the main entrance. Everybody in the room immediately stood up for a few seconds. Without delay, he ordered Amelia's attorney, the plaintiff lawyer, to proceed with the presentation of Amelia's case first and then to follow with the direct examination. This was followed by the cross-examination carried out by Abd's lawyer, but he had no objection.

The latter sat down, leaned over to his client, and murmured, "I have successfully negotiated with her lawyer and the kids' legal guardian to make you pay the sum of 100,000 French francs over a period of five years. In compensation, these two lawyers would not object to my demand that you'd have full custody of the boys with your wife's visiting privilege. I have spent many hours working out a final agreement, which was submitted to the judge last week. This afternoon session should be brief."

Subsequently, once Abd received an exorbitant bill from his attorney, he found out, through written communication with the regional lawyers association, that it had markedly surpassed the allowable cap imposed by the association and that the law in Esset District dictated the judge's decision with regard to the custody of the children of divorcing spouses; there was no need for negotiation on monetary compensation between both parties' lawyers. The children older than eight years were free to choose the parent they wanted to live with after the divorce.

Now, let's get back to the session in court. At that point, the attorney *ad litem* approached the judge's bench and quietly said something to him while pointing his finger to the report he had filed earlier on behalf of Emal and Yasir. Nobody in the room could hear a word out of this brief conversation. The judge quickly went over that particular assessment. It appeared as if he had read all the documents related to this divorce case before he came. He then proceeded to call the attention of all the lawyers in the room. "I want to see the doctor's youngest son alone in the chamber."

The guardian *ad litem* made a sign to Yasir to follow the judge's order. The latter, frightened, while directing his look to Amelia, slowly walked toward the judge. Then both disappeared behind the courtroom for at least ten minutes. An unusual anxious quietness reigned in the room. Both reappeared. This time Yasir went to sit on an empty chair next to his brother. Sitting back on his imposing mahogany chair, the judge solemnly swept his look from one side of the room to the other. "Before I pronounce my ruling, I want to hear both sides' rebuttal witnesses in the room, if any."

Abruptly, Mrs. Heireteid stood up and loudly declared that the disunity was the result of difference of ethnic background between spouses and not from social deviation. As soon as the latter sat down, Mrs. Lambert, while looking around her, defiantly insisted that she was in agreement with her friend Heireteid and that it would be a big mistake to let the father have the custody of the children. She also contended that Abd was an unsociable man who would have a great deal of difficulty in raising the children. Having no supporting witnesses, Abd decided not to represent himself as the *pro se* litigant. Being first time involved in a divorce trial, he didn't know that his lawyer could help him rebut the ladies' nonsensical comments. So, he sat motionless next to his sons.

Ignoring the comments made by these ladies, the judge continued, "Based on written materials submitted to me by both sides' attorneys, by the guardian *ad litem*, and especially on my sequestered talk with Yasir Rasulov, I have come to the following adjudication: Dr. Rasulov will have full custody of the children, and Mrs. Rasulov, the visiting right, meaning she will have the right to be alone with her children every other weekend. As far as the couple's assets are concerned, an agreement has been reached between the lawyers, and therefore, I have decided not to discuss this matter in public, for the sake of personal privacy."

Just at the moment when the judge had his last words, one could hear a commotion coming from where Amelia was flanked by her attorney and the paralegal. Mrs. Heireteid and Mrs. Lambert rushed to the site, took the sobbing Amelia with them in their car, and sped away almost unnoticed. Accompanied by Yasir and Emal, Abd headed toward the main entrance and then walked to the rusty two-door Citroën parked behind the courthouse.

As soon as all three sat down, Yasir on the back seat, Dad at the wheel, Emal angrily uttered these words: "I would spit at these two women's face had they been facing me at the exit door."

While leaning against the car door and pondering the events of the past nine months and the single parenthood's bewildering complexity which would be presented to him during the coming years, Abd simply replied, "We all have suffered for many years. With God's help, we should leave our past behind and start over a new life satisfactory not only to three of us but also to your mother inclusively. The outcome could have been worse or alternatively something very wrong could have happened to any one of us. So, be thankful to God and praise him through your daily prayers."

Abd understood and accepted the children's temporary frustration that came on during the divorce trial. The meaning of his life solely rested on the happiness that he tried to bring to his sons. He arranged with Amelia to have her keep Yasir during the first week after the trial and then drove with Emal to his newly purchased house in Odinard. Both slept on the living room floor that night. Within five days Abd managed to accouter the house first floor and his bedroom with secondhand furniture. Since Emal had returned to his boarding school, Abd concentrated alone on getting the upstairs small room, across the hall from his, ready to receive Yasir in less than a week. Hastily he applied a new and bright coat of paint to the walls of this room. The memories of joyous moments spent on a few Sunday afternoons, before the breakup of the family, with his son playing with the miniature train set, enticed him to decorate it with four photographs of vintage railroad steam-powered locomotives hung on both sides of the window looking over the neighbor's flower garden. The dusty old-looking ceiling light bulb, attached to two naked wires, was replaced by a dome light. In addition, Abd had a new maple single bed, a night table, and a bed lamp delivered to this room to make it attractive upon his son's arrival. The six-and-a-half-foot Steinway had to be delivered by movers specialized in moving expensive brands of pianos. It barely fit into the guest room on the first floor in which Emal slept each time he came home. A second maple single bed, similar to that of Yasir, was purchased a few weeks later for the older son. The deadline was met, and the house was ready for the occupation of a divorced man and his two preteen and teenage sons.

CHAPTER ELEVEN

The Most Difficult Single-Parent Life

That was the Sunday preceding Abd's resumption of seeing patients in his Odinard office. He and Yasir had hastily finished their lunch. They had planned to take a walk to the elementary school located one block away from their house, knowing that they would be able to see only the external aspect of the school complex. Abd wanted his son to be familiar for the first time with the shortest but safest route to and from the new school. Father and son put on their heavy winter coats. They locked the kitchen entrance door, descended one step to get to the empty breezeway, and then strolled to the school complex in the windy, cold afternoon of December. They managed to have a quick look at its well-organized interior through the windows.

On the following Monday morning, the newly hired mother-of-three secretary was alone in the office, taking calls. Abd went to school with his son and asked to be introduced to the school principal by the admission office lady. The latter was a very kind and helpful middle-aged lady to the newcomers in this industrial town. Abd revealed to her that he was a single parent and wished to know whether there was an after-school hour session to keep the children safe and under supervision while waiting to be picked up by members of their family. The answer was yes, giving Abd a great deal of hope in his search for ways to have Yasir constantly under the watchful eyes of an adult while he worked.

That evening after supper, Abd went over with his son all the aspects in connection with schooling. He taught the latter how to introduce himself in a friendly manner to all his fourth-grade classmates. They checked Yasir's waterproof school shoulder bag to be sure that the necessary school supplies were in place, and then both went to bed early. Abd had trouble falling asleep; he kept thinking about the missing role of a mother *vis-à-vis* the raising of underaged children. Unanswered questions, such as "From now on, who will pick up Yasir at school and then look after him while I am at work?" or "How can I find someone I could trust to stay with Yasir at night when I am called out to the hospital for an emergency?" haunted him for days. He became obsessed with the idea that no one but himself had to assume the transportation of his son after school hours to and from sites of regular extracurricular activities such as soccer practice, oboe lessons, and especially bimonthly trips to Foxeline to spend the weekend with his mother. But quickly he realized that alone, he would not be able to undertake other household tasks in addition to being a full-time medical doctor. Furthermore, he didn't want to become an overprotective parent. Instead, he chose to let his son acquire the normal growing-up independence without being under constant influence of either of the parents. The ideal solution would be the search for a person or persons who could assist him 24-7 or at least make himself or herself available, when needed, from the time of school dismissal in the afternoon until six in the morning of the next day, five days a week. But this approach would cost a good amount of money, and Abd had just started a new practice from scratch.

Yasir's first day in a new school and Abd's first day in the office were uneventful. That Monday morning, the secretary was alone in the office, taking calls from new patients who saw the ad of Abd's new medical practice in the local Sunday newspapers. Abd walked his son to school and returned to his office to catch up with reading of medical periodicals. He was called by the Odinard Hospital Emergency Department to see a few patients on public assistance, who used the ED for their medical care.

At three, Abd returned to school to pick up his son. As they walked to their car parked on the street, a lady, accompanied by a girl approximately Yasir's age, gave a friendly greeting, "Mister, you must be new in town. We have not seen you before."

"Yes, we arrived to town last week, and we are still trying to find our way around. My name is Abdulai Rasulov, or Abd for short, and Yasir is my son."

The lady reached out to shake Abd's hand. "Catherine Mathichée and my daughter, Adelle."

The girl interjected, "Yasir was introduced to our class this morning by a fifth-grade substitute teacher. Our regular teacher had to attend a one-day seminar. Like me, his favorite sport is soccer."

"If we could be of help to you, please call. My husband and I are usually at home after six."

After exchanging their telephone number, Abd drove his son home and then started to prepare dinner while Yasir was upstairs doing assigned homework. At the mealtime spent habitually at the kitchen table, quietly Abd asked his son about his first day in the new school; but as usual, his son didn't say much except these same words he had for months repeatedly used to spare his father from worrying: "I'll be okay, Dad. Don't worry."

Right after dinner, Abd took courage to call Catherine. Her husband answered the phone. Then he transferred the call to his wife. Catherine and Abd talked for a while on the phone. Smilingly, Abd hung up the handset and then called out to his son. "Starting tomorrow, you will be picked up every day in the morning by Mrs. Mathichée at seven. She will drive you and Adelle to school. At three, she will return to school to bring both of you home. You will stay at her house, do your homework, and wait for me to pick you up after office hours. She agreed to feed you at dinnertime in case I am detained by patients in the office or at the hospital."

This arrangement with the Mathichées had solved part of the huge concern Abd had on the care of his young son living alone with him. The most difficult aspect of this concern lay with the absence of an adult's pair of eyes on his son at night when he had to go to the hospital to see patients. Hiring a housekeeper was out of the question. Abd's income during the first two years was too small for such a luxury. There were no relatives in the area that he could count on to look after his son, who was still a minor. He seriously entertained the possibility of trying to reconcile with Amelia. At that point in time, Amelia was deeply involved in her relationship with Jean-Marie, the "friend of the family." People in the area saw them together in neighbor villages, in hunting cabins, and even at the town dump. Their gossip at town's public places about a doctor's wife and her new "friend" was the talk of the town. As a matter of fact, this man's wife was going through a severe depression caused by her husband's relationship with Amelia.

One afternoon, while still in his office and approximately a month after the divorce decree, Abd got a call from Jean-Marie's eldest son. "Doctor, can you do something to help my mother? She has not been sleeping, eating enough to sustain her normal weight, and crying day and night. Our family doctor told us that she is having a severe depression that needs to be urgently addressed. Can you talk to your wife and tell her about the destruction of our family unity caused by her condemnable relationship with my father? We would greatly appreciate if you could talk her into giving up her relationship with him."

Because he no longer had any jurisdiction on Amelia, Abd advised this man to take up his complaint with the court. Abd was faced with two alternatives. On one hand, such a grave situation should have deterred Abd from attempting to legally reverse the official "irreconcilable difference" listed on the divorce certificate and reunite with Amelia. On the other, because of his single parenthood, he alone must assume all household chores including cooking, cleaning, washing, grass mowing, and other minor routines in addition to having a full-time medical practice; he decided to go through with this reconciliation attempt, which could be the only solution, if successful. Even though Yasir repeatedly insinuated that his father must not remarry at least for a while, Abd was convinced that he could talk his son into accepting his mother again with the help from the local mental health service.

The very first thing he did was to get in touch with Biorn, Maurina's husband. He came to know Biorn after a few annual summer trips to Stockholm to see Amelia's mother. Abd, the two boys, and Amelia stopped by each year to spend a couple of days with Maurina and her husband in Karolinska suburb. Biorn and Abd had many common interests—music history, painting and sculpture, world political affairs, and medicine. They exchanged letters during the Christmas holiday season. Since Biorn was subspecialized in psychology, Abd had consulted him a few times during the year preceding the relocation to Odinard on his marriage difficulty. Biorn was a perfect counselor and friend to Abd.

Biorn believed that the marriage dissolution between Amelia and Abd shouldn't have happened and that the official divorce should be reversed back to a remarriage through reconciliation. He discussed this issue with a friend of his who happened to be a reputable psychiatrist affiliated with Karolinska Institute. The latter advised Biorn to invite Abd to his house, together with Maurina, Amelia's childhood girlfriend Stella, a practicing psychologist in Stockholm, and Yasir's godmother and Amelia herself if she agreed to the attempt of reconciliation. Biorn suggested that the psychiatrist be the leader of the session of discussion. Abd signed out for that last weekend in January to a local internist in solo practice in Odinard.

He flew to Karolinska and then spent the entire Saturday morning in the psychiatrist's office with Biorn and Maurina. The three men agreed on how to approach Amelia. But Maurina was not at all convinced that Amelia and Abd could ever live again together under the same roof, even after both had agreed to undergo lengthy and complicated psychoanalysis and therapy. She and Biorn had a serious disagreement on the subject. She contended that she knew the situation better than anybody else among the four sitting for hours in that office, as she just returned from a five-day trip to Foxeline to see her closest friend Amelia. Upon further inquiry by the psychiatrist, she revealed that she had met during her journey with several WLM activists, including Mrs. Heireteid, Mrs. Lambert, and Mrs. Rosewin, a music teacher recently arrived to the area from Canada.

That Saturday evening was crucial with regard to a last chance of reconciliation between the divorcees. It was seven o'clock, yet Stella had not arrived. Biorn proceeded to call Stella to find out whether she would be present at this meeting at his home. Stella could not be located anywhere. There was neither a telephone call nor a letter from her replying to the invitation. Amelia had not responded to the written request signed by the psychiatrist and Biorn to attend a "reunion" even though the letter was sent off a week earlier by express mail. Finally, Biorn decided to use the three-way telephone conference, hoping to let the psychiatrist explain to Amelia his professional advice. The phone rang at Amelia's home in Foxeline. Someone picked up the handset, but there was no human voice, only a breath sound. Abd, sitting next to Biorn with a phone handset to his ear, was anxiously waiting for Amelia's voice. A few seconds later, Amelia came to the phone. Biorn introduced the psychiatrist to her. The latter spent at least thirty minutes with her on the phone. One could detect her sobs off and on during the conversation. Very disappointed, the counselor turned to Abd and Biorn. "I am sorry. I was unable to persuade her to officially file a reversion of the divorce decree and start a dialogue of reconciliation with her former husband. She was adamant about the direction she took. She stated that she no longer had any feeling for her ex and that she is preoccupied by the image of another whom she gets along with much better. I am sorry."

The next day Abd flew back to Odinard. As he entered the house and before he was ready to go to the Mathichées' home to pick up his son, the phone rang. Jean-Marie's son was again frantic on the phone. "Dr. Rasulov, please help! My mother was urgently taken to the hospital in Foxeline this afternoon. She fainted when she heard my father say that he was going to file for divorce and marry your ex.

I know you no longer have any jurisdiction on her, but you can use your persuasive skill to convince her that her action could ruin my entire family. Please try, Dr. Rasulov. Thank you."

"I sympathize with you. As I had said last time, I am powerless in trying to rationalize with her. She has made up her mind about the new chapter of her life. I realize that it is a desperate circumstance, but I cannot be of any help to you and your mother. I am deeply sorry." That was the first Easter holiday for Yasir and Emal after their parents' separation. Abd drove Yasir to Foxeline for his bimonthly visit with his mother on Thursday evening. Emal, detained by an organizational meeting with his ski team, was picked up from the boarding school by a neighbor who happened to be in the area in the afternoon of that Good Friday. He spent some valuable time alone with his father on the following Saturday. They went to the Lutheran church service on Sunday. Then both went to a nearby family restaurant for their Easter brunch before heading in the direction of Foxeline to bring Yasir home. Father and son knocked at the garage side-door of their former home now occupied by Amelia. As the door opened, the family's favorite dog Lali was already there to greet Emal first with a soft bark followed by one-stroked licking of his palm, a gesture of happiness she conveyed to him every time he returned from school. But quickly Lali ran out to accost her approaching master she had not seen for several weeks with a repeated tender yelp while incessantly rubbing his pants with her head. Abd sensed right away that Lali missed him greatly, and vice versa. At that moment, Amelia, in casual attire, descended from the first floor, embraced Emal, then called out while holding her oldest son by his waist, "Yasir, the party you have been waiting for the whole day is here."

Within a couple of minutes, Yasir, with a facial expression of discontent, came down on the squeaking wooden staircase with his rucksack casually hanged on his left shoulder. He was about to join his brother standing next to Amelia on the basement floor. "Hi, Emal. Where is Dad?"

"He is here, outside of the door with Lali."

Amelia pulled Yasir over and squeezed her two sons' bodies against her sides for a few seconds, when Abd entered the house basement in company of Lali. Amelia had no intention of asking her just-arrived former husband and son to go upstairs for a few minute's rest, before heading back to Odinard. She embarrassingly then non-chalantly looked at Abd while slowly walking in the direction of the staircase. "Hey."

Suddenly, Jean-Marie, with a trembling voice while coming down from the upper floor with a couple of sheets of what appeared to be scrapped papers in his hand, yelled, "Yasir, don't forget to take your homework with you. Otherwise, you will find an excuse to return sooner than thirteen days from now. I can't tolerate any more your argumentative attitude."

Emal angrily pointed his finger to the face of his "former friend of the family" and impudently replied, "You have no right to talk rudely to my brother like that!"

"I have stooped as low as I could for months in dealing with you two, and now I have enough of your misbehavior."

Father and sons took turns to sadly stroke Lali's head, then walked to their car, heading home. That was the last time they saw Lali. She died of liver cancer at the end of that same year.

Once again at the wheel, Abd asked whether Yasir had spent a nice three-day Easter holiday with his mother. Not making a single comment during the two-hour drive, Abd attentively listened to what his two sons had to say. Forthrightly and defiantly, Emal uttered, "I wish I had a golf club with me when Jean-Marie made that stupid, uncalled-for indirect insinuation to Yasir. I could then use it to whack his head."

Sitting quietly behind his brother, Yasir related that he was "miserable" during the entire visit. "He behaved as if Mom is now his property. I believe, what had bothered him the most was that my presence had prevented him from staying alone with her during my visit. The guy left after midnight and showed up at the house already at dawn on two consecutive days, even before we had the chance to get out of bed. Noticeably, Lali growled at him every time he got close to Mom."

As the car approached Odinard, Abd somberly said to his sons, "You know, my life has been revolving around you two and myself for quite a while, as you are undoubtedly aware. I don't have enough words to express how much I love you two. You two are the only hope left for me. You are my life, and God is the witness. As long as you continue to keep up with your good work at school, I am happy. Don't worry about me. God is guiding me through the tough times."

Abd started to see more patients in the hospital as well as in his office, but he also became very preoccupied with finding a way to keep Yasir safe at home at night when he was called to the ED to see patients or to the nursery to care for sick newborns. The preteen boy was doing passably well in school. He and Adelle were members of the soccer team of the middle school. They did their homework together in the afternoon until he was picked up by his dad. The Mathichées, practicing Catholics, became Abd's good friends. They had empathy for the single-parent doctor. They treated Yasir like their own child. Catherine proposed to keep Yasir at their home during the week, and Abd graciously accepted the offer. Abd routinely stopped by to see his son every day after office hours. He missed his son in the evening after supper, and without his son, he had no incentive to cook anymore. As a result, he neglected to have nutritious meals. Ready-made TV dinners replaced freshly cooked meat and vegetables, but he kept up five-day-a-week physical exercise in the form of jogging as a way of preserving his sanity and endurance.

Yasir spent his first Christmas with his mom still living in the same house in Foxeline. He continued to hold a grudge against his former friend Jean-Marie, who spent most of his time at the house. But he remained obedient as far as bimonthly visits with his mother. During long weekend or holiday breaks, Emal, just turned seventeen, drove his brother to see their mother in Foxeline, and Abd did not have to worry about having to find appropriate transportation for them.

One afternoon, Abd's former classmate John Campbell showed up at the door. "I am attending the annual International Infectious Diseases Conference in Toulouse and wanted to bring you guys a surprise—me."

Abd rushed to the door and embraced his friend, whom he had not seen for almost ten years, although they kept in touch with each other two to three times a year through short written notes or phone calls.

John turned to Yasir and embraced him. "You have grown quite a bit since I saw you last in Paris, before your dad and mom moved to the Pyrenees region."

Abd took his friend and his son out for dinner. They barely finished eating when Abd's beeper went off twice. He knew that it was a call from the hospital ED. He excused himself and asked Yasir to walk back to the house with John. "It won't be too long. Give me an hour or even less."

Once back at home, John discreetly and gently asked Yasir how he was doing in school, whether he was happy living alone with his father. Purposely, John didn't want to bring into the conversation the notion of divorce and single parenthood. Yasir responded by saying that he was doing okay in school, that he had made friends with a good number of his classmates, enjoyed weekly soccer games with other middle-school teams, and in general was very happy except for some inconvenience for not being able to sleep in his own bed during the week. He volunteered to say that he had made a right choice. "I am glad I am living with my father. My bimonthly visits with my mom since their separation have reinforced my conviction that I made a wise decision."

John understood correctly that Yasir had denounced his mother's relationship with a married man. He was convinced that the boy was much happier than he had anticipated before coming. Proudly, Yasir let John know that he would be thirteen in eighteen months; then he would be old enough to be safely left alone at home day and night.

Thirty-five years later, when the two old friends saw each other for the last time, John reminded Abd again that Yasir was genuinely happy and felt protected when he was living alone with his father and then during the years after his father was remarried. After many years that had gone by, Abd still vividly remembered those short evening walks on the weekends around the block before bedtime with Yasir. He had been fully convinced that his young son unconditionally loved him. This feeling had been indeed echoed in Yasir's dream that one day, when he had earned enough cash through his summer job as a vendor assistant to a vegetable stand owner, he would buy a small paddle boat to go fishing alone with his father.

One Saturday morning, at breakfast, Yasir sadly looked at his father. "Dad, can I be truthful with you? The Mathichées have been admirably nice to me since you accepted to let them have me stay at their home, and Adelle and I are getting along very well, but I miss you so much at night and often I have been having trouble falling asleep. Can I stay home with you at night from now on? I have no problem with having you drag me to the hospital at night when you get called out. I am sure I would be able to sleep somewhere in the building, waiting for you to wake me up and take me back to my room you took pains to warmly decorate for me."

Abd's tears welled up in his eyes at Yasir's plea. So he agreed to go along with his son's supplication. The first test of the new arrangement between father and son took place a week later. It was a few minutes before one o'clock in the morning of Friday. The phone rang in Abd's bedroom. The night nurse informed him that the obstetrician on call had made a decision to urgently deliver by caesarian section a preeclamptic woman in labor and wanted to be assisted by a medical doctor familiar with newborn resuscitation. Abd woke up his son who was still in deep sleep after playing hard as attacker in a soccer game at school that afternoon. Both dressed up quickly, got into the Citroën, and then headed toward the hospital. The ED was still crowded with waiting patients and their family members. They passed the busy crowd and then approached the medical library two doors away.

Two females in gray gowns and a male in a long white coat were sitting at the huge table, reading. Abd leaned toward the man. "Hi, Dr. Marchant. Do you mind if I let my son stay here while I am attending a C-section?"

The latter shook his head and plunged back into his reading. In a hurry, Abd pulled together three chairs at the far corner of the library, improvising a temporary uncomfortable bed for Yasir to sleep on while he was in the operating room. They got back into the car and drove home about an hour later. The next day, Saturday, Yasir got up at ten o'clock, tired. But at least he had altogether more than eight hours of sleep. As Abd's practice was getting busier, he was called out more often at night. After a while, he realized that getting his son out of his sleep and dragging him to the hospital at night was not a permanent solution until Yasir reached his thirteenth birthday. The idea of hiring a person to sleep over at night five days a week became more realistic in his mind. He decided to discuss this idea with the Mathichées, who happened to know a family, members of their church, with a twenty-three-year-old daughter named Anna, engaged to a policeman, who might be interested to help. This young lady lived half a block away from Abd's home. There was no problem for her to come to the house and be with Yasir when Abd was called out at night. That was a real relief for Abd when this person accepted to take the job. She proposed the financial compensation, and Abd accepted it as such. The safety issue for his son was finally resolved, but Abd must continue to do all domestic chores mentioned earlier.

Yasir wanted to assist his father with dishwashing and floor vacuuming, but Abd rarely accepted his son's extra hand. He wanted his son to concentrate on homework and spend time with a few selected friends during the weekend. He sent his son to his room at eight thirty every night after quickly going over his homework so that the boy could have enough sleep; but himself, he never had the chance to go to bed before midnight. Dishwashing, kitchen cleanup, and table setting for the next morning had to be done at the end of the day. Sadly, it had become inhuman for having to assume alone all household chores in addition to a full-time medical practice for a long period of three years. Despite regular physical exercise, insomnia and fibromyalgia/myofascial pain syndrome returned over the next several months.

In addition to these setbacks, the professional relationship between Abd and other primary care physicians gradually deteriorated. Abd's double specialty and his unusual compassion attracted not only a large number of new patients, but also family members of colleagues specialized in other medical fields. As a result, envy and jealousy quickly developed among a few of his primary care colleagues practicing as GPs or pediatricians. None of them had a subspecialty. Odinard was a small city and therefore not able to support subspecialized doctors like Abd. As a matter of fact, he was the first one of this kind in Odinard. Furthermore, he was a foreigner of different ethnicity, and small-town mentality bred unfounded, strange, or obscure and contradictory rumors, which were current at the hospital. But Abd avoided responding to these hearsays and gossip, and eventually the whole mess calmed down.

Abd was having persistent dull pain on the left side of his lower jaw for several weeks. Finally, he developed swelling and redness of the cheek over the painful area. He looked in the mirror with his mouth wide-open. Greenish pussy discharge oozed out from around the second lower left molar. He knew right away that it was a dental abscess that needed to be taken care of as soon as possible. He went to see a local dentist on the same day. The latter took x-rays of his two jaws. The result was astounding. Abd had many dental cavities and decay that required a course of treatment with penicillin followed by root canal work on at least four teeth. The dentist's words resurrected memories of his childhood years in Bamyan when beet sugar was the only source of calories available to sustain children's growth and of the lack of dental hygiene during a long period of famine. Abd began the penicillin course of treatment that same afternoon.

The following week he drove to the boarding school to pick up Emal, who started his midterm school break. Once in the car, the teenager imploringly looked at his father. "Dad, the school nurse told me and a few other kids that we have the so-called dental malocclusion. She explained to us that the teeth are misaligned and that we need to see a pediatric dentist, but she didn't say why."

That same evening, Abd sat down his two sons and then examined their mouths. He confirmed the diagnosis made by the nurse. "Indeed, you two have malocclusion, a pediatric dental problem frequently mentioned these days by dentists. I will try to make an appointment for you two to see Dr. Vaillancourt, the only certified pediatric dentist in this area. Sorry, I should have paid more attention to your teeth, but at least you have healthy teeth and it is a perfect time to straighten them out. You should be thankful to your mom for reminding you to brush your teeth after each meal."

Emal and Yasir were seen the week after by Dr. Vaillancourt, who suggested the standard treatment of malocclusion—wearing a dental brace for at least eighteen months. He explained to Abd that this entity had been frequently observed among children of mixed races and informed him that the long-term outcome of untreated dental malocclusion could be devastating. Without hesitation, Abd made another appointment for the children to receive the braces. Before leaving the dentist's office, the receptionist handed him a bill amounting to 7,200 French francs per child. The fee included materials, labor, and quarterly adjustment of the braces; and it could be paid in full within three months without interest. Sadly, all expenses related to health care fortuitously came all at once, and he had no way to come up with enough money to pay for the root canal work and the children's braces at this point of his career. He was already in debt to his eyeballs with the mortgage on the house and Emal's private high school tuition. Yet his income from his medical practice remained sluggish. He was caring for a large percentage of patients on public assistance, but the government reimbursement for their care was barely sufficient for the office nurse's salary. Abd was already deep in debt; therefore, incurring additional expenses was out of the question. Since his world had been revolving around his two sons, his mother, and his sister Nabeela and nothing else, he decided that the priority of care should go first to his sons, even though he was told that the root canal work on him had to be done urgently before the bad teeth became irretrievable and that the two-week course of treatment with penicillin was only to keep the infection under control. Being a specialist in the field of infectious diseases, Abd wholeheartedly agreed with his dentist on this subject. But without the financial means, Abd had no choice other than wait until he saved enough to pay for his dental work.

Six weeks later, while doing a written project together with Adelle, Yasir learned from Catherine Mathichée the sacrifice his father had made. He rushed home, went upstairs, closed his door, and sobbed. He worried about his father's overwork that would undoubtedly lead to a health setback. He was fully aware of the multifaceted complex problems related to the post-divorce phase and his father's assumption of a new single-parenthood responsibility. Nevertheless, his anxiety strengthened further the love he had for his father. Heartbrokenly, Yasir's overall anxiety and concern about the unknown facing him, his father, and his brother during the next few years had an adverse effect on his schooling. His winter semester report card showed a sliding, from a previous C+ to a worrisome D- with an F in math and physics. He felt bad and apologized to his father for his poor school performance. Abd knew that his son definitely needed tutoring on these two subjects. He used compassionate words of encouragement to save his son from regressing back into depression. Luckily, the same twenty-three-year-old Anna, who had been coming to stay with Yasir at night when Abd had to go to the hospital, was willing to take on the additional responsibility of transporting Yasir at the end of the day, twice a week, to the tutoring teacher in math and physics. The bimonthly oboe private lesson with a freelance musician located five kilometers from home was scheduled for Friday night, and Abd managed to provide the transportation.

Life went on peacefully as usual at the Rasulovs' home. Abd relentlessly continued with the time-consuming house chores as he had been doing for the last two and a half years. His office practice and his hospital patient care progressively gained more public recognition. There had been a complete harmony between father and sons. Abd was content and happy; he managed to overcome all difficulties inherent to single-parenthood and to fulfil all his paternal obligations *vis-à-vis* his two sons. Unfortunately, the peaceful home atmosphere was suddenly interrupted by Abd's sickness. He developed an acute urinary tract infection (UTI)[5] that landed him in the hospital for an overnight stay, followed by two weeks of convalescence. He felt weak and had trouble tolerating the medication prescribed. He knew that prolonged overwork, lack of sleep, and poor diet could weaken the immune system that, in turn, could easily succumb to the invasion of germs causing serious infections. So he decided to take it easy for a few weeks. Even though the relationship between the fourteen in-town primary care colleagues and Abd had considerably improved, he couldn't find a single one in Odinard to cover for him. They were in group practice, and their contract excluded them from temporarily taking care of out-of-the-setting patients. Abd had to be content with the help from a solo practitioner in a neighboring town, thirteen kilometers away.

Yasir's life was further affected by his dad's illness. Abd learned from the grapevine that his son had poor concentration and was observed to have episodes of daydreams in class. His year-end report card showed no improvement. That was a bleak moment for the entire family. Abd felt that he had failed his two sons and single parenthood should be the last resort for a divorcee. In order to find some relief, even just as a transient solution, Abd signed out to his colleague solo practitioner for a week and drove to Cap d'Adge, Languedoc-Roussillon, to pay a visit to his brother Ali, who was in town on vacation and whom he had not seen for several years. This trip had dual purposes—get some rest for himself and the first acquaintance with Ali's family for his two boys. Abd always had a deep sense of bonding between members of his extended family.

During the four-hour trip to Cap d'Adge, father and sons thoroughly enjoyed the beautiful landscape of the southern mountainous French country. Abd took this rare opportunity, being alone with his two sons at the same time, to discreetly discuss in general terms about education, profession, job, etc. He pointed out to his sons a fact that is undeniable by society: financial wealth doesn't make your fellow man respect and esteem a person, but higher education does. In this connection, very likely the following sentence found in Abd's memoir reflects his personal conviction on this matter: "Sons, I'll do everything possible financially in order for you to get a doctorate or at least a master's degree, even if I will have to work ten additional years past the age of retirement of sixty-five; and I have no objection to see you work, even as a street sweeper, to make a living thereafter. My life experience has taught me that a certificate of higher education is the equivalent of an expensive life insurance policy. I am sure you understand what I mean."

June 25 was a nice, warm day of that year. Abd signed out to the neighbor town solo practitioner for a couple of hours and drove to the boarding school to bring his oldest son home for the summer break. While their father was at work, Yasir went over the hard life he was living with Abd without the presence of a female figure in the household. He conveyed to his brother his apprehensiveness about their father's declining health and its adverse effect on his own school performance. "Emal, I have been having trouble concentrating on everything I do, especially in class, and I don't know what to do about it. Even though Dad continues to be very forgiving and cheerful to me despite my poor school performance, I sense that he is suffering from the precarious way of life he is enduring. Lately, I have been having second thoughts about Dad's remaining single. As you know, I have been afraid that Dad would possibly make another mistake in getting married again too soon after his divorce. But I don't believe at the age of fifty-one, he will be able to carry on much longer the hardship of his daily life as a single parent until we permanently leave our nest."

Somberly, Emal looked straight, purposelessly into space. "I am sorry for not being able to be of any assistance to you two these last three years. I feel very guilty for having my education in a private school with a very expensive tuition that Dad has to pay. However, there is a smidgen of hope in this regard. Recently, upon reception of a supporting letter from Dr. Naguda, the school administrator is seriously considering the possibility of granting me a full scholarship for the two remaining years. This was confidentially told to me by Mr. Einucle. Personally, I think we should encourage Dad to remarry, given the fact that he had made, shortly after the divorce decree was announced, an attempt of reconciliation with Mom through Biorn and his friend psychiatrist, but failed. My biggest concern is whether he would be able to get an annulment of his first marriage from the Catholic Church. So, let's discuss face-to-face this matter with him as soon as we can get him to sit down for a few minutes."

Even though he was encouraged by his two sons to bring into his lonely life a new female figure, part of Abd remained hopeful, while the sane part was apprehensive about the direction this recommendation would take him. The children's performance in school, the high school and college tuitions, and their future were just some of the subjects Abd was mulling over again and again for weeks. In the end, he decided to have a partner to share his busy life. But what it would take to establish a connection with a woman to start with was not an easy task. He was too busy with his medical practice and with time-consuming routine house chores. He had no free time to socialize. The idea of looking back into his recent past experience with women working at the last two hospitals appeared logical to him.

The memory of Lillian, the receptionist at the Lazerat Hospital information desk, came to his mind. He placed a call to that hospital and was told that Lillian had been remarried to a colonel in the French Army and left town last fall. Abd was sad and regretful for the missed opportunity. Then he thought about two divorced nurses at the Odinard Hospital. Both had teenage children. One was the hospital night supervisor, and her eldest son was a close friend of Yasir. The other was a night-shift registered nurse at the level 2 hospital nursery intensive care unit (NICU). Both knew that Abd was a single parent, and both were very "pleasant" to him at the workplace. Because Abd was frequently called to the obstetric department or nursery at night for urgent care, he met both quite often.

In connection with this new challenge, it would be interesting for the reader to know more about Abd's humane natural disposition, besides his perspicacity, resoluteness, self-control, humbleness, and especially his spiritual mindedness, just to name a few. All these distinguishing traits were also found in an earlier paragraph he wrote in his diary about the relationship between him and Charmina; but the following story precisely reflects the man's conviction, determination, gentlemanliness, and undeniable moral strength.

Six months had passed since Abd filed the divorce paper. The people in the towns of Foxeline and Lazerat were shocked at the publication of Amelia's divorce filing in the local newspapers. They were wondering why such an unhappy outcome could put an end to the reputation of the used-to-be "model" family of the region. They had not seen the doctor, his wife, and the two boys together attending Sunday Mass at the Lazerat Catholic Church for quite a while. Then, an unexpected opportunity presented to Abd while he was secretly in the middle of his preparation to leave town.

On that Monday of mid-October, temperatures across the Mid-Pyrenees were five to ten degrees above normal. That year the unusual extended seasonal warm air delayed the foliage peak, and the stone maple trees on the ground of Lazerat Hospital remained a deep, verdant green. On his way to the hospital front entrance from the parked Citroën, Abd's blue windproof hooded jacket was spotted with a few quick-melting snowflakes. After stepping in under the canopy, going through the revolving door, he clumsily tried to peel off his coat while walking to the hospital information desk.

Alone at the marble counter, receptionist Lillian jovially greeted, "Good morning, Dr. Abdulai. How are you? You seem to have your arm stuck in your coat sleeve. May I help you?"

"That would be nice if you could hold my medical bag for a moment while I try to use my two free hands to take off my heavy jacket. Thank you."

Lillian got close to Abd to grab the heavy leather bag from his right hand. Her left hand, probably not unintentionally, touched his. "Your hand is freezing cold. Please step inside, behind the counter, and warm your hands with my hidden portable electric heater before you go to the nursery. You may share it with me. I don't mind. By the way, the mother of a newborn delivered during the night has asked you to be the baby's doctor."

Abd was struck by her suspiciously inquisitive set of blue eyes. She was exceptionally cordial that morning. At that right moment, he reminded himself of the announcement in the local newspapers three weeks ago; undoubtedly the majority of the hospital employees were fully aware of his pending official separation. Up until now, Abd had been keeping himself socially distant from young female hospital employees, being a family man, a practicing Christian well respected by the community. He had seen Lillian numerous times at the information desk but had not so far paid attention to this gorgeous, half-Danish, half-French woman. He instantaneously devoured her beauty by taking a swift couple of minutes, while rubbing his hands above the heater, deciphering her clean facial lines partially sheltered behind tufts of dark-blond hair harmoniously ornamenting her slender, well-developed body wrapped in a fitted white blouse and a knee-high pleated checkered pencil skirt.

Lillian, getting a little close to the doctor, softly uttered these words, "I am sorry to hear the news. What can I do to cheer you up?" Abd was somewhat surprised by Lillian's spontaneity but found a genuine charm in her manner. "How are you and your family?"

"My children have been illness-free for a while, thank God."

Just at that moment, Lillian, looking down embarrassingly to the clipboard listing the name of patients scheduled for surgery on that day, continued, "I lost my husband almost two years ago. Probably you were out of town when this happened."

"What happened?"

"As you probably know, André worked out of town in commercial building construction. He usually left home early Monday morning to return Thursday night and spend the rest of the week with us. An arctic blast spread through the entire area, and the roads on George Hill pass were covered with black ice during the entire week. By daybreak on that Friday, the highway patrol found his truck front end almost split in half by a roadside electric post."

"I am sorry, Lillian."

"My children need a father figure, and myself, a life companion. Since you know in and out of the medical circle many people, can I ask you to keep both eyes and ears opened to a possible still-single gentleman?"

Abd wasn't sure whether Lillian's daring request was directly aimed at him, but this was a real possibility, given the fact that she and he were in two unusual family circumstances, the current friendly atmosphere, and the captivating tone of her voice.

Abd thanked her for letting him use the heater, grabbed his medical bag, and then before walking to the nursery, peered at the blushing face of the pretty young woman. "I'll be happy to look into it, just for you, Lillian. Will you be able to meet that imagined person somewhere out of town on a first date for the sake of privacy?"

"I am willing to take a day or two off to go anywhere as long as I receive a notice a couple of days ahead so that I would have ample time to find a substitute." Lillian cheerfully gazed at the doctor.

By insinuating about the possibility of a meeting with her alone, Abd wanted to test her real intention to be certain that he had not misread her mind, realizing that he was twenty years older than her. During the entire following week, his thoughts were wandering around the possibility of a remarriage with a full-bloomed mature young woman shortly after the divorce. He dreamed of a union with a mother of two young children who was welcoming a single parent of the opposite sex with two sons. However, he realized at the same time that he was still faced with at least two main obstacles—legally he was still married to Amelia and was still waiting for the court to finalize the divorce decree. Secondly, as a Catholic he ought to go through a lengthy process of application for Vatican annulment plus a strenuous prenuptial education. Sadly, he had to place his dream of again having a happy family for the second time on the back burner for an indefinite period. But Abd believed that he should remain friendly to Lillian and continue to keep her in mind for a possible future joint venture. Knowing that Abd was a proud man, one wouldn't be flabbergasted to see this trait tied to his sense of cautiousness. Not surprisingly, Abd arrived earlier than usual to the Lazerat Hospital five days later. This time he wanted to advance to Lillian a fictitious scenario, projected from his current personal difficult phase of life, in order to determine once and for all whether she was truly interested in getting to know him.

As he passed through the revolving door, Lillian greeted him as usual with a smile. "Good morning, Dr. Rasulov. You are early today. But currently you have no inpatients."

As he approached the information counter, Abd elatedly replied, "I have to look for a couple of articles in the library. By the way, I might have good news for you, Lillian."

"Really, Doc? What is it?"

"I happen to know a gentleman who had gone through a very traumatic divorce last spring. He is slowly recovering from it and is looking to start a new life in a different town not far from here. He has the custody of his two children, whom he loves dearly. The only obstacle is that he might be too old for you. He has a stable job. Are you surprised if I say to you that this man knows this area very well and I got the impression that he has seen you before?"

"How old is he?"

"Late forties to early fifties, somewhere in that age range. If you are interested, I can quickly find out his real age."

"I have no problem with getting to know any available mature single man in that age range."

Abd was getting a little more specific this time. "Would you be willing to have a first date with this 'old man' somewhere between here and Murat? If you are serious about this adventure, I will talk to him. I am sure he will be delighted to meet with you in a locale that provides you two with a relaxed and friendly atmosphere."

"As you surely know, I always trust your judgment. I'll be delighted to. I can't wait for that first meeting. Please go ahead with your plan. Thank you."

Ten days had passed, and Abd was very busy during this interval with at least a dozen tasks related to the pending relocation to Odinard. The end of November was marked by frozen deciduous multicolor leaves scattered on the roads leading to Lazerat Hospital. He started his office hours that day with full confidence. He felt totally relieved, knowing unequivocally that Lillian's initial request for help was specifically directed to himself and not to another man. At lunchtime, Abd had to go back to the hospital to see one of his patients admitted before noon via the ED with pneumonia.

Bundled up in a heavy winter coat, Abd was approaching the information desk and was pleasantly greeted by Lillian and her coworker. As he proceeded to walk to the medical/surgical ward, Lillian called his attention, "Dr. Abdulai, are you aware that your coat shows a partial detachment of its bottom seam?" Abd slowed down his walk and pulled up the right flap of his eight-year-old outer garment to the level of his eyes. There was indeed a piece of ragged fabric hanging down from its hem. "You may leave your coat with me if you wish. By the time that you finish your admission workup and initiate the treatment of your new patient, it will be waiting for you here, fully repaired."

Abd, who could not resist Lillian's offer, joyfully replied while peeling off the heavy winter coat with the young woman's help, "Thank you very much, Lillian. It's very sweet of you." Abd quickly disappeared behind the three-mirror-paneled wall reflecting Lillian's body neatly swathed in a fitting dark blue-colored satin outfit. About an hour later, Abd reappeared to find his coat, hung on the back of a chair adjacent to Lillian, neatly repaired and brushed. He left the hospital to go back to his office, joyfully thinking of the caring pretty young lady. Circumstances favoring the rapprochement of Lillian and Abd were mounting. The doctor was no longer walking past the information desk in a hurry. Lately, he had been looking forward to seeing Lillian's radiant face each time he came to the hospital. Their reciprocal glance at each other with a discreet smile met almost every day Lillian was on duty. Soon, an unexpected encounter reinforced the magic, spontaneous, and agreeable feeling between a man and a woman. The darkness was slowly enveloping the entire region at four thirty on that Sunday afternoon of late November. The church bell ended its hourly toll at the stroke of five. Abd quietly entered the Catholic church side door. He reverently knelt at the far end of the pew, made a brief routine sign of the cross, and then sat down in the poorly lit back pew of the church nave. With his forehead rested against both half-folded hands, he knelt and recited his prayer in silence and closed eyes.

Suddenly, he felt a barely discernible movement of the bench that was immediately followed by a faint child's voice. "Is it okay to sit here, Mom?" An absolute quietness reigned over the entire empty church after the earlier scheduled Sunday evening Mass. The flickering lights on the votive candle rack were the only nonhuman activities. Once getting up from his kneeling position, Abd took a quick look in the direction of the voice heard before. He recognized the silhouette of a woman wearing a dark shawl over her head and accompanying two young children. Kneeling, all three were in silent prayer. At the far end of the pew Abd looked at his wristwatch, when loudly the church bell rang from its bell tower the third and last time of the day at six, summoning the Christian faithful to recite the Lord's Prayer. Suddenly he heard once again the voice of the same child. "The doctor, Mom." He stood up, solemnly knelt at the altar, and then quietly exited the side door. Outside, the icy gusts of wind flung occasional flakes of snow into Abd's face.

Before he crossed the narrow copper stone-paved road to reach his parked Citroën, the woman he saw in the church approached him. "Good evening, Dr. Abdulai. Are you still working on Sunday evening? Our daughter was quick in recognizing you. How are you?"

Bearing down his look at the two nice and quiet children, Abd thanked her. "I had to admit to the medical ward an elderly lady this late afternoon. What a coincidence! Glad to know that religiously speaking your family and I are practicing Christianity the same way. We are in communion with God anywhere and at any time."

"The temperature is dropping quickly, and the country roads might become icy as the night falls. So please drive carefully, Doc!"

While driving on the eighteen-kilometer stretch of hilly winding road in the direction of his home in Foxeline, Abd vividly remembered the words "Please drive carefully, Doc," which made him realize that perhaps there must be a third person out there who had expressed concern for his safety besides his two sons. Then serious thoughts invaded his natural analytical propensity. He had to seriously take into consideration two situations that could conceivably lead him to change the entire plan he had made months before he filed for divorce. He reasoned with himself by clearly laying out in his mind and side by side two distinct alternatives; the first one dealt with Lillian, and the second with his two sons. He realized that Lillian was truly unique. She was a very caring person, young and pretty, and the aspect that gave him a great deal of reassurance for a long-lasting marriage was her devotion to God. He believed that all these three attributes were the most relevant when a woman or a man is in search for a life partner. But he only knew the surface layer of her life. The other deep layers remained unknown and required additional regular contacts with her. The assessment of this alternative would demand time. Additionally, Abd always wanted to do things lawfully; he must wait until the divorce decree was issued before he could legally look for a new partner. The situation in connection with his two sons on the other hand was clear-cut, as he knew them from birth and therefore required no further hesitation. Indeed, the boys knew in detail the reasons for their pending parental separation, the suffering involving the whole family, and yet, they still unquestionably wanted to be under their father's custody after the divorce. Alternatively, Abd gave some serious thoughts about bringing into his two sons' life and his own a widow with two children; but the unknown element that was worrisome to him could—he reasoned—derail the peace of single parenthood with his sons he had been dreaming of. He didn't want to take that chance. Furthermore, through Emal, Yasir had repeatedly, during the last three years, expressed his concern about his dad's possible hasty remarriage. Yet the idea of abandoning Yasir and Emal to a foster parent setting or of letting Amelia and Jean-Marie have them and run away with another woman like a large percentage of men did was beyond his imagination. He considered this act as selfish and cowardly.

In the end, Abd decided not to further the idea of committing himself to a young woman with a bright future. Instead, he wanted to remain friendly to her without the slightest moral commitment. The next step to sentimentally disengage with Lillian wasn't easy to achieve. Abd had to find a way that was not only logical but also least traumatic to both. One early morning he appeared at the hospital information desk and found Lillian just walking in. He took courage to painfully announce to her that his—fictitious—friend had found a partner in Bayonne City and then quickly walked away with a somber, regretful, sad, and disappointed facial expression. Disappearing fast behind the mirror-paneled wall, he chose not to look over his shoulder at her undoubtedly doleful face.

Since Abd had let pass a quasi-superb opportunity to unite with a widow and her two well-disciplined toddlers three years earlier, and since he had steadfastly convinced himself that the union with divorcees having teenage children from their ex-spouse could interfere with the peace and love he was having with his two sons, it became quite obvious that he had to find a woman who was still single and had never been married before. Now that his two sons had wanted him to remarry, he initiated the search using the most rational and practical approach to find, he hoped, a lifelong partner of the opposite sex.

Six months later, and after exchanging letters with a good number of singles via an out-of-town nonprofit religious dating organization, he finally decided on a forty-two-year-old secretary who had never been married. Her name was Martine. She came from a hardworking middle-class French family in Rennes, France Bretagne. The civil wedding took place at the lady's hometown courthouse, followed by a simple reception at which Emal and Yasir, respectively on piano and oboe, played in duet the Pachelbel Canon in D Wedding Prelude. Four months later Abd finally got his annulment from Rome and had a traditional Catholic wedding ceremony performed by a priest after four weeks of doing the marriage prep program at his parish. Martine adjusted quickly to her new role of wife and mother.

CHAPTER TWELVE

Small House with a Solid Foundation Was About to Crumble

From the kitchen, Martine called out to Yasir still upstairs in his room, "Are you ready? It's twenty-five to half past seven."

"I'll be right down."

Since she became Mrs. Rasulov a month ago, Martine had been driving Yasir and Adelle to school every other day, sharing this chore with Catherine Mathichée. While spending a lot of time during the day looking for a new job in town, she comfortably filled her role of a housewife, alleviating her husband's household burden of the last three years. At the end of the day, she was physically exhausted and realized that no one person alone could assume all the tasks her husband had done before her arrival without assistance. But she was happy thinking that she could help a preteen who needed a maternal figure, share the life with a highly educated compassionate professional man, and especially self-assured that her marriage had a solid foundation—their love for each other through fervent piety.

The unemployment rate at the time was over 16 percent in Odinard and surrounding areas. It took Martine several weeks before she could find a job. She worked as a staff nurse on the night shift at a nursing home. It was managed by two Austrian Dominican sisters who came to France two decades earlier in search for an exceptional fervent religious life. She loved her job, even though sleeping during the day after taking care of routine household chores and working in the thick of the night wasn't the most desirable for her. She was a hardworking person. At 6:30 a.m. she came home from the "home." After a quick wash-off, she drove Adelle and Yasir to school every other morning, and subsequently every three days each week once she was able to make an arrangement with another family to car pool two more of Yasir's classmates. On the day when she didn't have to drive the children to school, she already got up after a six-hour daytime sleep. Then she went shopping for food after trying to keep the house in good order to spare her husband from having to be burdened with nonprofessional chores. Before going to work at 9:00 p.m. she made sure to feed the whole family with a healthy supper and to clean up after the meal. She took care of the family laundry and vacuumed the house every three to four days. She didn't want Yasir to assist her. "You must concentrate on studying to catch up with your first-year high school workload," she said to him each time he offered to lend her a hand to do her routine simple tasks in the house. On weekends, she took Yasir to soccer practice and oboe lessons. She never failed to drive him bimonthly to Foxeline to visit with his mother as the divorce court had stipulated. Yasir, by this time, was thirteen and a half and was able to be left alone when his stepmother worked at the home at night and his father was called out to the hospital. All house chores heretofore assumed by Abd were taken over by Martine, including the services provided by Anna, who had been hired to transport or stay with Yasir at night when his father was called to the hospital. Yet not a single complaint or lament was heard coming from her. But there was a definite setback with regard to her general health. She put on over nine kilograms, or 19.8

pounds, within a year. Her husband suspected that long hours sitting at her working desk night after night in addition to incessant bedside care of the elderly residents, daytime sleep affecting her circadian rhythms, deprivation of relaxation, and total lack of physical exercise constituted chronic stress that induced changes in her overall cortisol metabolism, which in turn caused her truncal obesity. This was a great concern for the couple, but no immediate remedy could be used to slow down her stress-induced increasing appetite. Martine's devotion to her husband and stepchildren was beyond the duty of any average newlywed woman. Gradually Yasir started to realize how lucky he was to have a maternal figure looking after his welfare. He had been slow in accepting Martine as a substitute mother due to his pessimistic view of life during his childhood years, but eventually he became affectionate to her, signaling a new bond between them. Emal, away in college, had little contact with Martine, but her regular telephone calls to his dormitory during weekends had reassured him that she had brought to his father and his brother a healthier lifestyle.

On Thursday morning at 6:55 of the sunny last day of spring, Yasir just finished his bacon and egg dish that Martine hurriedly prepared upon her return from the home. He was thumping up the squeaking wood staircase, getting ready to be picked up for school, when his stepmother exclaimed, "I want to remind you that you have to spend this weekend with your mom. I will drive you to Foxeline right after school, as I am not on duty the next two nights."

"No, I am not going, and I don't have to…"

"But you have to obey the court order, her right to be with you every second weekend, remember?"

"She doesn't love me and my brother anymore. She had refused to reconcile with Dad two years ago, and now she wants to marry her boyfriend as soon as this guy will be legally divorced from his wife."

In the meantime, Amelia left her boyfriend Jean-Marie for unknown reasons and was subsequently introduced to a local merchant widower, Serge, a hardware store owner, by the WLM ladies. They got married five months after Martine and Abd's church wedding. The relationship between the two couples was correct but superficial. Yasir had no reservation as to his biologic mother's new life but remained closer to his dad and Martine. He had become less reluctant to go to Foxeline every other weekend but was not too eager spending the whole weekend with his new stepfather. The reason he gave was, "He [Serge] intercepted every call I made to my mother." He preferred to hang around with his high school friends in Odinard. Everybody, including Emal, seemed to be content with the final outcome of the divorce and remarriage. Martine continued to be stupendously dedicated to her husband and the two stepchildren. She just entered into the second year of her marriage. Abd's practice was getting busier, but the combined income from husband and wife was barely enough to support the family of four. Abd had already paid a total of 88,000 French francs borrowed from two banks for Emal's first two years' tuition in a private high school upon his relocation to Odinard. Thanks to Dr. Naguda's intervention and this school's administration for the award of the remaining two-year full scholarship to Emal. Now, they were facing another financial hurdle—Emal was about to start his first year in college. After three exhausting months of searching for a college suitable to his vocation, Emal was accepted not only to one of the most prestigious private liberal arts schools in Carcassonne, Region of Languedoc Roussillon, but also to half a dozen of other less known but fairly reputable state colleges in the Regions of Limousin, Auvergne, and Aquitaine, whose tuitions were more affordable to low middle-class French families. However, Emal wanted to go to the private college in Carcassonne, giving the following explanation as reason. Graduates from Carcassonne would have a better chance to get enrolled at Hautes Etudes Commerciales, HEC Paris," the distinguished postdoctoral business school of France.

Abd and Martine were happy with Emal's serious intention of pursuing a future business career. But the Carcassonne college exorbitant tuition was beyond the Rasulov family's means. Even though they were already in heavy debt with the house mortgage and the loan to pay for expenses incurred at the start of the new medical practice in Odinard, the couple had to find a way to pay for Emal's private college tuition. The majority of low middle-class fathers wouldn't pay a dime for their children's college expenses. They would leave up to them to finance themselves if their children wanted to go to state colleges, let alone to expensive institutions like the one in Carcassonne. Martine volunteered to use up the entire dowry of over 100,000 French francs she brought with her when she got married and to take overtime work at the home to generate extra earnings as supplements to an additional commercial bank loan at 12.5 percent interest. The total amount of money husband and wife came up with was adequate for the payment of the four-year college expenses amounting to 64,000 French francs annually. The couple felt that spending money on their children's education was a good investment for their future, and they didn't expect any in-kind repayment from them. Abd had been trying to instill, since their early childhood, in Emal's and Yasir's minds that a certificate or a diploma is comparable to an insurance policy guaranteeing them a future decent job. Neither Abd nor Martine had set terms or conditions when they decided to let Emal attend the costly college in Carcassonne, and Yasir, another slightly less expensive private liberal arts school four years later. However, they anticipated at least some sort of expression of heartfelt gratitude from them once the children grew up and were on their own. Luckily, Yasir was still in tuition-free public school, and his father and stepmother didn't have to worry about his college expenses for four more years. The family financial issue was at least temporarily resolved, and life went on uneventfully. Abd's medical practice was getting larger and appreciably well-known to the entire region.

It was time for Abd to introduce Martine to his extended family members and to give his own family a vacation, but an arrangement had to be made to find coverage for his practice. In addition, a request for Martine's vacation time that coincided with the children's summer break had to be submitted several weeks in advance to the governing sisters of the home. Fortuitously, around the same summer interval, Zekirullah announced his unanticipated trip to Geneva, Switzerland, to attend an international conference on the health of children living in developing countries. Seven months earlier, Dr. Zekirullah was named as Afghanistan deputy minister of health after the death of his partner, Dr. Faisal, and the dissolution of their medical practice in Tupchi. The two brothers talked over an anticipated family reunion somewhere in France. They got in touch with Ali in Vienna, Austria, Nabeela, and her husband, Feda, in Reims, and the wealthy Aamir and his second wife in Aix-en-Provence. Aamir offered to open his luxurious five-bedroom house to all his siblings' families for the scheduled five-day reunion.

On the first day of gathering, arguments broke out between Zekirullah and Aamir. At times, they threw insulting comments to each other. Later on, Abd learned from Ali that these two had not been getting along too well already for the last few years. Ali and Abd took pains trying to reconcile the two brothers, but their effort was in vain. Instead, they were accused by Aamir for being impartial, meaning taking sides with Zekirullah. Except Nabeela and her husband, Feda, the rest of reunion attendees left on the second day after their arrival. The first family reunion became the only one, a very brief and the very last one. From that meeting on, Aamir showed his lack of cooperation in every issue related to the extended Rasulov family. His unusual attitude made him stand out as a "black sheep"—his own words. For no reason, he frequently became resentful toward his three older brothers on trivial family matters. He convinced himself that these three ganged up to belittle him.

In the meantime, Grandma Elaha became a live-in nanny for her youngest son Aamir's family. While living on the income derived from the French aid for Afghan refugees program, supplemented by Abd's and Amelia's monthly financial assistance and occasionally by that of Zekirullah, she looked after Aamir's third child while both parents worked. She prepared daily delectable meals for the entire family that was composed of the couple, two teen girls from Aamir's first marriage, and the baby. Elaha was by then over seventy-five and started to have some early signs of cardiac ailment. Abd found out about Elaha's health problems through telephone conversations with her and handwritten messages she regularly sent to him. Everybody in the extended family tended to stay away from Aamir except Nabeela and her husband for reasons to be discussed later. Even though busy with her daily household chores, Elaha managed to keep in touch and occasionally played a few card games with her Afghan relatives living nearby. Aamir and his second wife through marriage arrangement, for unknown reasons, failed to convey to Abd their mother's health matters in an informative way, possibly because they thought doctors in Aix-en-Provence were more knowledgeable than his own brother academically oriented in internal medicine or possibly because of Aamir's simple desire to ignore Abd. But Abd recognized that he was also partially at fault for his lack of regularly watching over Elaha's cardiac illness by phone calls. He was too emotionally affected by his marital problem during that same period. He remained regretful for the rest of his life on this matter.

Aamir's abnormal behavior was directed mainly to his three older brothers, namely, the eldest Zekirullah, Ali, and Abd. He was distrustful of every idea, opinion, and action that came from them. On the other hand, he agreed with everything Nabeela and her husband said. Instead of being happy and proud with either of his older brothers' accomplishments, the estranged Aamir remained suspicious and even resentful toward the three older brothers he pejoratively called "the trio." Even though being a civil engineer like Ali, who graduated from L'Ecole Superieure d'Electricite de Paris, a prestigious postgraduate engineering school, Aamir never made an effort to express his admiration for his brother's achievement. Instead, he had been eager to quarrel with him and took sides with Nabeela each time she had recurrent arguments with Ali about the way she treated the latter's son, her nephew, who had spent four years under the same roof in Reims with Grandma Elaha and her. Shockingly, Aamir had adopted over the years a more aggressive attitude toward Zekirullah, especially after the latter became the Afghan minister of health. At one point, he openly questioned, defied, and even challenged the customary Afghan role of the eldest brother who was supposed to look after the welfare of his younger siblings. Since Zekirullah was the oldest son of the Rasulov extended family, and not surprisingly, he was at odds with Aamir on a variety of subjects. The relationship between Aamir and Abd was not any better. Aamir criticized his brother for being too Westernized, married twice to white women, sympathized with Christianity, socialized only with non-Afghan refugee crowds, being absorbed into Western arts and music, and last but not least, adopted the habit of using knife and fork, abandoning the Arabic custom of sitting on the floor and eating with fingers. But he was not satisfied with these trivial differences of way of life that separated him from Abd. Since Zekirullah lived in Kabul and Ali was the poorest of all, Abd was his main target for constant criticism. He wanted to know how expensive the house was that Abd lived in, where Abd's family went for vacation, how Emal and Yasir could go to expensive private colleges—his three daughters were sent to public state universities—after Abd's relocation to Odinard and started from scratch a new medical practice. Since he was rich and through lavish expenditure in dinners and gifts, he lured to his side many poor middle-class Afghan refugees throughout France and made them his cronies. Nabeela and Feda voluntarily joined in without having to be coerced, as they had issues with Ali's son many years earlier. Through spying upon each other, these bought-out individuals arrived to supply Aamir with detailed information on a large percentage of his countryman's families. The families of Aamir's siblings made no exception. The extraordinary personality of Aamir will be further illustrated in the next chapter.

One day in early spring, when Ali was struggling with his mentally ill wife at the Vienna General Hospital, a telephone call came through the information desk receptionist. "Are you Mr. Ali Rasulov?" she said. "A phone call for you from France. Please keep the line open. I will direct the call to your room. Room 18B, right?" Aamir was on the phone, inquiring about Ali's wife's illness. Ali thanked his brother for his brotherly concern. But Aamir kept talking. Without being asked, he brought up again the old dispute Ali had with his sister Nabeela about the treatment his son was subjected to while the latter was still living with her in Reims. Aamir insisted that Ali had "exaggerated the whole thing" and that Amelia—yes, Amelia—had agreed with him and Nabeela that his son was not a "misfit." Ali was shocked by Aamir's contention but started to wonder why the latter had volunteered to say that he had taken a special trip to Foxeline to see his own brother's divorced wife Amelia and her newlywed husband Serge, carrying with him ten pounds of lobster as a gift. Ali found that Aamir's reconnection with his brother Abd's ex-wife was completely out of line, and this behavior was totally in conflict not only with Afghan tradition but also with civilized Western societies. Ali had noticed for quite a while that Aamir was envious of his brother Abd's intellectualism and accomplishment and of Zekirullah's attainment of the status of minister of health.

The difference of personality between siblings was not limited to one family or one generation.[8] Emal and his brother's dispositions were noteworthy since their early childhood. He talked well, using intelligent responses when he had a conversation with adults. He impressed his maternal grandmother each time Abd and his family returned to Sweden for vacation. In contrast, Yasir started to show his tendency to be "whiny"—Grandma's word—at early age, when he couldn't keep up with his alert and quick-responding brother. Unfortunately, their Swedish grandmother spent more time and paid more attention to Emal in preference to Yasir, who became openly frustrated. The latter felt rejected by his own grandmother, who discreetly expressed her opinion to Amelia that Emal was more Swedish in appearance and Yasir predominantly Arabic. As the boys were still toddlers, Emal gradually became temperamentally domineering. He picked at his sibling verbally and physically through repeated pinching. Abd tried to teach him that he should be gentle in dealing with children younger than him, especially with Yasir. He worried that Emal might bully younger students in school. The over-and-over rehashed urge from his dad fell on Emal's deaf ears. One day, at the age of seven, Emal kept incessantly teasing his brother for over half an hour while having dinner. Frustrated, Abd got up from the table, took Emal to his room, and gave him a spanking. That was the first and the only time Abd ever had his hand on one of his children. The domineering attitude seemed to entrench permanently in Emal's personality. The following anecdote illustrated the dominance he had over his younger brother during his entire life.

Spring break of his second year at Carcassonne was another opportunity for Emal to spend a couple of days at their Odinard home with his father and his brother, and the rest of the week with his mother in Foxeline. Abd took a few hours away from work on that Saturday and went out with his two sons for a tennis game.

After having a cup of coffee and a plate of tasty French pastries at a nearby shop, they started the game with laughs and jokes. Abd was happy with the prospect of being able to spend a good part of the weekend with his two sons after signing out to his regular colleague to take over incoming emergency calls from the hospital and from his patients. Father and sons took turns playing two against one because they couldn't find a fourth player that morning. The boys couldn't win the tennis match despite their effort. Abd had not played since the family moved to Foxeline but still could deliver his formidable backhand ball with power and precision. Yasir didn't take the game seriously, thinking it was just an opportunity to create a moment of relaxation for his father. For him winning or losing the game to his father was inconsequential. Emal, on the other hand, wanted to show that he was good at any sport. He had every intention to beat his father by at least two games. Before going home, he proposed to finally declare as the winner the person who closed the set with the winning ball. Yasir kept laughing and joking while playing. He made one mistake after another. Emal yelled at his brother, "Shape up or ship out." The last return ball delivered by Yasir was a foot beyond the baseline. Dad won the set at seven-to-five. Angrily, Emal violently smashed the balls against the net with his racquet. Ending the morning game, Abd quietly walked to the other side of the court, pulled his two sons together, and tightly hugged them while uttering, "Just pure luck for me. You two played much better than I did. How often had we played together, and from now on, when will we have another chance to play again? I love you two." From the bottom of his heart he knew that his two sons were crazy about each other from the time they were still toddlers.

Emal, now in his third year at Carcassonne College, was getting scanty with his bimonthly routine calls home, and yet his phone bills were entirely paid by Abd and Martine. They attributed this increasingly sparse communication to Emal's studious effort with school subjects he had to concentrate on. For this reason, they didn't make anything out of it.

Then one day near his third-year summer break, he was found at eight in the morning sitting quietly at the doorsteps of the Odinard house when Martine opened the front door to bring in the local daily newspaper before she went to bed. "What are you doing here so early?" She looked at her stepson, astonished.

He quickly replied, "I came home directly from school with the school bus carrying the school soccer team to Pamier, and from there I hitchhiked. I want to celebrate Dad's retirement next week." Approximately a month later, a lady who used to be Abd's neighbor in Foxeline came to his office for her daughter's annual checkup. She haphazardly mentioned to Abd how glad she was that she had seen his oldest son again a few weeks earlier, after almost three years. She described him as having "grown to be an adult, almost as tall as the man he walked side by side with." She meant to say Jean-Marie. That same evening, Abd told Martine "not to believe every word Emal said from now on." The couple no longer had any doubt about their suspicion after the following scenario. Emal came home for his summer vacation. He was trying to find an odd job to make some pocket money. That was Saturday afternoon. Father and sons decided to go shopping for food, alleviating Martine's routine trip to the market. At the local grocery store parking lot, Yasir volunteered to go alone to purchase all items on the shopping list his father handed to him. He wanted to let Abd and Emal talk about schooling and projected plans for his brother after college graduation while they were sitting in the rusty old Citroën.

Abd started to say to his oldest son how hard it was for him to be a single parent during the three previous years until Martine came into the picture. Without hesitation, Emal interjected, "I had nothing to do with your divorce, and I don't want to hear anything having to do with the past." In retrospect, that was the very first sign of a switch in Emal's bonding with his father. From there on, this young man gradually became from seemingly aloof to outright coldly interactive with Abd and Martine. During the same period and for the next few more years, Yasir remained very attached to his father and stepmother.

Emal graduated from Carcassonne with a passing grade and decided not to pursue further the postgraduate education. This decision eventually had a determinant effect on the relationship he had with his close high school and college friends. The discrepancy of postgraduate education attainment between them was the explanation of the deterioration of old friendships. He quickly found a low-level office job in the food sale business in Strasbourg and within two years got married to a former student who also graduated from Carcassonne College. Martine and Abd borrowed 40,000 French francs and gave it to them as a wedding present. Emal's wife, Ënerod, wanted to become a paralegal technician specializing in the national social equality promoted by the leftist secular incumbent government, instead of looking for a teaching job, as she had majored in foreign languages in college. In order to obtain a certificate in this political field, she had to take a crash course that lasted at least one year. But the couple had no money. Emal called his father and asked whether he could borrow 15,200 French francs for his wife to matriculate at a local private law school. Martine called her husband at work and talked over with him about Emal's request and then went to their bank to get a loan, which was wired to the newlywed couple on the same day. Emal wrote a nice letter, but there was only a single handwritten sentence from Ënerod at the bottom of the typed message: "Thank you for your help." Bewildered, Abd and Martine continued for many years after to wonder why Emal didn't ask for assistance from the financially much better-off Amelia and Serge at the time. Eventually, Yasir let his father know that Amelia's several-million French-franc assets in Sweden was strictly controlled by her husband Serge. Abd and Martine were very proud of the young couple when friends and acquaintances asked about their children's whereabouts. They ostentatiously boasted how nice their daughter-in-law Ënerod was each time when they talked about grown-up children that had left home and were on their own. They did it on purpose, yet they could not detect even a smidgen of warm feeling toward them from Ënerod. Patiently they wanted to let time resolve this perhaps unfounded suspicion.

Almost thirteen months had passed since Emal's wedding and he still had not contemplated a visit to Odinard to see his aging father now in the midsixties. At this point in time, both Martine and Abd needed a vacation. They decided to take a trip by regional train across the country from Odinard to Strasbourg to see Emal and his enigmatic wife. Ënerod and Emal were on the train platform glancing at each window of passing second-class cars that progressively slowed down and then finally came to a grinding halt. Emal helped his father with the suitcase. Due to his osteoarthritic joint disease, Abd walked behind at some distance from the young couple on their way to the parked car across the street from the imposing Strasbourg railroad station. Leaning toward Abd, Martine whispered to her husband's ears, "It wasn't a warm embrace that I had expected to receive from her since their wedding. We will see in the next couple of days." The next day happened to be Emal's birthday. While helping Emal move the table and a few chairs to make room for three couples sitting, the third one being his college classmate friend Jennie and her boyfriend, Abd noted that the nine-hundred-square-foot apartment, two blocks away from the twelfth-century Strasbourg Cathedral, also known as Strasbourg Minter, was tastefully furbished with used but clean furniture. However, what attracted Martine's and Abd's attention the most was the well-preserved prewar upright Blüthner piano that was worth over fifteen thousand francs. Abd didn't want to ask how his son got it, thinking why he had to have a second piano, as his six-and-half-foot Steinway, recently professionally appraised for over 180,000 francs, was still in the Odinard house. This huge instrument had been moved twice by companies specialized in relocation of professional Steinway pianos. Emal wanted his father to keep this expensive musical instrument until he had a good job and could afford to move to a house that had enough room to accommodate it. But Abd knew right away the answer without having to struggle with his imagination. The young couple still owed Martine and Abd a total of 27,200 French francs; and due to their financial status, Ënerod's parents couldn't afford to acquire such a luxurious instrument for their son-in-law. It wasn't too difficult for the visiting couple to quickly figure out the source of money needed to acquire the upright antique. The visit with Emal and Ënerod gave the couple some rest; but there was no obvious improvement of their relationship with their daughter-in-law.

It was around eight in the evening when Abd and Martine received a phone call from Emal announcing the birth of their daughter, Azalee, at the Strasbourg General Hospital. She was the product of thirty-nine-and-a-half-week gestation. Mother and child were doing well at delivery, but the obstetrician wanted to keep the patient an extra day in the hospital for observation due to a mild hemorrhage after the placenta was evacuated. The newborn took to breast fairly well. At the end of the second day in the hospital, the baby started to regurgitate after each nursing episode. Soon regurgitation turned into outright forceful vomiting. Emal called his dad to report what was going on with his beautiful seven-pound and three-ounce brown-haired and hazel-eyed daughter. Abd asked whether he could talk directly with the mother to get more detailed description of the vomiting problem. Email handed the phone handset to his wife, but she refused to talk to her father-in-law, saying that she was too tired. Back on the phone with Emal, Abd learned that the baby had a dark-green meconium stool the day before and had a few more small and lighter yellow bowel movements on that day. The newborn had good muscle tone and appeared to be, at times, alert between feedings. She had no fever and was able to comfortably rest on her mother's abdomen or in her bassinet. Abd was glad that the possibility of bowel obstruction due to newborn small gut malrotation or large gut intussusception was almost with certainty ruled out. However, he entertained the likelihood of infantile gastroesophageal reflux disease (GERD), which is a fairly common, transient, and most of the time a benign illness in newborns with a complete recovery within a couple of months if recognized and promptly treated. Abd suggested for Emal to call in a neonatologist for consultation and advice. He followed his father's advice but decided first to discuss his father's suggestion with Ënerod. The latter talked on the phone for a few minutes with her college friend obstetrician in practice in St-Malo, Bretagne. The next day, the baby was thoroughly examined by a female neonatologist. She confirmed the telephone diagnosis made by Abd and started to implement without delay the treatment of GERD while baby and mother were still hospitalized. Initially there were a few recurrent mild vomiting episodes after discharge from the hospital, but her illness was fully recovered within sixth months, as predicted.

The following discreet observation that broke Martine's heart of gold dated back approximately two years. Before she made the Strasbourg vacation trip with her husband, she went to a local jewelry store and bought a Sterling silver bracelet after she learned from Emal that his blond wife in general disliked gold ornaments and preferred to dress in black with "standing out" silver jewels. Martine could not afford to buy for herself such an expensive—relative to her salary—ornament. She took it with her as a wedding gift. She wanted to build a good relationship with a new member of her husband's family. She believed in making the first step to show the young woman that she cared. At the first dinner at the Strasbourg apartment, Martine handed the box containing the bracelet while looking at Ënerod's left wrist. "I hope you like it. If you don't, I can bring it back to the store and make an exchange for something else you have in mind that would go well with your beautiful dresses." The young lady host was wearing for the evening a bracelet similar in size, shape, and material. She took a glance at Martine's gift, uttered a soft and trifling, "Thank you," and then quickly put it aside. The only difference between the two ornaments was the more classic engraved relief on that of Martine's. Subsequently, and each time she saw Ënerod, Martine had never seen her wearing the gift bracelet. At her sixtieth birthday, when she and her husband were invited—a rare event—to Emal's new home in Grenoble, French Alps, for "celebration," thirty months after the seniors had arrived there, again she saw Ënerod wearing her own bracelet and not the one she bought in Odinard. Even though profoundly disappointed, Martine continued to praise her husband's daughter-in-law every time her friends asked about her family. She hoped that the cold relationship with Ënerod would eventually improve once the latter had her first child. Only an infinitesimal shred of hope remained in her mind, and that was the offshoot of wishful thinking, not rational.

By this time, Dr. Rasulov and his wife Martine had been living in Grenoble for almost three years. A shocking incident was about to happen to them. He was working out of town, and she was still holding her nursing job at a local assisted-living facility. They were not too happy with the rowdy and inconsiderate couple occupying the apartment above them. They decided to look toward the southern part of the city for a two-bedroom single home in a new development area. They found a house still under construction that fitted well with their budget and needs. The saleslady took their name, and they promised to think it over while expressing their favorable first impression in terms of location, floor layout, construction materials, etc. On the same evening, Martine phoned Ënerod to find out how the baby Azalee and the rest of the family were doing. They were still living in Strasbourg. Emal was away on business. During the phone conversation, Martine casually mentioned that she and her husband had found the house mentioned above and might be interested in buying it. Ënerod told her that Emal was offered to be brought back to Grenoble by his firm to fill the newly created position as vice president and that the couple was thrilled with the prospect of moving back to "the city they considered home." The couple had lived for a short time in Grenoble when Emal was employed by another much less known business firm. Martine delicately asked Ënerod how far her to-be-purchased home should be from their future residence but got no answer. Instead, the latter related to Martine that she and her husband had recently looked at a few new home developments on the south side of Grenoble; even though Emal's employment contract had not been signed and sealed. She mentioned that a saleslady had asked her and Emal whether they were relatives of another couple of the same name Rasulov who had, a few days earlier, expressed interest in a smaller two-bedroom model still under construction, located a half block away and on the same development. Approximately a week later, Emal made a "business" trip to Grenoble. At the end of his journey and before flying back to Strasbourg, he dropped in to see his father and stepmother at their apartment. The couple was delighted to see Emal. At lunch, they praised and congratulated him for his outstanding professional achievement.

When Abd was about to get up from the table and have the dessert and coffee served in the family room, Emal's facial expression suddenly changed. "I have to be truthful with both of you. Ënerod and I and your granddaughter need some 'space.'"

Martine, having kept in mind the unanswered question she posed to Ënerod the week before, looked straight in Emal's eyes. "My parents have taught me and my siblings how parents should relate to their grown-up children, especially when dealing with the ones who are married. Based on that teaching, I have delicately advanced our concern to Ënerod on the subject of distance between your future residence and our future home once you two will move back to town. In other words, unlike some grandparents, we don't want to stick our nose into our children's affairs."

Very determined with his tone of voice, Emal replied without hesitance, "If you decide to buy the two-bedroom house near Belvédère golf course, I will have to forfeit the 40,000-franc deposit and turn down the job offered to return to Grenoble. Ënerod doesn't have a good feeling about the whole matter."

Very disappointed, Martine immediately vented her frustration. "Your father and I, with our broker's help, had looked at this possibility last fall, many months before we learned from your own wife that you might be relocated back to town. We didn't know that you had looked at the same housing development. Sorry for having inconvenienced you two."

Three weeks later, Abd and Martine received a long letter from Emal, who was about to move his family to Grenoble. He tried very hard to convince his elders that they had "misunderstood" him and his wife, that he never said "Don't move to the vicinity of Belvédère golf course," but rather to another development where the price of homes was much less expensive and therefore more affordable. The reality was that he and Yasir had already figured out that their father didn't have enough savings for a comfortable retirement after having spent all incomes derived from the medical practice, from Martine's wage and dowry, and banks' loans. In the same letter, he also stated that his wife Ënerod had been behaving as a good daughter-in-law since he married her and that she was looking forward to having her daughter Azalee frequently in touch with grandparents Martine and Abd. He closed his letter by stating that it was a "terrible burden" his father had placed on him and his brother to "constantly doubt [them] and [their] intentions." The elder Rasulovs looked at each other, shook their heads, and bitterly smiled before putting down the letter. They still vividly remembered the rare and unexpected telephone call from Emal, four years earlier while they were still living in Odinard, recommending them not to buy property within the metropolitan Grenoble but rather a "more affordable" retirement patio home in the town Villard three quarters of an hour drive from Grenoble. Possibly, at the time, the young couple was dwelling on the notion of "potential toxic in-laws" living next door. It wasn't too difficult to read the young couple's mind after Abd and Martine had the unpleasant encounter with Emal on his business visit to Grenoble and his following contradictory letter mentioned above.

As a result of the overt cold relationship with Emal and Ënerod, the senior Rasulovs intentionally bought their next homes in two different sectors of the busy city of Grenoble, far enough from their son's home. In contrast, without a single exception, all of Abd's old colleagues and friends living in France or in neighboring European countries were enjoying the presence of their children living in the nearby or even on the same street. These retirees or semi-retirees had ample opportunities to see their grandchildren during their twilight years of retirement. Those who had been keeping up with new medical awareness either took care of these youngsters themselves or gave valuable experienced advice to their parents. Abd and Martine were totally deprived of this type of rapprochement. Instead they were kept out of all medical decision making when their only grandchild was sick with a bout of urinary tract infection (UTI)[5] shortly before her second birthday. It was a long story about this incident that there is no need for the writer to dwell on, but needless to say, Abd had to practically twist the child's parents' arm to have her seen by a professor expert in this delicate and complex field of infantile UTI. Ënerod believed that a casual follow-up by the child's pediatrician was more than adequate. Abd took pains to arrange a meeting with the professor who explained to Ënerod the necessary follow-up tests to be done once the infection was under control to ascertain that a congenital urinary tract malformation was unambiguously ruled out. Abd's genuine concern over his granddaughter's UTI was based on the following basic knowledge. If the anatomical structure of the urinary tract was demonstrated to be normal on imaging tests and yet the patient continues to have repeated UTIs, as this has happened to one of the blood-related immediate relatives of Azalee, the cause of the disease is not fully established; and therefore, maintenance antibiotic therapy is not the final curative solution. Abd believed that the possibility of a "functional" abnormality of the urinary tract lining might explain the recurrence of UTIs. Interestingly, almost thirty years later, scientists have come up with a very plausible explanation that confirms the suggestion made by Abd.[5] Since the communication with Azalee's parents had been extremely limited and finally ended up in a complete unilateral disconnection, Abd and Martine had no idea whether Azalee had undergone the recommended post-infection investigational tests and whether she subsequently had repeated UTIs.

The following examples further illustrated Ënerod's haughty attitude toward Martine and Abd. This set of grandparents adored their granddaughter Azalee whose parents lived only a twenty-five-minute drive from her grandparents; yet she was allowed to visit with them only thirteen times from the time she was born until she was eleven years old. With four exceptions when she was allowed to stay overnight with her grandparents in the Grenoble house, each of her visits lasted no more than a few short hours. When she was permitted to spend the night with Martine and Abd, the visit was restricted to less than fifteen hours. The child was brought to her grandparents' home after her father's working hours—Ënerod didn't have to work and stayed home to care for her only child—and on the next day, around eight in the morning, her parents already knocked at the door wanting to pick her up. Weekends made no exception. The restriction of visiting time extended also to occasional invitations to their house that Emal and Ënerod made on the occasions of birthday or Christmas holiday. On that specified day, Emal never failed to insist that Abd and Martine arrive only after four in the afternoon, and not before. He repeatedly turned down Martine's offer to come earlier to help Ënerod prepare the dinner. He also refused to let the grandparents watch and play with the toddler Azalee while her parents got ready to sit down at the dining table. Yet Azalee had mentioned in passing that she had spent several days in the company of her other two sets of grandparents who had come at least twice a year and stayed at her parents' house in Grenoble. Martine had the desire to see her beloved Azalee as often as she was allowed to do so. In furtherance to her wish, she proposed to Ënerod to let her babysit Azalee at any time of the day including weekends, as she had substantial unused vacation times. The latter replied that they had contracted with a "professional" babysitter. Not being able to convince Ënerod and Emal that even though not blood-related to Azalee, she truly loved her and liked to see her as frequently as possible, Martine offered to take mother and daughter out for lunch on her day off. After repeating the offer over a period of several months, finally Ënerod accepted. Bringing along a toy as a present for the loving little girl, Martine went out and spent a pleasant time *a-trois* in a restaurant chosen by the five-year-old Azalee, who expressively showed her deep affection for her step-grandmother. Eleven months later Ënerod reciprocated by inviting Martine out for lunch, and Azalee greatly rejoiced seeing Grandma Martine again. That was the last lunch *a-trois* Martine ever had with Ënerod. Subsequent to that restaurant meeting, Azalee's mother always found an excuse to turn down repeated invitations from Martine. Can one imagine how Martine felt about being snubbed by the wife of her husband's oldest son? The reader would easily recognize Ënerod's standoffish attitude as this writing continues.

Going back to the last few years of living in Odinard. Tired and exhausted by long years of busy medical practice, Abd entertained the idea of retirement at the age of sixty-six. He sold his practice and moved to Grenoble, where lived a couple of old friends who still exercised their medical profession part-time. One of these two was Abd's best man at his first wedding in Karolinska. But because of his meager savings, Abd had to supplement Martine's earnings with income derived from *locum tenens* work and from institutions that invited him as a teaching guest in infectious diseases. Consequently, he had to travel on average two weeks per month to several faraway cities in almost all French arrondissements. This type of work gave him some professional satisfaction with teaching and lecturing, but most of the time, nothing but headache and disappointment with his locum tenens assignments to private groups of medical practitioners. However, Abd had no choice. He needed to build up a retirement savings after having to spend every dime of his office-practice income and all the money he borrowed from banks to defray his two sons' private schooling and college expenses during the years of private medical practice. These nine long years of work away from home put a lot of stress on Martine, as she worried a great deal about her husband's overall hardship he had to put up with in order to generate the necessary savings for a frugal but comfortable enough living condition during the remaining golden years in Grenoble.

By now Abd had reached his seventy-second birthday. Before quitting his travel for work, Abd decided to make, here and there, two-to-three-week trips to developing countries to provide free humanitarian medical service to the poor and the needy. He anticipated that working with these underprivileged and preoccupation with their health day after day would steer his mind away from the sadness of being progressively isolated by his two sons. To a certain extent, this assumption turned out to be true. Blending in with these destitute and caring for them gave him the true sense of carrying out the Lord's work. Initially he joined organized groups to go to Papua New Guinea, Bolivia, Cambodia, and the Philippines; but subsequently he undertook solo trips after he had learned from previous assignments that intermingling with natives while providing medical assistance was more interesting and satisfactory, as he was able to put himself in their shoes to appreciate the hardship of poverty they had to endure. Surprisingly, Abd had not acquired any of the local bacterial infectious diseases—quite a few of them were resistant to antimicrobials—he was exposed to during these trips, except once, when Martine joined him for their tour to deliver doctor service, nursing care, and medicines to an Eastern European country. Both, husband and wife, developed an itching skin rash consisting of bumps and blisters on their wrists two days prior to boarding a night train via Budapest to go home. With his naked eyes, Abd recognized right away that the rash was scabies, a very contagious disease commonly seen in several developed countries of the Western Hemisphere. On the same day, the initial clinical diagnosis was confirmed by microscopic examination at the local hospital of the scrapings taken from skin lesions on Abd's wrists. Application of topical sulfur ointment on the entire body's skin surface after a soapy warm bath was immediately implemented while the senior couple isolated themselves in a hotel. This time-consuming treatment regimen was repeated every day for three consecutive days until the itching was abated and the rash had dried out. They boarded the train, heading for Grenoble on the fourth day. Soon this temporary setback became history. A few months later both husband and wife resumed their medical missions.

During the past four years, by then seventy-six years old, Abd was suffering from severe osteoarthritic disease of both knees. The pain was only partially relieved by repeated steroid injections, whose effect was transient at best. Walking around the block became a difficult chore. The only remedy left was to undergo a total knee replacement, a tedious surgical procedure undertaken only by a handful of French orthopedic surgeons at the time. Fortunately, Abd was able to discuss this operation with a doctor specialized in this field. The latter had his training at one of the university hospitals in Paris and recently relocated to Grenoble where ski injuries of all sorts were common. Abd was thoroughly checked by the internist and the cardiologist working as a team with the operating surgeon. The surgery went well, and there were no apparent immediate complications in the operating room. However, Abd was not that lucky, even though he was operated on by a reputable doctor. On the second postoperative day, Abd felt dizzy and very tired and appeared to be confused. Blood tests revealed that he had lost almost half of his blood volume and had to be transfused with three pints of blood. But this was not the end of his ordeal. That same evening the painful calf below the operated knee turned red, swollen, and had the appearance and the consistency of a large summer oversized sausage. The on-call internist quickly checked him over and then immediately wheeled him to the x-ray room on a stretcher. A blood clot had developed inside the affected calf. A hematologist was called in, and urgent treatment to dissolve the clot before it migrated to the lungs or to the brain was implemented without delay. Abd had to be kept three extra days at the hospital for continuing treatment to completely dissolve the blood clot and for close observation. After discharge and for the next ten days, he had to be kept on blood-thinning medication injected by a visiting nurse. That was a close call.

On three consecutive days during his father's hospitalization, Emal came to the hospital to see his father after his office hours. He expressed a great deal of concern when he and Martine realized that the "old man" was confused and "sleepy" after having developed the steady but invisible profound hemorrhage. But Martine received no call, no visit, and no well-wishing card from their daughter-in-law Ënerod during the entire ordeal.

Several months later, somehow the subject of "Dad's illness" came up during one of those rare telephone conversations Emal made from Grenoble airport while waiting for his flight departure. She conveyed to him her disappointment for Ënerod's lack of sympathy for the father of her husband at a time when life or death was at a fleeting moment. Emal hastily replied, "She [Ënerod] was on vacation with Azalee at her parents' home during that week, but don't you remember, I was visiting with Dad every day, and she had in person brought to you two a cooked dish upon her return to town a week later? Don't you think that was good enough from her part?" Martine's heart sobbed, and she became speechless. Subsequently the contact between the parents and the only married son amounted to no more than a couple of calls from the latter per year; and the calls were made from his office or from the Grenoble airport. It appeared as if he tried to avoid talking to his father or to his stepmother from home. His routine words at the opening of these brief conversations, before his inquiry or lack thereof about how the seniors were doing, were always the same. "I have been so busy with out-of-town pitching for new business contracts…" But Martine did not want to give up completely. She wrote a short note to Emal suggesting him to meet on one-to-one basis with his father on a neutral ground and try to find a way to improve their relationship. Emal accepted Martine's recommendation. Father and son met in the Grenoble People Park at the indicated day, place, and time. The atmosphere was cold from the start. As soon as they sat down on a freshly repainted green bench away from the busy alleys, Abd brought up the past events leading to his divorce, not with the intention of putting blame on his ex-wife, but rather to explain why he had to arrive to this painful decision. While reminding Emal that he had chosen, without being coaxed by anybody, to live with his father after the legal separation, Abd asked his son why he had gradually but steadily become estranged since he got married. He was responded to by a few minutes of embarrassing silence from the part of his son.

With remorse, the father pronounced his *mea culpa*; then the son sternly looked at him. "I don't want to hear anything that has to do with the past if you two want to remain in touch with me and my brother." This is a common theme: the initiator's attempt of setting boundaries for the estranger is well-known to the investigators in the field of mental health. The purpose for the initiator is to maintain limited contact with the victim of estrangement, as the initiator is unwilling to agree to a reconciliation.[6]

Abd got up from the bench, saying, "Thanks for your effort. Not much else I could do to repair our damaged relationship. Goodbye." From that day on, and for many years after, Emal repeatedly labeled his father as "condescending, arrogant, irate, hypocritical, and out-right hostile" in a few of his rare correspondences or telephone conversations he had with Abd and Martine.

To understand the gravity of the abrupt severance of relationship between Emal and his brother on one side and with Abd and Martine on the other, this writer has to at least touch upon the gradual transformation of Yasir's attitude. As briefly mentioned earlier, unlike his older brother, he was not the favorite nor was he equally loved by his Swedish grandmother from his early childhood on. Ironically, as he grew older, his physical appearance was gradually leaning toward that of Europeans. But he remained the underdog throughout his entire life, while his brother, the dominant figure among the two of them. He was recognized already from birth by people around him that he was a child with a mild and gentle manner. He demonstrated to be of service to everyone he was in contact with, a responsible, polite, and respectful teen by the time he started his first year of high school. Everybody liked him. Because of these qualities, instead of concentrating on studying, he took too much time out of his three last college years. As a result, he experienced setbacks in learning and eventually was barely able to pass his final bachelor exam at Nantes College, another fairly reputable private school where he had spent four years. Yet his father had identified his intellectual capacity as early as his budding childhood years. This observation was later confirmed and reinforced by brilliant reports he made on his scientific research works. Abd concluded that his younger son was a "late bloomer" like himself.

To be realistic, the reader should also see the other side of the coin. Hence, the most basic and relevant trait of Yasir's personality needs to be brought up for discussion. He had trouble formulating his own opinions. Instead, he was too easily persuaded and ended up becoming a follower instead of an initiator of a new idea, a personal viewpoint, or even a trivial, simple proposal. But when his father and stepmother insinuated that he was not an independent thinker, he got very angry. The submission of his personal thoughts to that of others eventually led him to come up with unfounded, bizarre, and even laughable stories. The chronological events covering the phase of his life extending from the time of his parents' official separation to the time he joined in with his brother to shun his father and his stepmother will illustrate the profound transformation of his relationship toward the latter. Probably the reader still recalls Yasir's spontaneous revelation to John Campbell of his new life when he was still living alone with his father after the divorce. At the time, Yasir's feeling could be summarized in these few words: He (Yasir) "had made a right choice" and "I [Yasir] am glad I am living with my father…" As it was already mentioned earlier, Yasir was very protective of his father right after the divorce. He didn't want to hear anything that was related to his father's personal life. He was afraid that his father would "make another mistake" by getting married again, but this fear was understandable in the mind of a preteen. He had no hesitation of repeatedly conveying this fear to Emal for the next three years. He was well aware of the hardship his father had to endure at least during the three years preceding the arrival of Martine into his life. Almost every day, at the dinner table, he repeatedly asked how his father was doing and whether he himself was placing too much burden on the latter. He accorded genuine attention to his father's health, in terms of workload, sleep adequacy, and physical exercise requirement. There was no doubt in anyone's mind that Yasir's over-all concern over his father's daily life that this preteen had a true love, not pity, for the latter. This was remarkable in view of the fact that the young man's life was torn apart by his parents' divorce; and yet, while being exposed to distressful circumstances, he was still able to grapple with the sense of fairness and face the reality of life. His behavior during his high school years was impeccable. He never had his father and stepmother worried of his whereabouts. Each morn-ing, he outlined to them his schedule for the day before he went to school. Yasir's conduct in college was absolutely irreproachable. He hung out with classmates whose family shared the same values as did Martine and Abd. He called home regularly to express his con-cern over his poor school performance and fear of betraying their love and trust. After his college graduation and during the next two years living alone while working in a biological research lab in the city of Nantes, Yasir continued to exhibit his natural attachment to the parental nest he had chosen to detach himself from. Despite the distance, he managed to divide his number of visits equally between Foxeline and Odinard during weekends and earned vacation days. Abd and Martine reciprocated their love for Yasir by occasionally driving to Nantes to see him and to keep an eye on his lonely first time in a big city. They discreetly supplemented his meager income with gift cash or foods until he found a better-paying job in Paris twenty-seven months later. In order to save money and at the same time have an opportunity to be alone with his son, Abd signed out his practice to a colleague, rented a van, and in the company of his youngster, they drove Yasir's household belongings from Nantes to the capital of France. On their way to the new city, they leisurely made several stops for food and for visits of renowned historic French memorials and shrines. They freely discussed about the painful past, and Yasir repeatedly insisted that his father should never put blame solely on himself for the unavoidable ending of his first union. Not only the new employment with an institution doing interesting research in the deterioration of the planet by human waste, but also the expanded social life in this city of light was very pleasing to this young man. But neither the new job nor the new lifestyle did lead Yasir to neglect his gratitude toward his father and his stepmother. He called home every month to inquire about their health, to share with them about new knowledge in the pollution of water, soil, planted crops, and therefore consumed foods. He discussed with his father the possible association of contaminated foods with antibiotics used for the enhancement of production of animals grown for meat consumption and human intractable diseases. He ended each phone call with, "I love you two very much." There were no adequate words to describe the intimate reciprocal love all three had for the next few more years until Abd and Martine moved to Tarbes, also in Mid-Pyrenees, where they built a farmhouse intended for Abd's retirement. For the next three years, probably due to the distance, Yasir's visits with his father and stepmother in Tarbes were limited to only once a year, either during the French Labor Day or Christmas holidays. He alternated these visits between Tarbes and Foxeline, where his mother lived. Socially, he was surrounded by friends of both sexes and from all parts of the world. He dated at least half a dozen ladies working in private or governmental institutions but didn't seem to become serious with any one of them.

This was the twenty-third of December, two years after Abd and Martine moved to Grenoble. Martine hastily swallowed her breakfast before rushing out, going to work in a nursing home. Abd just put down his telephone handset, concluding a conversation with his placement service agency about a two-week out-of-town assignment.

While putting on her winter coat, Martine made the following remark: "Only two days until Christmas, yet we haven't heard from Yasir. Since he left home and went out on his own almost ten years ago, he has been very prompt in letting us know in advance the date of his arrival to town, the day of his visit with us, and that with his brother's family. Have you noted that he has not called us as often and as regularly as usual and his sparse calls tend to be brief and less inquiring after than in the past several years? Of note, since the last Christmas, unlike on previous years, Emal has stopped letting us know whether his family remained in town during the holiday and whether he and his wife had the intention of having Christmas Eve dinner with us and his brother. So far this year, neither Emal nor Ënerod has told us about their holiday plan. Do you have an explanation for this coincidence, dear? I think I have an idea about your two boys' change of attitude toward me and you."

Convincingly, Abd responded, "I have made the same observation. I can only surmise that the grown-up children, in a small number of families across the land, have adopted a different attitude toward their biological parents, especially when they are married and have an additional obligation toward their in-laws. For those who are still single, they are too busy with their search for a girlfriend or a life mate and therefore paid less attention to their aging elders. In both instances, the biological parents' life becomes a secondary concern for them.

"Furthermore, in a case of divorce like mine, the relationship between each set of grandparents and a grandchild is most of the time totally different, depending on the daughter-in-law's or the son-in-law's interconnection with their spousal family. In other words, the grandchild's relationship with his/her grandparents is strictly under the control of the child's parents. But this controlled tie might change after the grandchild reaches adulthood. Quite different from the old days, grandparents nowadays have no shared jurisdiction on their grandchildren anymore. But this unusual situation is rarely encountered in a stable family unit made up of individuals whose upbringing was based on faith, love, and fairness.

"Go down the list of all our French, German, Austrian, Belgian, Swiss, and Scandinavian friends' families and that of my relatives in Afghanistan, you will find no grown-up children among those families having such a bizarre relationship with their parents like ours. Three generations of humans live in harmony, and the grandchildren benefit the grandparents' experience and wit during the seniors' golden years. Honey, to start with, just think back about the commendable relationship between you, your five siblings, and your parents before and after you grew up and had your own family.

"Let's take a couple more examples to illustrate this remarkable bonding in many family settings that we know. You met my Austrian old friend Ikrid a couple of times, right? Her second son took over his father's business after the latter suddenly passed away. He lives next door to Ikrid, and his wife comes every single day to routinely see her, making sure that Grandma is okay. During the day, when the young couple is at work, Ikrid looks after their two-year-old daughter. At three thirty in the afternoon, Ikrid walks to the school a couple of blocks away with the baby and brings her two older grandsons to her home. She gives them a snack, reads, and plays with them until their parents pick them up. Ikrid's oldest son is the director of a physical therapy business and lives in Salzburg. He comes home every second weekend to see Mama. Ikrid's youngest son is a middle-school teacher and lives in Vienna. He has been engaged to a high school classmate for almost a year and has been talking of a pending wedding this coming summer. He takes the three-hour train from Vienna and comes home twice a month to be with Ikrid during the weekend.

"The second example is right here in town. You know David Butterfield, right? You probably remember, he was in training with me during our residency at Oxford General Hospital. He has been in private practice but also a part-time instructor in pediatric allergy and immunology for over thirty years at the Grenoble University. His son, whom Emal had met once many years ago, was a graduate from Paris Medical School. He also has a PhD degree in medical sciences. After the completion of his long years of training, this man was offered by several reputable French universities to stay in academic medicine and do research and teaching. Instead, this young doctor chose to join a large group of medical practice and settle in Grenoble to be near his parents. Every time I think about our situation, I scratch my head, wondering why we are so unlucky. But I think you and I have a very good idea why this is happening to us."

The couple's intuitive insight and perception was initially considered as presumptive, but subsequent unpleasant incident-laden relationships with Emal and Yasir accentuated as the years passed by. Martine, always ready for damage repair through her conviction about God's love and forgiveness, proposed a meeting to put to rest several possible misunderstandings between children and parents. To show that Ënerod had been, and still as far as she was concerned, remained as a close member of the extended family, Martine insisted that she should be involved in all discussion and therefore should attend the meeting. Emal agreed to bring his wife along. On the convened day, Yasir, arrived from Paris, showed up alone with his brother at the hotel room reserved by Martine. The absence of Ënerod bothered Martine a great deal, but she purposely avoided mentioning her name during the entire meeting that lasted barely two hours.

The very first thing the two young adults jointly said was, "We don't want to talk about any subject dealing with the past, specifically the divorce. We want to discuss only matters that have connection with the future."

Their father, without hesitation and without making comments, replied, "The future is a continuation of the past going through the present. We don't see how you two can intentionally put aside events of the past and address only issues of the future that have not yet happened." Ironically, Yasir and Emal brought up at the end of the meeting their "bad" childhood experience by recounting the mockery and ridicule they were subjected to because of their non-French last name.

Before leaving the meeting room, Emal looked at Martine and Abd, saying, "Nothing was accomplished." The meeting failed to encourage the rapprochement between the involved parties.

Since the last time Yasir called almost nine months ago, there had been no more routine communication by mail or by phone with Abd and Martine. Then suddenly the phone rang. That was Yasir, who appeared quite agitated. "I want to talk to Dad."

Martine handed the handset over to her husband, who said, "Glad that you called. How are you? Haven't heard from you for months! Are you okay?"

Continuing to appear upset, Abd's younger son shouted, "I don't want you to interfere with my education and my personal life from now on. Okay?"

"What do you mean?"

"You know what I mean. Without talking to me, you went behind my back and called several institutions looking for employment for me. Then you proceeded to call at least five universities, trying to find a study program for me after you were unable to find an employment for me."

"Yes, I did make quite a few calls to inquire about possible new employments suitable to your education and experience, as you had said more than once that you would eventually leave Paris to move to another city near the ocean. Yes, I worry about your future and I want to help you. Is it a crime to have a noble intention to help someone, let alone your own son? Remember, you wrote on your Christmas card the year after you graduated from college that you 'want to eventually go back to a graduate school and get a more advanced degree than your brother did'? Purposely I did not mention our surname, your given name, or mine. Instead, I used Martine's family name and the nickname of her brother to do the inquiry. So, be assured that nobody would even have a faint idea for whom I had made these inquiries."

The explanation for Yasir being so upset was rather simple. Even though Emal had been consulted by his father and had agreed to let the latter make these querying calls, he later denied that he had indeed said "no harm to get info, but in the end, it is Yasir's decision," referring to any decision about a new employment or matriculation for his study toward a master's degree. How could Yasir not be angry at their old man when his brother had turned around and told him that their father had made these phone calls specifically on his behalf instead of reassuring him that was just an anonymous preliminary information-gathering process? Since Abd was always concerned for his son's future due to a lack of advanced education beyond the bachelor's degree, he constantly made an effort to instill in him the notion of "a certificate of achievement or a postgraduate certificate after college is equivalent to buying an additional life insurance."

In order to fulfill their dream of seeing Yasir having a stable, interesting, and well-paid job not too far in the future, Martine came up with an idea that was shared with pleasure by her husband. She wrote a long letter to Yasir, who was still living and working in Paris.

She suggested that he take out at least two years from working for a living and come and live with his semiretiring father and still-working stepmother. She outlined in detail how her proposed cohabitation could work out smoothly while Yasir went back to school full-time for a master's degree. She offered to have the unfinished basement of their house in Grenoble remodeled with additional new amenities for bathing and cooking or alternatively to share meals with the senior couple, who was more than happy to pay for Yasir's school tuition. In other words, Martine and Abd wanted to totally support Yasir financially as long as he would want to achieve his goal: get at least a *cum laude* attached to his master's degree.

Within less than one week's time, Yasir called to say that he had decided to decline Martine's offer. From that day on, instead of being kinder and appreciative, Yasir gradually showed his anger against the senior couple for reasons that remained obscure to the day when they consulted the very first psychologist. Intrigued by Yasir's change of attitude, Abd and Martine were trying to be initially calm and patient, but Yasir became more and more insolent on the phone. He constantly interrupted his father's effort to voice his personal opinion with words like "why," "so what," and "wrong." He aggravated the latter by repeatedly interjecting before his father or his stepmother could finish a sentence. He showed extreme impatience, raised his voice, giving the impression that he was mad. After a few more similar sessions on the phone over a period of several months, Abd decided to handle Yasir's telephone conversation differently. He shouted back each time Yasir started to become disrespectful, showing his younger son that he was no longer willing to tolerate his contemptuous behavior. He didn't think that this approach was very effective in bringing back the most loving relationship he had had with his son, but he thought it must certainly stop any attempt of intimidation. The father and son relationship had all ingredients to deteriorate further, especially when Abd and Martine were devastated by the following two unexpected, unbelievable anecdotes of Yasir.

Thirteen years after Yasir had left his paternal nest to live alone in Paris, he came up with a new forthright accusation that his father had "forbidden" him to travel through Chile, the South American country frequently in turmoil with political unrest, during his exploratory study on the manmade pollution of the planet. He was promptly reminded that no parents would impose on their children any thought or action after they left home and are on their own; and if they worry about the possible risks their children might run while undertaking a new adventure, they might just give some warning because they care. But forbid a thirty-four-year-old son to undertake something that has to do with his career was certainly not within the realm of their jurisdiction. Furthermore, Yasir could not reconcile the accusation he made with the fact that Abd and Martine had given him 1,200 French francs to help him defray some of his expenses during the trip. Despite these controversies, Yasir continued to claim, year after year, that indeed his father had "forbidden" him.

Phone calls from Yasir gradually became almost nonexistent, but his rough manner on the phone remained unabated over the next several years. Then one day, he responded to a call from Martine inquiring on his general health and the progress of his evening schooling toward the master's degree, a gesture of caring, as most mothers do. The conversation ended with another new accusation. This time, it was "Dad" again. "Eight years ago, during a gathering at Emal's home in Grenoble for Christmas Eve celebration, I witnessed an angry confrontation Dad had with Azalee, who was playing on the floor with toys she just received as gifts from several members of the extended family." He emphatically placed the blame on his father for being rude and intolerant toward the little girl. Martine told him that it was not possible that such an unpleasant encounter could take place between his father and his four-year-old niece and that she and her husband were rarely allowed to see Azalee, who adored the shunned grandparent couple. She asked Yasir why an old man who loved his granddaughter dearly had to choose Christmas Eve to fight with her. Martine reminded Yasir that she was sitting at his father's side during the entire evening, and if what he had claimed was true, she would have indisputably known of these events. "I was there too, and I saw it," Yasir insisted. Martine realized that her stepson had some sort of emotional problem. Less than a year later, Abd and Martine were told by Emal that Yasir was under intensive psychoanalysis and that the couple should never again "argue" with his brother.

Martine couldn't put up anymore with Emal's fabrication and distortion during the rare telephone conversations he had with her and her husband. She pointed out to him that on one occasion he had started himself to talk politics with his father and not the other way around and that she was also on the phone during the entire phone call he initiated himself. She reminded him that he had been a staunch junior member of the French Conservative Party until he married Ënerod, who, ironically, was at the other end of the French political spectrum. She replied to a long note Emal sent to rebuke his father for getting "angry about politics" during the previous phone conversation. "Again, you distorted the whole conversation. I was there and I can testify [to] the fact that your father talked to you in a calm fashion and hung up the phone as usual. He did not 'slam' down the phone as you had incorrectly written at the end of the paragraph five [of your note]. I should point out to you that Yasir had adopted the same approach as yours, i.e., no contact with us for months, using the same excuse that your father 'gets angry on the phone' and ignoring that both of us have experienced Yasir's anger several times on the phone or in person."

Martine brought up another instance where Abd was so frustrated with the way his two sons were treating him. She quoted a sentence taken out from a letter Abd wrote to Yasir: "From now on I wish to detach myself 'sentimentally and emotionally' from you two (Emal and Yasir) and Emal's family." She explained to him that his dad "obviously hoped to spare the remaining component, namely, the 'formal' contact either by phone or by letter." Then she added, "You interpreted those words of your father as to 'never call again.' You see, it is very easy for you to take his words out of context without trying to wholly understand the meaning of his words." Within the same context, Martine did not hesitate to confront Emal for having said that they were "being endlessly attacked by Dad for every single bad thing in the world, for the shots he's taking at Ënerod and her parents." Without further comments on this statement, she replied, "This is preposterous."

In her desire to continue reasoning with Emal, Martine quoted the latter's frivolous sentence, "Dad has to be right in every single thing there is and cannot tolerate any conflicting point of view or opinion." To these foolish words, she responded, "That is your take on it. I know your father would be satisfied and content if you two [meaning Emal and Yasir] agreed to bring up the past, as sad as this may be, for discussion. Many events have happened during that period that you and Yasir are not aware of, as your father did not want them to interfere with your schooling. Judgment cannot be accurate if one does not know the whole story." Then Martine went on to quote once more Emal's words: "It appears there is no apparent way to end this with Dad that I can see." To these much less accusatory words, Martine replied, "Yes, I can see a way. This could be achieved if you and Yasir stop accusing us, exaggerating or putting words in our mouths, and decided to respond to specific questions that had been raised by us these years. There would be no resolution in sight if one party continues to ignore these specific questions."

Referring to an incident that took place on the Christmas Eve when Martine and Abd drove Yasir to his brother's house, Martine reminded Emal that she and his dad would feel very uneasy if they accepted to come in his house that evening, after Emal had humiliated his father by calling him names the day before on the phone. To prove that she and her husband were tolerant and peace-loving parents, regardless of the children's repetitive verbal abuse, she wrote, "However, we definitely had shown our correct etiquette by wishing all three [Emal, Ënerod, and Azalee] of you a 'Merry Christmas' and hugging you, which was genuine."

Martine went on with her rational argument about being socially isolated from the rest of the "extended" family. She and her husband believed that this unilateral detachment had started sometime after his marriage to Ënerod but became quite obvious after Azalee was born. Emal must be embarrassed when he read, "Emal, how can you allow Azalee to spend days and weeks with your in-laws or with your mother and Serge; but we could not have her stay with us more than twenty-four hours, once every two to three years? Answer me that! I feel we are discriminated against."

At the end of her letter to Emal, Martine revealed that she and his father had seen four mental health specialists since his and his brother's estrangement had become evident to her. She closed her letter with, "It is time for you, Emal, to reach out for someone who can professionally give us help in finding a solution to heal all of our wounds."

It appeared that the bitter relationship between the senior Rasulovs and their adult children was not enough to haunt them day and night.

Another unexpected and disturbing news came from Vienna. While still frustrated by Aamir's repeated lack of cooperation in dealing with his three older brothers, Ali dropped a bombshell. He sent a brief note telling Zekirullah a shattering piece of news that one of his former students, and also his distant nephew, had reported to him the following story. Instead of informing his oldest brother his intention of compiling the Rasulov family tree book, as most of the middle and younger children in an Afghan society would do, Aamir sent out to all his relatives living in exile anywhere in the world the copy of the draft of his compilation, asking them for possible additional missing information and for a final approval. This action taken in secrecy by Aamir *vis-à-vis* his older brothers was bad enough, but what bothered their nephew the most was the book paragraph describing the life of Haashim Rasulov. Aamir contended that his father, yes, his father Haashim, had an affair with his mother's aunt during the second evacuation from Bamyan when intensive battles between Afghan warlords' troops took place. At the end of the written note, Ali wrote: "An unexpected anger all of a sudden swelled up in my heart when I read our nephew's lines." Thankfully, Haashim's reputation for being a righteous man with an impeccable morality was not easily shaken by nasty innuendo coming from his own son.

The above invented bizarre story wasn't rebellious enough for Aamir. He needed more attention-seeking approaches. One of those was the spread of the rumor that Abd owed a poor relative living in Tupchi money and failed to repay the borrowed sum and that eventually Aamir himself had to pay out of his pocket the debt on Abd's behalf. In order to clear himself of the false accusation, Abd obtained from this relative a written statement denying that she had ever loaned any money to him; but rather, she had regularly received financial assistance from him.

"It is quite obvious to the reader that Aamir was indeed a mendacious and nefarious individual," Abd wrote in his diary the week before he died.

CHAPTER THIRTEEN

Enough Is Enough

Three more long years of total disconnection with his two sons had passed, and Abd just turned sixty-nine. While endlessly concentrating on providing medical and financial assistance to the poor and the needy overseas, Abd came up with the idea of showing to his two sons, born and raised in France, and his wife, descendant of an old Gallic family, his roots. With trepidation, he wrote to Yasir and Emal asking them if they were interested in knowing their father's birthplace. With some enthusiasm, both wanted to accompany their father and their stepmother to take a weekly flight from Paris to Kabul, then from there by bus to Bamyan. Within twenty-four hours, Emal replied to his father, "Thanks, Dad, for wanting to introduce us to your native country. I want to bring Ënerod and Azalee along if you have no objection. Can we plan on going there during Azalee's summer vacation? Using my awarded mileage, I will upgrade your plane tickets to business class so that you two could be comfortable during the fourteen-hour flight through Vienna. I will take care of the cost of Yasir's ticket."

Yasir offered to accompany Abd and Martine, wanting to assist the old couple in getting in and out of the bus, the train, and the boat. Since he could take only one week away from work, he agreed to make a quick extra trip by boat with them to the hiding site the Rasulov family had used in the past as a hideout during the intensive battles between the warlords. They planned to hire a boat captain to get there after visiting the old Bamyan house where Omira, after the immigration of Grandma Elaha and Nabeela to France, continued to share cohabitation with Faiz. The trip seemed to be well planned, and everybody was looking forward to seeing Abd's birthplace and for Martine, Emal, and Yasir to meet the remaining members of the Rasulov extended family for the first time. Thirteen days before the departure date, Emal called Martine at work while Abd was out of town to attend an annual medical congress. He informed her that he had to change his entire travel plan, citing that Ënerod had a second thought about the trip to an "unknown land" and that she didn't want her daughter Azalee to go on the trip without her. Emal once again talked on behalf of his brother, "Because of his workload and evening schooling, Yasir will not be able to accompany you two as planned. He will be travelling with me on the same plane, and we will be meeting you two in a hotel at Kabul airport. He and I will terminate the trip earlier and fly back to Paris on the fifth day. Call me at my office, as soon as you have a few free minutes and we will go over the new travel itinerary."

Abd and Martine were disappointed by the decision made by Ënerod, but neither of them was caught by surprise. Before the departure date, Yasir called Martine to give his excuse why he had decided to take the same flight with his brother instead of accompanying the aging couple as he had offered. "The schedule of my evening class has changed, and therefore I will have to alter my week of vacation time accordingly. We will be arriving two days later in Kabul, but I will not have enough time to make the boat trip." When they finally met at the Kabul airport hotel, Yasir inadvertently showed to Abd his printed-out flight schedule. Discreetly, Abd read the words "Business Class" at the top of it.

By the time Martine and the aging Abd arrived in Bamyan, they were physically exhausted after the long fifteen-hour flight on an old prop-jet plane, in coach class and with three connections before arriving to the destination. Abd, determined to show Martine the mountainous hideout cave his family had used in the past, hired a boat owner to get them there while waiting for the arrival of the boys. The river trip was pleasant, but Abd was profoundly disappointed by the condition of the cave which was defaced by repeated acts of vandalism.

Finally came the day when the visitors from France, in company of Faiz, started their visit to the Bamyan valley. They squeezed themselves into a reconditioned used Russian van and headed toward the provincial capital. They drove to the cave-laden sandstone cliff to see the two UNESCO-listed giant Buddha statues, the male Salsal and the small female Shamama.[7]

Abd had his first opportunity to recreate the image of an old Afghan Buddhist woman, in disguise, gathering deadwood for fire on her way to worship Buddha represented by these huge statues. That woman was nobody else but the boys' own grandmother Elaha. After spending a good hour at this site, Yasir took over the wheel and drove to Tupchi to visit the Rasulov family private cemetery. The van was left at the foothill, and all five climbed to an isolated platform where they located several dirt mounds, each with a tennis racket-size flat stone planted on top. A three-by-five-foot rectangular flat piece of marble with inscription in Arabic letters and enclosed in an iron fence was the centerpiece of the graveyard. Under the two words in bold characters, "Rasulov Family," three names were engraved on this stone slab: great-grandfather Kareem and his wife Waida to the left, and Haashim Rasulov, followed by an empty space to the right. A few feet from this enclosure was a series of four more freshly built mounds, each with also a planted flat stone on which the names of four Rasulov children still alive were engraved. From left to right the names on each mound were in Arabic: Aamir Rasulov, Ali Rasulov, Nabeela Rasulov, and Abdulai Rasulov. But what stood out was the words in Latin alphabet, "Amelia Englund," inscribed on the same stone and immediately under the two words "Abdulai Rasulov." This discovery shocked not only Martine but also Emal and Yasir.

Totally bewildered, Abd turned to Faiz. "Have you seen these empty tombs and this engraved name of my divorced wife the last time you came here?"

"My last visit to our ancestral burial plot was six months ago. The area now occupied by these new tombs was then still vacant. There was nothing but dirt and gravel. If you want to find out who had these graves built, we can go to see the town elders. If they are not there, then we can get the answer from the gravestone markers' shop located right at the entrance of Tuti Koshteh town, on Route A77."

They got back in the van and returned to Tupchi but could not locate any of the two designated town representatives. Driving eastwardly, the van suddenly slowed down, then stopped in front of an open yard dotted with various-sized unpolished flat natural stone pieces. The whole crowd entered a mud-bricked, corrugated-roof building when a slouching old bearded man casually glanced at Faiz. "From Taloquan Funeral Home?"

"Not really, but perhaps you can help. Are you, by any chance, the builder of the four recent empty graves at the Rasulov plot?"

"You are talking to him. What do you want to know?"

"We wish to know who had commissioned you to do the work."

"A man showed up one evening approximately four months ago. He handed me an envelope containing a sheet of paper showing a neatly drawn sketch and two additional pages giving detailed instruction on the erection of the four graves with stone markers. He introduced himself as a representative of the Rasulov family who was selected to take care of the project. He paid me cash, almost twice as much as the price I quoted him, and said, "I will be back in a couple of months to inspect your work."

The bearded man proudly added, "Frankly, I had no problem to finish the job, except the difficulty with which I had to work with the Latin alphabet on the last tombstone."

It wasn't difficult for the visitors from France to figure out who had built these four empty graves and for what reason. Their conviction was further reinforced by the notice Ali and Abd received from Zekirullah twenty-one months later. At the time, Zekirullah was living in Kabul, only 130 kilometers from Tupchi. Therefore, he was very much aware of events that frequently happened in his birthplace. Since he was the oldest son of Haashim and Elaha Rasulov, he tried to fulfill his role of surrogate parent and assumed authority over his younger siblings while looking after their welfare. Ali and Abd, the middle two children of the family, appeared to be easily adjustable, cooperative, patient, and good at bringing occasional conflicts between siblings to resolution. As a result, they got along well with Zekirullah. They shared common thoughts and often came up with joint plans of action with the latter. The youngest son of the family, Aamir, on the other hand, constantly exhibited his rebellious attitude, especially toward his oldest brothers.[8] He wanted to show not only to all his siblings but also to the villagers in the Tupchi-Bamyan area that he was his own man and that he distinguished himself from his older brothers. In order to achieve this end, he used his wealth to lure his sister Nabeela and her husband Feda and many village elders to his side. They considered and obeyed him as a warlord living abroad.

In the letter, Zekirullah recounted the various twists and turns he encountered in dealing with Aamir since their mother Elaha passed away. He cited the following difficulties he had to deal with Aamir. Approximately one year after her burial, the oldest brother together with the two middle siblings proposed to move her ashes buried at an Afghan cemetery in Aix-en-Provence to Tupchi. Aamir objected, saying that "Ma's children should keep 'her' next to his in-laws' burial plots so that they could continue to play cards in heaven." Three and a half years had passed and Zekirullah had retired from his ministerial post. At the age of eighty-four, and with a slowly declining health, he worried about the unresolved issue of repatriation of Elaha's remains. He wrote to Ali and Abd, asking them to come up with a new proposition, enticing Aamir to change his mind.

Since his two older brothers were not in physical shape to bring the remains back to their homeland, Abd volunteered to assume the entire project as follows. Using his own savings and taking time out of his humanitarian mission trips overseas, he would go first to Aix-en-Provence to unearth Elaha's ashes with the help of Ali. From there, he would fly to Kabul, carrying with him the urn containing the ashes. Zekirullah would wait for him at Kabul airport; then the two brothers would go by car to Tupchi cemetery. Once again Aamir turned down his three older brothers' proposition. This time he used this excuse: "I am eleven years younger than Abd, and I will repatriate Ma before I become totally disabled. In the meantime, my wife and my children will take turns to bring flowers to her tomb weekly."

In the same year, on the Buddha enlightenment day, Ali and Abd met at the site of Elaha's tomb. To their surprise, there were no flowers, not even an empty flowerpot at her grave site. Instead, the two brothers spent time weeding around it. In mid-December of that year, Zekirullah received a handwritten note from the daughter of his maternal aunt, the one who brought a cooked carp to the Rasulov family several years earlier. The latter asked Zekirullah whether he knew anything about Abd's plan to bring Elaha's ashes to Tupchi cemetery. She quoted a couple of sentences in a letter Aamir had sent a few days earlier to the village representatives: "Abd wanted to bring our mother's remains home, but he will leave the urn at a Kabul airport hotel for 'someone else,' a stranger to all of us, to take it over from there. I worry that the urn might be in the hands of an untrustworthy individual. I want you to be aware of this." Seized by anger, immediately Zekirullah called his cousin while still holding the letter with his trembling hand. "You should know by now, Aamir is a chronic liar. He is very good at distorting the truth and fabricating stories. Abd, Ali, and I had worked out the plan of repatriation. We never mentioned the word 'hotel' in the written proposition we submitted to Aamir. Ali had agreed to help Abd unearth the urn at the Aix-en-Provence cemetery. Then alone with the urn, Abd will fly to Kabul where I will meet him at the airport. From there, he and I will drive to Tupchi. I have made a special arrangement with the owner of the tombstone yard in Tuti Koshteh, and the urn will be buried next to my father's site on the same afternoon. At no time will my mother's ashes be unattended during the entire journey. Unfortunately, Aamir had refused to go along with our plan. This was the third time that he contemptuously rejected our joint plan of repatriation of my mother's remains. Aamir has been behaving like the oldest son of my parents. He wants badly to usurp my role. Please let all our relatives know the truth when you have the chance." In the early spring of the following year, without informing his three older brothers, Aamir brought Elaha's ashes to Tupchi cemetery in company of Nabeela and Feda. They had the remains buried under the slab next to Haashim's grave. The burial ceremony was carried out in the presence of the two designated village elders and several local distant relatives who were afterward treated with a lavish festive meal under a huge erected tent. At the conclusion of the ceremony, each of the attendees reverently bowed to Aamir after receiving a light-blue envelope containing, as usual, money.

Up until this point in time, Martine had tried not to interfere with the relationship between her husband and his two sons, except for a few rare verbal corrections she made when Abd's words were misunderstood or intentionally distorted by the latter. She was no longer able to tolerate the unjust treatment her husband received for years from Yasir and Emal. Sensing that her husband was reaching his seventy-year mark and was still not able to understand the reason(s) of the unilateral disconnection and the "forced" estrangement, respectively from his children and his only grandchild after he had done so much for them, Martine decided it was time for her to voice her personal opinion by writing a long letter to Emal. Here are the most significant points she brought up, going over each and every issue that had made her husband's genuine paternal love for his sons to become nothing but "venom"—the word used by both estranged grown-up individuals. In the poignant letter, she let Emal know that she read all correspondence his father had sent to or received from him and Yasir, and therefore, she was not only fully aware of the conflict between father and sons but also shared his views.

"Your name-calling, referring to your Dad [bully, animosity, endless anger, and venom] was appalling to me," she wrote. She pointed out to him that he was very good at taking out of the context her and her husband's general discussion by removing words or expressions like *if*, *whether*, and *wonder whether* each time he quoted his father's saying. She argued that these words did not imply "a statement of fact," but rather simply raise "a possibility."

Martine did not hesitate to rebuke Emal's incessant complaint that "he [his father] 'constantly' sends letters and emails that try to shame [a word also frequently used by Yasir during that same period] me" by reminding him that his father had sent only a single personal letter to his office and two trivial innocuous replying emails during a period of two years. "See, you exaggerate!" she wrote.

With regard to the intervention of three psychologists and one psychiatrist to find a solution to the family feud, Martine asked Emal why he never got back, not once but twice, to the very first counselor who had wanted to set up a meeting of all involved family members for the purpose of a possible reconciliation. He responded, "I had not received a second call from anybody," after his father and Martine, three years later, had requested that the same psychologist try again to talk Emal into a dialogue between all five persons embroiled in the family strife.

To demonstrate to Emal that he had departed from the reality and facts to assume in writing that his father was "convinced" that he (Emal) was "bad," and "it never ends," she responded by saying that these last three words "give the reader the impression that your father has been 'constantly' after you two. It is not true at all! Why? Because you rarely talk to him, write to him, or see him. When have you ever invited him to go with you to a ballgame, fishing, to a movie or just take a ride? Never!" As a matter of fact, while living only an hour and half from the best ski resort in the Grenoble area, and during a period of eighteen years, Emal had invited his father and stepmother to spend a winter vacation with his family only once. This two-night get-together took place at a ski apartment owned by the company he worked for. Martine did not forget the only Sunday brunch at Emal's private golf club on the occasion of Azalee's third birthday. This invitation took place exactly one week after Emal and his family had accepted to have a dinner elaborately prepared by her in honor of the little girl's natal day.

The suspicion that Yasir had joined his brother to relentlessly criticize their father was reflected in the following words Martine addressed to Emal. "Prove to me, from your father's letters to you or to your brother, that he (your father) has been constantly 'hostile' and 'angry' with you two. You quote the word 'crimes.' We have seen or heard the same word used by your brother himself in the past two to three years. Interestingly enough, the two words 'shame me' used in the second paragraph (of your letter) were also used by your brother either on the phone with me or in his letters to your father. I wonder why? Neither one of us has ever used the words 'crimes' or 'shame me.' Do not put words into our mouths. It is not necessary from you two to come up with these harsh words in order to build your case."

To disagree with Emal about his statement "Nothing we can do" [he referred to the occasional reciprocal invitations for dinner made by him and Ënerod] is ever good enough," Martine continued, "You know we are not the type of people who would see a deeply rooted family conflict resolved by getting together just for dinner. We find that strategy extremely meaningless and superficial. Some other gestures to show love and concern are required."

Martine did not hesitate to question Emal's (and Yasir's evidently) motive for their repeated refusal to sit down with her and her husband and to discuss issues that might have connection with the predivorce phase. With sternness, she replied to Emal's statement "It is never clear what you or Dad want us to do or say that make things right" with subtle but implying sentences: "Yes, we know, and you know too, the explanation why you two have steadfastly refused to go back in the past and answer why you two have drastically changed your opinion about your father. That is what we are 'trying to accomplish.' We know why. Your father had already mentioned it in paragraph three (of his last letter). There is no need to repeat it here." By this time, Martine and Abd had already seen a psychiatrist and the psychologist who had tried to set up an initial dialogue, but without success. Both of these counselors had ruled out every possible cause of the strife, except one that still needed to be verified through a friend of Abd living in Karolinska.

She raised an embarrassing question to her husband's two sons. "Let me ask you, where and how would you and your brother be now, if both of you had chosen to live (after the divorce) with your mother and Jean-Marie? Recently, Yasir said to me he is not sure if he would have chosen to live with your father if he had to do it over again. That was enough for me to question why he didn't go to live with your mother instead of with your father. Your father did everything he could to prevent you two from living in an immoral and criminal environment, whether or not your father had problems with your mother. I do not see any connection with your saying, '... not of our making as kids.' At the time, the *Foxeline Daily* newspaper reported that Jean-Marie was indicted for having stolen guns from collectors and for stealing from local people who gave him money for investment. Were you two aware of this report?"

To address Emal's complaint of the lack of effort from the part of Martine and Abd to communicate, Martine wrote, "You complain we didn't notify you when we moved to a new place and when Dad was sick and had to be admitted to the hospital. You labeled this as a 'communication' issue. Months went by and neither one of you had called or written to us. Therefore, we assumed you didn't care. Had you and Yasir tried to get in touch with us on a regular basis, you would have known of these happenings."

By this time, Martine knew that she could expect nothing but poor excuses, exaggerations, manipulation, ingratitude, falsehood, and meanness from her two stepsons. During the last year and half or so, Yasir continued to send Abd and Martine on occasions of birthday, Mother's Day, and Father's Day greeting cards. At the end of these greeting cards, Yasir repeatedly wrote, "I love you two." But in the next letter to Abd and Martine a few weeks later, he contradicted himself with words and sentences like, "How hypocritical" his father was, "I tried everything I could last year not to stoke this 'venom' you sent my way," or "You [his dad] are so angry inside yourself," and many more. Consequently, he could hardly put a dent in Martine's effort to improve her relation and that of her husband with her stepson. The following anecdote finally convinced Martine that she should give up hope of bringing back any relationship with her two stepsons, no matter how superficial it could be.

Without notice, Abd and Martine arrived by train to Paris with the intension of seeing Yasir by surprise. They had thought that such an improvised visit, even just for a few hours, would prove that they still loved him and therefore didn't mind to make a long trip to see him after he had turned down their invitation to come for a visit with them in Grenoble three years earlier. That was Saturday at noontime. Once the senior couple had checked in the hotel, Martine placed a call to Yasir announcing that they were in town and wanted to see him.

She was extremely careful with her words on the phone and calmly said, "Sorry for not informing you in advance of our arrival to town for the weekend. We don't want to interfere with your weekend commitments. But it would be wonderful if you could see us, even just for a few minutes, anywhere you want. We will take the subway and get there in time."

Right away, Yasir showed signs of indignation. "You two are going to screw up all my weekend plans. I have to go to work in the lab for a few hours this afternoon. This evening I have to meet someone to discuss a research project. Sunday morning, I am supposed to meet with a professor to discuss with him some aspects related to the evening course I am taking. I don't know how I can squeeze in a visit with you two before you take the afternoon train to go back. Why are you trying to complicate the whole thing by not letting me know the date of your arrival in advance? I hate to be surprised like this. Will see if I can make it. Bye."

One could detect the anger in the tone of his voice. Three hours later Yasir called back, saying that he would make an effort to see the couple, but the meeting had to be held outside of the hotel, not in the hotel lobby or in their room. Martine insisted that the hotel was located on a busy thoroughfare and the inherent traffic noise wouldn't be suitable for a short visit with him. Eventually he gave in and reluctantly accepted to come to the hotel. Yasir showed up that Sunday afternoon at their hotel room.

Martine and Abd greeted him at the door, "So glad to see you after quite a few years."

He refused to sit down, having a resentful and unfriendly facial expression. Leaning his back against the edges of the commode while standing, he repeated the same question he already had raised earlier on the phone, "Why do you have to make everything so difficult by coming to town without advance notice?"

Convinced that he might run the risk of igniting the old verbal confrontations he had with his son, Abd purposely let Martine do the talking with Yasir. The latter was not too eager to respond to questions on his work or his study toward his master's degree. Deliberately, Martine left out the social aspect of her stepson's life. Then he became enraged when she said to him, "You are a coward for having steadfastly refused to tell us why you and your brother have chosen to disconnect with us these past years without giving an explanation."

At this point, he approached his sitting stepmother while pointing his index finger in her face. "Don't you dare ever say that word [he meant the word *coward*] again to me." He then turned around, furiously mumbled a few words, forcefully slammed the door, and then left. Martine and Abd could hear his heavy footsteps in the corridor. That was last time they saw him in person.

Martine came home that afternoon from her biweekly shopping for food. She almost tripped over the rough cement walkway to the house while trying to figure out who had sent a letter from Sweden, which she just retrieved from the mailbox. She handed it to her husband, who was having trouble getting up from the reclining chair due to his worsening osteoarthritic knee. The Stockholm-postmarked envelope came from his friend. The much-awaited friendly letter was accompanied, in addition to an invoice from a lawyer, by a separate brief statement with these words: "Her [Amelia's] total asset has grown to over twenty-eight million French francs, and there have been no others who claimed as secondary beneficiaries."

The unilateral disconnections from Emal and Yasir were announced to Martine and Abd by letters that were postdated two days apart. Because of the lengthy and the accusatory tone of Emal's note to justify his as well as his wife's desire to terminate the relationship with his father and Martine, the latter decided to keep in her own pocket-sized notebook for future reference some of the most intolerable excerpts from the infamous disengagement letter her stepson wrote to his elders.

The true story went like this. Azalee just turned eleven. She was a perfect only child who was among the top three in her class, gifted in solo recital of violin and piano pieces of classical music, excellent performer in school theatrical plays, and well behaved everywhere she went or with whom she talked to. But because of the strained relationship between her parents and her paternal grandfather Abd and his wife Martine, she had not been allowed to be in touch with the latter for over two and a half years. The previous two annual Grandparents' Day visits with her at her private school were "reserved" by Emal for her maternal set of grandparents on one year and for the other set of paternal grandmother Amelia and her husband Serge the year after. The school customarily invited all grandparents each year to spend a couple of lunch hours alone with their grandchildren in order to keep the seniors abreast of the youngsters' school performance and perhaps to entice them to make contributions. But these two sets of Azalee's grandparents had no plans to make a trip to Grenoble that year. Therefore, her parents had no other excuses but agreed to let Martine and her husband Abd spend the two-hour visit with Azalee on this occasion that had taken place five weeks before that coming Christmas. The senior couple showed up on time at school, and both were warmly greeted by Azalee with her usual tight hugs. The latter joyfully took her grandparents to her classroom, showed them the various tools used by her teachers for teaching, taught them how to play children's games, and then they went to the school dining room for lunch accompanied by two of her classmates. These two students had no grandparents visit with them on that day.

While at the table, Abd leaned toward his granddaughter and murmured, "Have you been attending church services on a regular basis since we last accompanied you and your parents to the Sunday Mass five years ago?"

Azalee was well aware that Martine and Abd were devoted practicing Christians. Hesitantly and with her pair of innocent eyes staring at the far window, while her left index finger was scratching her head, she replied, "We don't go to church anymore during the school year. We attend church services only on Christmas Eve or Christmas Day, Good Friday, or Easter Sunday."

One of Azalee's classmates volunteered to add, "My parents have not been taking me and my two brothers to church for quite some time."

After lunch, while holding Martine's hand and delightfully talking about her principal role in the next school play, Azalee led Abd and Martine to the school library famous for its large collection of embossed religious books that dated back to the early 1700s. Before returning to her afternoon classes, she walked the old couple to their car, gave each of them a tight hug, and waved at them while walking back to the school building. The two hours spent with their grand-daughter were refreshing to Abd and Martine and remained their highlight of that winter and for the subsequent years. Unfortunately, Azalee's parents didn't want to recognize that their only child had a wonderful bond with her spurned set of grandparents.

Here are some of the excerpts taken out of the abovementioned disengagement letter of Emal and Ënerod that Martine carried in her handbag for many years after. "It's a shame that you missed an opportunity to see a great year she is having in fifth grade. It's a shame you clearly didn't take advantage of the time to engage her as the eleven-year-old that she is. And instead decided to be 'selfish' and advocate for an agenda which isn't hers nor that she understands… deliberate intention on your part to use a day with her for your own gain but entirely at Azalee's expense." Abd had indeed said to Azalee at the lunch table that his inquiry should be kept "as a secret," a common, casual, and harmless word frequently used to express the intimacy and love when grandparents are in contact with their off-spring. Unfortunately, Emal made this minor issue a mountain out of a molehill with this sentence: "To tell her [Azalee] that she needed to keep your conversation with her 'a secret' from us and not to tell us is objectionable behavior that violates all child psychology and 'strange danger' guidelines (thankfully she's had that training at school and thus didn't hesitate to speak with us). It's disappointing to think an adult would do that to a child, much less a grandparent to a granddaughter." Emal's and Ënerod's final excuse to permanently sever their filial kinship with Abd and Martine was clearly reflected in the following subparagraph of Emal's letter: "Despite the differences we may have with you, we have never once said a single disparaging word or thought about either of you to Azalee, since that would be inappropriate in our view. But after this Grandparents' Day incident where it is very clear that you are not going to behave in a similar fashion, and instead used your time with Azalee to try to manipulate her feelings and perceptions, we have elected to disengage with you and will not allow you to have unsupervised visitation with Azalee. Many things have been said between us all over the years on both sides that are regrettable and hurtful, and that is a consequence as adults that we all have to live with. But we will not allow that hurt to extend to Azalee...we will protect her from that unnecessary hurt and damage at all costs." These excerpts illustrated the young couple's intentional reconstruction of the events that had taken place during Martine's and her husband's visit on the Grandparents' Day three months earlier. One wonders why Azalee's parents had to distort the whole story, if not for a very specific purpose—to build up a case in order to justifiably shun them forever and at the same time to befittingly side with Amelia, ignoring completely her past three major blunders leading to the divorce.

CHAPTER FOURTEEN

The Search for Answers Abruptly Ended

Azalee had graduated from her high school *magna cum laude*. She was about to start the first semester of her freshman year at Carcassonne College. She majored in arts and music. During a lecture on the influence of renown Baroque through classical music composers on their offspring, she suddenly realized that she had been seeing her paternal remarried grandmother Amelia and her second husband, Serge, as well as her maternal grandparents several times annually during the last eight years. In contrast, she had not seen or heard from her paternal grandfather Abdulai and his second wife, Martine, since she was eleven. She searched for an explanation, thinking that she had been too busy with her high school education, then with college entry applications followed by preparation for living away from home in the historic city of Carcassonne. The addition of a few gatherings with senior high school classmates to say goodbye after graduation had further interfered with her mental search for the said explanation. But she wasn't satisfied with these excuses and felt guilty. However, an unusual circumstance was about to ignite her curiosity in finding the real cause of her being kept away for so long from Grandma Martine and Grandpa Abd, whom she dearly loved.

Chance had led her to share her college dormitory room with the granddaughter of a French government dignitary that year. This young woman, named Charlotte, majored in biology and psychology. They shared many common interests, among them, music and painting. They got along so well to the point that they called each other "sister A" and "sister C" instead of "hey you," commonly heard among roommates in boarding schools. They confided to each other everything from their childhood slap-on-the-wrist types of misbehavior, all the way to their secret teenage love.

One Saturday after finishing their jointly prepared lunch, both were drinking coffee, comfortably relaxing in their upholstered chairs in the space-limited dormitory living room. While holding her opened book entitled *Family Bond between Generations*, and with an inquisitive pair of eyes, Charlotte looked at her dozing roommate. "Any divorces among members of your extended family?"

Azalee, half awake and somewhat surprised, replied, "Yes, why?"

"I am reading the chapter on divorce and its effect on the normal social relationship between members of the extended family."

"What kind of effect? Must not be very good, is it? Are there cases of separation or divorce in your family?"

"Not within the two previous generations and my generation that I know of. My grandparents on both maternal and paternal sides never talked about corporal or sacramental separation during our annual family reunions, and therefore, I didn't really know much about this broken relationship between two spouses until I started reading this book, which is part of my assigned reading that goes with my two-semester psychology course. Do you have a personal experience with a divorce through the court?"

"Yes, I do, but rather vague at best."

"It would be very helpful to my study on the subject if you could share with me your experience. However, I don't want to rekindle painful memories if you have gone through them and they have caused you suffering."

Without hesitation, Azalee calmly replied, "I don't mind talking about my limited personal experience, and perhaps I can learn from you the proper way of interaction between family members and extended relatives through marriage. My paternal grandfather and his first wife were divorced through a court order thirty-six years ago, and the hurtful effect has been felt ever since throughout the living members of two generations."

"Have you ever been told the reason(s) for such a dramatic separation by anyone? Are the divorcees remarried and happy? And where do you and your parents stand *vis-a-vis* your divorced grandparents? Are the relationships between your parents and these two—I assume remarried—sets of grandparents equal socially and emotionally?"

"According to my dad, my paternal grandparents ended up in a bitter divorce after seventeen years of an apparently unhappy marriage. I was born almost ten years after their permanent separation. My parents haven't told me much about it. But among old photographs, receipts, bank account statements fortuitously found in the house basement while I was looking for my father's old piano musical sheets, I came across a divorce court order paper on which both names of my paternal grandparents were listed. The divorce decree stipulated that Grandpa Abdulai had full custody of my father and my uncle Yasir, but my grandmother Amelia had regular scheduled visiting rights.

"Subsequently, I confronted my father for more details on his life after his parents were divorced, but he kept repeatedly saying, 'I will tell you more when you enter adulthood.' He tried to duck my questions time after time and appeared to be embarrassed each time I brought up the issue. In retrospect, I realized that my parents have had and still have a totally different relationship with my paternal grandfather Abdulai and his second wife, Martine, in comparison to the other set of paternal grandmother Amelia and her second husband, Serge. As I was still a toddler, my parents had always preferred not to let me spend as much time with Grandpa Abd and Grandma Martine, yet they dearly love me and I love them from the bottom of my heart. I never could stay with them alone more than fifteen hours each time I visited with them. As a growing-up child, I appreciated Grandpa Abd's knowledge in science, religion, music, world history, geography, and basic health issues. By the way, he is for higher education, and he himself is a medical doctor with two specialties who had gone several times to developing countries to provide humanitarian medical services.

"In contrast, I was left for days alone with my grandma Amelia and her husband, Serge, or with my maternal grandparents. These two last couples had been coming at least twice a year and stayed at my parents' home for at least a week to ten days. I still remember the only time when Grandma Martine and Grandpa Abd—who lived only twenty-five minutes away from us—were asked on short notice to babysit me while my parents had to urgently go somewhere. I was then five years old. Since I was born until now, I could count the number of my overnight visits with Grandpa Abd and Grandma Martine with less than the five fingers on my hand.

"The following observation might be interesting to you. I have repeatedly tried to know more about my grandmother Amelia's background, but she was uninformative about it. Through my uncle Yasir, I learned that Grandma Amelia had not seen her father again after her parents were divorced when she was eleven years old. Subsequently, when she was still married to my grandfather Abdulai, he encouraged her to reconnect with her father, but she steadfastly refused."

"Based on your surname, which is not typical French, there must be some difference of ethnicity among members of your family. Do you believe that this unusual family discord was the result of difference of cultures?"

"I don't believe so, now that I am older and that I can closely observe and reason in a rational manner. Even though he was born in Afghanistan and raised Buddhist, Grandpa Abd has lived more than three quarters of his life in Judeo-Christian culture-based countries. Furthermore, he converted himself to Catholicism through reading and long years of contact with Christians. Now that you have almost finished reading your psychology book, you should be able to suggest to me some explanation why I have not been given the opportunity to know and to enjoy the precious relationship I am supposed to benefit from one particular set of grandparents during their golden years. I am anxious to get your opinion on a subject that has been bothering me since I started my senior high school year."

"To be certain that my opinion is objective and meaningful to you, I do need more information on the structural aspect of your extended family, the cause of the divorce you had alluded to, the possible involvement of outsiders into the interrelationship between immediate living relatives that make up your two preceding generations. Perhaps unanticipated relevant information might pop up as we discuss this complicated issue."

"So please go ahead and ask me the questions that might help you and me find the right answer to a topic that has been besetting me for quite some time."

"Do your dad and your mom have siblings?"

"Yes, my mom has an older brother who is very smart and a high achiever. But through the grapevine, I learned that they never got along well since their childhood. My dad's brother is a very nice and a smart man too, but unfortunately, he is too easily influenced by good talkers, especially by one of those within his extended family. He doesn't seem to be interested in giving his personal opinion on many familial issues. But when it comes to the field of outdoor sports, he has proven to be a leader. In this connection, he has been repeatedly exhibiting his physical endurance as well as his organizational skills. As a matter of fact, he had received special mentions and recognition by local as well as national authorities for many strenuous and dangerous solo mountain biking trips in many countries around the world and for his exemplary use of his bike to commute between his home and his workplace."

"How often do your parents and your uncle see Dr. Abdulai and his wife Martine? Is your uncle Yasir married?"

"My uncle Yasir is still single. The last time my parents had contact with Grandpa Abd and Grandma Martine was on the Christmas Eve that followed my eleventh birthday. Grandma Martine drove Uncle Yasir to our house for him to spend the rest of the holiday with us. The doorbell rang. My parents and I ran to the front door. We exchanged Christmas wishes. My dad invited Grandpa and Grandma to come in. I saw Grandma pulling her husband by the sleeve while Grandpa uttered, 'Not appropriate this time. No, thank you.' Both husband and wife turned around, got back in their car, and drove away. I sensed that there was something very wrong that had happened between them earlier. That was last time I saw my loving paternal grandfather and his adorable wife."

"How about extended relatives of your grandmother Amelia and your grandfather Abd?"

"Like me, Grandma Amelia is the only child. I wasn't born when her mother living in Sweden passed away. I don't think she has any more relatives in that country with whom she is keeping in touch. Grandpa Abd has several siblings. With two exceptions, the rest of his siblings live with their family in this country, either in exile or as refugees. I overheard a couple of times the name Aamir mentioned during my parents' conversation on Grandma Amelia and Grandpa Serge, but I have never met the man."

"Who is Aamir?" Charlotte inquisitively asked.

"He is the youngest brother of Grandpa Abd and is the only member of the Rasulov family who had opted to establish a friendly relationship through regular and friendly contacts with Grandma Amelia and Grandpa Serge."

"Do you know whether this bizarre relationship between the brother of your grandfather and this latter's divorced spouse was the continuation of an old friendship or a new alliance for a specific purpose?"

"Good question! My parents tend to switch the subject each time I brought up issues involving Grandma Martine and Grandpa Abd. But with bits and pieces I gathered from talking to my mother, I learned that during the seventeen years of marriage to Grandpa Abd, Grandma Amelia had met Aamir only once, when the latter's first wedding through marriage arrangement took place somewhere in Normandy."

"Very interesting." Charlotte shook her head, smiling.

"It's your turn. Tell me a little about your parents and grandparents," Azalee quietly queried.

"I come from a small family. My parents just celebrated their twenty-fifth wedding anniversary last month. My sister Julie, five years older than I am, a college graduate, is married to a province legislator. I knew very little about my maternal grandparents as they both died before I was five, and they lived a few hours by train away from us. On the other hand, I still remember the wonderful time my sister and I were enjoying my paternal grandparents' weekly visits, as they lived only two blocks away from us. We have been and remain very close. We celebrate Christmas, New Year, and Easter together after attending church services, and we never fail to remember each other's birthday with greeting cards and telephone calls. I come from an old French family, and we are practicing Catholicism."

"Tell me more about your faith, a subject that I am constantly struggling with since my last meeting with Grandma Martine and Grandpa Abd when I was eleven on the Grandparents' Day organized every year by the school."

"As most of the young adults do, I was searching for the meaning of life during the last part of my high school senior year. At the moment, an antireligion movement was organized by a few of my classmates. These secular ultraleft students managed to carry out meetings to disseminate their cause. I attended a few of these gatherings. But in the end, I realized that they were advocating wealth distribution and dependency on the government rather than on God. That was the end of my search. I have become more fervent ever since."

"I am not that lucky. I feel that there is an imbalance in the way I am encouraged to deal with my three sets of grandparents and it is time for me to look into this matter and try to find an answer. The word *religion* has ceased to be mentioned in my family since the last time I saw Grandpa Abd and Grandma Martine."

"I would hope your anticipation will be more active than your retrospect. I hate to tell you this, but that maladroit relationship between your paternal grandmother and the extended relative Aamir you mentioned earlier needs to be scrutinized."

The conversation between Charlotte and Azalee finally ended when it was getting dark outside and it was time for them to reach into the refrigerator for a light supper before going to bed.

Bitten by the integrity bug after spending that Saturday afternoon with her roommate Charlotte, Azalee was determined to pursue her desire to find out the reason for which her grandfather Abd and step-grandmother Martine were forsaken by her parents and her uncle Yasir since that Christmas Eve. Away from home, exposed to several students' independent opinions, and liberated from the enclosing walls of self-centeredness, of bias judgment, and especially of political correctness, Azalee gradually developed a deep sense of fairness.

Two weeks before going home on Christmas and New Year holidays, ending her first semester of study at Carcassonne College, Azalee sent a note to Grandma Martine, asking whether she could give an idea why there had been a total disconnection between the two Rasulov families for over eight years. She specifically requested that Martine send a response to her dorm address, and "NOT at my [her parents'] home."

Without making comments, Martine wrote back, "Thanks, darling. Grandpa and I had given up hope of hearing from you again after these long years. Now that you suddenly decide to write to us, I am going to send you two letters written by your father, we think, as his explanation for the unilateral cutoff. Give serious thoughts to every word and every sentence in these correspondences. You may share any part of the letters' contents with your friends in school, if you wish. If you want more information, we would be more than willing to let you read multiple documents related to this unfortunate disconnection. Since you have asked about our health, I am going to say just a few words. I just turned seventy-four, and we celebrated Grandpa's birthday exactly six months ago by the day. We have been having quite a few old-age medical problems like the majority of seniors do. I am okay, but Grandpa has been seen lately by several doctors at Grenoble University Hospital for weight loss and fatigue. Darling, no matter how you feel about us, our love for you has not changed." In her replying note, Martine enclosed the copies of Emal's last two letters written just before Abd's two sons decided not to have any more contact with the senior couple. The excerpts of these two letters were already enumerated in chapter 12.

So far Abd and Martine had seen a total of four mental health specialists hoping to find the cause for the filial rejections, but none of them could come up with a clear-cut explanation why Emal and Yasir had decided to take a stance against them after they were living with Abd and Martine as custodial parents for over ten years, from their preteen years all the way until they finished their college study and left home. These psychoanalysts, one by one, approached the hostility almost the same way. They started with a detailed history taking, which was followed by their scrutiny of the two-inch-thick file of documents related to the family discord Martine and Abd brought along at each session for reference.

As already mentioned in a previous chapter, the very first counseling Abd and Martine received came from a female psychiatrist Abd met at a medical congress in Grenoble, but no follow-up visits were possible with her due to the logistic problems. She had her practice in Brest, Brittany, several hundred kilometers away from Grenoble. However, the two words *spousal bribery* the psychiatrist had mentioned to them had a profound impact on their search for the cause of the filial disconnection. Additionally, the couple learned from the psychoanalyst another experience: the "fatherless phenomenon." She quoted an editorial article in a French newspaper showing evidences of double-digit increase in the divorce rate during the preceding decade. Because of the universally known detrimental effects of parental divorce on minor children, the French government was very concerned for the children's welfare. As a result of the governmental attempt to remedy this social ill, the nonworking spouses—the great majority of them was women—received substantial financial assistance and therefore didn't have to work. Consequently, it was rather more beneficial to become single parents depending strictly on the government's handouts. These women had the least concern for the social stigma associated with divorce. This concept of dependency led to the alarming increased rate of women filing for divorce against their husbands; and it was not uncommon during that period to observe the fatherless situation perpetuate for two to three consecutive generations. The consequence of this fatherless phenomenon was disastrous. Many single mothers from all walks of life, at any cost and perhaps for pride and revenge or both, dictated to their minor as well as to their adult children a total disconnection with their father through promises for financial rewards or resort to unfounded fabricated stories to undermine their divorced husbands. After this only meeting with the female psychoanalyst, Martine and Abd were convinced that the WLM undoubtedly had its profound influence on the birth of the single-parenthood anomaly. Tragically, in many cases, children from broken families never saw or had any contact with their biologic father again after the parental separation.

The next counselor was one of the three well-respected, reputable psychologists within the Grenoble medical circle. He was the one who had tried to set up a meeting with all individuals involved in the conflict. Unfortunately, his idea of a possible reconciliation got nowhere due to Emal's refusal to join in for discussion in his presence as the moderator. He suspected that Emal and Yasir had more than one reason to sever all contacts with their father and their stepmother. He believed that their uncle Aamir's strange relationship with their mother had definitely a bearing on their abrupt decision to disown their old man. This psychologist contended that if they cited a specific story fabricated by their uncle Aamir about their father as the cause for disowning, they would run the risk for having to provide at least circumstantial, if not concrete, evidence. "Therefore, a vague accusation without cause followed by the severance of relationship with the senior couple would be safe for them," said this counselor on his last telephone call to Abd and Martine. He strongly believed that the other reason was "clearly financial." He ended the conversation with, "I agree with your previous psychiatrist. The whopping asset in Sweden is the culprit. There is no doubt about it."

The third psychologist, a female social worker with a PhD degree and specialized in family issues, was able to partially make Yasir talk a little. But the latter continued to be vague in conveying to her his reason for shunning his father and his stepmother. He said to her, "My father's childhood is the issue, but my counselor

315

advised me not to elaborate further." After several failed attempts to ask him the permission to directly talk to his counselor, Yasir dodged her request, "My psychologist advised me to postpone any further discussion with you on this matter." Frustrated, this counselor gave up and terminated her work with Abd and Martine, saying, "This is an impasse after two-plus years of serious attempt. Nothing else I could do 'to go forward,' as long as they [Yasir and Emal] continue to remain uncooperative. I am sorry for not being able to help you."

The fourth and the last counselor, a specialist in ostracism, estrangement, shunning, and other forms of disconnection between parents and children, took the whole morning to go over the two-inch-thick file of documents during the first psychoanalytic session. (The reader will find more details on this subject by going on the website.[6])

He raised many questions during his scrutiny of the documentary materials. Martine and Abd had five two-hour conferences with him within a month. In the end, he concluded that there were three main causes that jointly bred the bad blood between Abd and his two sons. It was quite obvious that Abd's ex-wife, Amelia, needed to find a way to bring her two grown-up sons to her side. In a sense, it was revenge from her part, because Abd was given total custody of the boys by the court. In order to convince her sons that their father was not as good a person as they had thought, she must find a way to show that her three blunders, because of which she was not given the custody of the children after the divorce, were within the realm of social tolerance in France at the time. She easily found the person who could help her with her primary objective of winning the two grown-up sons over her side through malicious story fabrication, lies, deceit, and duplicity, even though she had met that individual only once many years ago—Mr. Aamir Rasulov, the wealthy brother of her ex-husband who happened to be the "black sheep" of the extended Rasulov family. This counselor arrived to his conclusion by saying to his clients Abd and Martine, "I found that the unconventional rapprochement between Amelia and Aamir rather freakish. Obviously, they need each other to achieve their devious end. As I see it, all ingredients necessary to persuade her two sons and achieve her goal were waiting for her. These are her large asset in Sweden, her vain-glorious former brother-in-law who would do anything that could undermine his own brother that he despises, the unfriendly attitude of the wife of one of her sons, and their eagerness to ignore the sacrifice made by their father until they were on their own. I am not at all surprised when I read the pages documenting that her former brother-in-law Aamir came to Foxeline with ten pounds of lobster to wine and dine with the doctor's ex-wife and her husband. With all due respect to you, Dr. Rasulov, may I say that your brother is not only a mendacious but also a nefarious person. This is a very rare situation dealing with the reversal of attitude by two adult children after they were spared from the deleterious effect of divorce by the custodial father, who singlehandedly cared for them and gave each of them an expensive education. Unfortunately, all the sacrifice made by their father didn't mean much to them anymore once they became aware that a large monetary inheritance from their mother was waiting for them. I sympathize with you, but I feel I am a mediator who is not able to help you get past this impasse, as long as your two sons remain unresponsive to your request for an explanation of the vague accusation they use as an excuse to disconnect with you two. Bad blood in the family these days because of money is not uncommon, but severing a relationship with your own parents without giving a cause is almost unheard of. I am very sorry for not being able to be of any further help to you." Abd and Martine thanked him for having come up with the main cause of the strife.

After the commencement celebration of her freshman college year and before leaving for summer break, Azalee wrote to Martine, asking whether it would be all right for her to pay Grandma and Grandpa a visit sometime during the next two months of vacation. Totally excited, Martine immediately sent Azalee a postcard with, "Of course, we would be delighted to see our granddaughter at her convenience. If you have never been told where our house is located, please call. Here is our phone number…" Three weeks later, Azalee showed up at eight o'clock on a Saturday morning at the senior couple's residence. Martine came to the door, quite happy by the surprised visit of a grown-up young lady she last saw eight and half years earlier. They embraced, and a few drops of tear seeped down their cheeks.

Azalee anxiously asked, "Is Grandpa home?"

"Grandpa was admitted to the university hospital this past Wednesday for a workup on his anemia, weight loss, and fatigue. I see him every day after work. Who brought you here?"

"I told my mom that I am going to spend probably the whole day at the library, searching for references on Baroque musical composers for my school assigned writing. I took public transportation. She was about to leave home to meet with her two former classmates when I left."

"I see. You don't want your parents to know that you were on your way to see us. What will happen to your relationship with them if they will find out that you have visited with us?"

"Grandma, I am a fully grown-up person, and it is only natural for me to raise questions and to find answers, especially when dealing with people I love yet I have not been encouraged or permitted to keep in touch with them for almost a decade. I think I am justified not to tell my parents, whom I love dearly, everything I carry in my heart."

After sitting down to have a quick breakfast, Azalee solemnly asked, "Can I see the thick file of documents you had referred to in your letter? I'll try my best to go over the entire file before heading home. I want to be home prior to her return. Since my dad is away on business until Thursday, my mom wants to skip cooking this evening and to take me out for dinner at five. So I should be at the bus station no later than four o'clock."

"Make yourself comfortable on the couch. You may lie down if you like. I will bring it to you right away for your scrutiny. You may ask any question you want. As far as your trip back home, I'll be glad to drop you off at a safe place a block or so away from your home, okay?"

"Grandma, when will I be able to see Grandpa?"

"Grandpa was supposed to come home last night after the hospital gastroenterologist finished examining his digestive system. But because of the bowel preparation for endoscopy was not adequate, the nurses had to prolong the cleaning process further, and he will undergo the procedure one more time this later afternoon. As you can imagine, all hospital services are drastically reduced on Saturday. After the endoscopic examination, which is carried out under general anesthesia, he will have to be kept in the recovery room for a couple more hours. Probably I will be able to pick him up around eight this evening. He will still be groggy for a few more hours after that. Since you have to leave here at around four, I am afraid you will not be able to see Grandpa this time. As I had told you in my letter, Grandpa has not been doing well lately health-wise. Can you make an effort to see him as soon as possible?"

"My parents want me to accompany them during their vacation trip to Bali at the end of July. Frankly, I don't want to join them, as I want to have some time alone for myself, but I don't want to disappoint them either. So, I will try to see him after the trip and before I return to school at the end of August. Okay, Grandma?"

Martine sensed that her husband was affected by a serious illness of some sort, but she thought he didn't want to sadden her with the results of the recent investigation at the hospital by a team of medical specialists. Abd was requested to return to the office of the hematologist-oncologist five days after his discharge from the hospital. He was sad but not at all surprised when he was told that he had *chronic myelogenous leukemia* (CML), a form of cancer affecting the bone marrow and the blood-forming cells at the start, and then, over time, spreading to other parts of the body. This type of leukemia mainly affects adults. The patient with CML may have no symptoms for months or even years as the cancer cells spread slowly at the onset of the disease. However, CML can suddenly change its course, from slow growth to a rapid invasion of practically all organs in the body. Before the introduction of the tyrosine kinase receptor inhibitor imatinib Gleevec in 2001[9] for the treatment, the survival rate of patients with CML was only three to seven years.[10]

Based on this general medical information, and since he was doing well after the treatment of his anemia, Abd decided to do a solo "tour de France" by car, followed by a brief visit to his brother Ali in Vienna and ended up in Bamyan with Zekirullah for a few weeks. He figured out that this itinerary was the most convenient way to enjoy the beauty of his adoptive country. Furthermore, he contemplated that the combination of a pleasure trip with visits to two brothers he had not seen for several years might turn out to be the last chance for him to relive his childhood and see his birthplace. He was hoping to return to Grenoble to rejoin his beloved Martine within less than a year, before the possible onset of the accelerated and blastic phase of CML leading to his demise.[11]

In order to minimize Martine's fear for his being alone during the entire trip from Grenoble through Foxeline, Odinard, Toulouse, Bordeaux, La Rochelle, Nantes, Rennes, Paris, Basel, Munich, and finally to Vienna, where he would leave his old Citroën with Ali then reach Bamyan by public transportation, he told Martine that his fatigue, dizziness, and pallor were due to the common old age pernicious anemia in lieu of CML. He reassured her that he would finish his initial course of treatment consisting of daily injection of vitamin B12 for seven consecutive days, followed by a weekly injection for four more weeks before he started the trip. He comforted her that the following required monthly injection would be given to him first at the Vienna General Hospital and subsequently by his brother Zekirullah. By the time when Abd had received the necessary number of vitamin B12 shots and ready to start his long trip, the cold weather of the late part of November was already felt on the alluvial plain of Isere and Drac Rivers where Grenoble lies.

On that memorable day, Martine got the permission to stay home from work to say goodbye to her husband. She got up early to pack his lunch and prepare his breakfast. They embraced for several minutes while they softly wept into their chests. Finally, they let their arms go free. Abd walked to his fourteen-year-old but still running well Citroën, looking back to his wife with a somber look. He sat down at the wheel, rolled down the glass window, waved at her, and then drove away. Sadly, that was the last time Martine saw her husband alive.

After over a week visiting the several beautiful old French cities along the way, Abd finally arrived in Paris. He parked his car in the outskirts of the city, at Hotel Le Piémont, where he spent three nights. One morning he took the metro, got off at Porte d'Italie Metro Station, and walked to University Paris Sud—Faculté de Médecine, where he used to work. His former boss Professor Duvier's black-and-white picture was still on the wall, but he could not recognize anyone among the staff he used to work with. He regretted having left the academic medicine he had been highly successful in. Afterward, he spent the entire day at Musée du Louvre and was satiated with the French impressionist painting artists. Due to his illness, he tired himself out too quickly and had to sit down several times on outdoor benches. On the third day, he quietly sat for hours on a pew a couple of rows behind the transept of Cathédrale Notre Dame, reading the Bible and listening to the chime of its hourly carillon. Abd started out his departure from Paris on the fourth day when he was caught by the unexpected snowstorm that grounded him at Hôtel de la Gare, where he met his companion of voyage, Hans.

Azalee showed up on the Advent Sunday, approximately a month after her first visit, at Martine's house and appeared quite anxious after she embraced her grandma. "How are you?"

"You are keeping your promise. You are back. I am glad. How was your trip to Bali?"

"I'll tell you later. Is Grandpa here this time?"

"Take your coat off and hand it to me. Sit down next to the fireplace on Grandpa's chair facing mine. I will bring you some hot cider to warm you up. I'll be right back."

While listening to the crackling sound of and watching the burning firewood, Azalee right away sensed that Abd wasn't at home. Martine returned a few minutes later with a pitcher of hot cider. "You remember I told you that Grandpa had not been well for the last several months. In the end, the doctors found out that he has 'pernicious anemia,' so he told me. He got the initial five-week treatment that made him 'feel much better,' he insists. Then he decided he wanted to make a trip alone to his homeland partially by car and by public transportation from Vienna after visiting with his brother Ali. He said he wanted to see many famous old French cities during the trip before he becomes 'too old to travel.' Since I have to work to make a living, I could not accompany him for several months. He left three weeks ago. Of course, I worry a great deal about him being alone during so many months, but I could not go against his wish. He must be somewhere in Germany or Austria by now. His absence is a hardship for me, darling. Do your parents know that you were coming here today?"

"No. They left yesterday morning to spend a long weekend with my mom's parents and will not be home until Monday evening. I was supposed to finish my assigned work I told you about, but suddenly I changed my mind, thinking this weekend is a good opportunity for me to finish reading the file. Furthermore, I had briefly related to Charlotte my last visit with you, how I had missed my sick grandpa and what I have discovered so far after I read the first half of the entire document you two are chronologically keeping in two folders. Charlotte encouraged me to go back and finish reading its second half and continue to postpone my judgment until I go through the entire document. I told her that I hate to keep my action in secrecy and that I have never lied to my parents. She said, by looking into the cause of the unilateral filial disconnection and its implication, I am searching for justice and this action supersedes the fear of lying to 'someone you love and respect.' She was very inquisitive about a possible 'extended family relative' who, for whatever reason, had been infusing controversies, fabricated stories, or even outright lies into the relationship between my parents and you two. I told her that she had correctly suspected this likely possibility many months ago, when she and I first moved into the same dormitory room, by telling her that the name Aamir, my grandfather's youngest brother, had been repeatedly mentioned throughout the first half of the thick file of documents that I went through."

Martine suddenly turned her attention to the sound of the town clock that began to strike and chime at midmorning; then she turned to Azalee. "I am going to attend the nine-thirty Mass. You are welcome to stay home and read the remainder of the file. Just carefully lock the door. I will be back by no later than eleven and will bring some French pastry."

"Grandma, I want to go with you to church. I have not gone to a church service since I was in my sophomore high school year when my parents attended their last Christmas Eve Lutheran service. I envy Charlotte's Christian faith and the peace and love between members of her extended family. Being the only child of a wealthy businessman, I have traveled to many foreign countries on vacation with my parents since I was a toddler. I excel in school. I can fairly well play the piano in an ensemble or give a solo violin performance at my high school senior year commencement. I thoroughly enjoy impressionists' paintings. I love skiing. My parents have been giving me everything I want, and yet I started to feel that something is missing in my life since the first day of my freshman year in college. Grandma, I am determined more than ever to find the meaning of my life in God. Can you help me?"

With joy Azalee accompanied Martine. They walked with their arms entwined to the small two-hundred-year-old Catholic church around the corner. Martine was so delighted to see her step-grand-daughter reverently kneel at the communion rail, make the sign of the cross after receiving the host while solemnly looking at the oversized wooden crucifix behind the altar. When the service ended, instead of following the stream of worshippers to exit the crowded nave, Azalee asked Martine to remain sitting a little longer on the pew, listening to the postlude religious music of Vivaldi played on the church organ. On the way home after the Mass, Azalee revealed to Grandma that she was enrolled in a one-semester weekly Bible study course at school and that she had finished the second class, "Part A: God as Creator (God the Father)." She confided to Martine that many students in the religious class were way ahead of her in their knowledge of Christianity, but because of her intense and purposeful interest in the subject, she was certain that she would be well informed about the Creator as much as the rest of the class by the end of "Part C: God as Enabler (God the Holy Spirit)."

They quickly stopped at the neighborhood bakery. After Sunday brunch, Azalee plunged back into her reading of the remaining two-inch-thick folder. She repeatedly asked Grandma for details of the circumstances bound to reported events, of unclear or too fictitious as stories or unrealistic assumptions made by individuals mentioned in the document. By dinnertime she wasn't able to finish reading the last twenty sheets of "Folder II." Martine offered her to stay overnight, and she joyously accepted. Martine didn't want to see her go home and be alone until Monday evening, before the return of Emal and Ënerod. They moved from the dining room to the fireplace after a sumptuous dinner Martine took almost two hours to prepare for her intelligent, talented, honest, and youthful visitor with a very bright future.

While Azalee was clumsily rekindling the smoldering logs in the fire box, Martine reminded the latter by counting on her fingers. "Our last meal with you alone and Grandpa at our home on 17 Rue Tilleul on the east side of town, believe or not, was twelve years ago when your parents brought you to us for an overnight stay. We were still renting and the multiple-apartment rental complex had an outdoor swimming pool. It was mid-July. You spent at least three hours with us in the pool. You swam like a fish, and before you left on the next morning, you waved at us from your dad's car saying loudly, 'I'll be back soon.' But sadly, we had to wait until your last month's visit. Do you still remember those wonderful hours you spent with us, darling?"

Azalee turned around, with tears running down her cheeks, approached Martine, and tightly hugged her for several minutes. "Grandma, I am truly sorry. For many years, my life has not been under my own control. You and Grandpa must know that I love you two from the bottom of my heart, and I want you two to know that I am an adult now."

That Sunday night, Azalee slept on Abd's vacant twin bed in the master's bedroom. Both ladies sat up against the headboard and talked for hours until past midnight. Before Martine took out the worn-out leather-covered black Bible from her night table and read Psalm 18 before falling asleep, she turned to Azalee, who was still fully awake.

"Grandpa and I are keeping a few things that were in connection with your father's and your uncle Yasir's growing-up period. We found them while packing before we moved to this house. But because both have unilaterally severed their relation with us, we have been waiting for the right opportunity to turn over to them or to you these childhood memorabilia. Among them are their awarded Bible and Certificate of Confirmation from the Lutheran churches, one in Foxeline and the other in Odinard, at the completion of their catechism study."

Azalee got up from the dining room table then slowly walked to the living room while taking a quick glance at her wristwatch. "Grandma, it's already five after four. I must go home before my parents return from their trip. Please stay there and rest. I will catch the 4:25 bus and will be dropped just a half block from our house. Don't worry. It's still daylight."

"Absolutely not. I will drive you home and will make sure that everything is okay in the house before I leave you."

Martine quickly put on her coat and her shoes, briefly combed her gray hair tufts, and then both drove the old Peugeot out of the garage, heading toward Grenoble Heights, where Ënerod and Emal's house, valued at over a million, was located. Before entering the residence and while sitting in the car, Martine turned to Azalee. "Did you make anything out of your reading of the documents?"

"Certainly, Grandma. I have now a better idea of what was the cause of the sad relationship between you two and my parents. I think I have found the source of all troubles, and I must be very thankful to Charlotte for having suggested that I should pay attention to a possible 'extended relative' involved in family affairs of other peaceful living individuals. What attracted my attention was the unilateral disconnection with you two by my parents and Uncle Yasir since I just turned eleven, yet you two are still waiting to know why your two stepsons don't want to have anything to do anymore with you and Grandpa. Additionally, I paid a great deal of attention to the unusual relationship between Aamir and Grandma Amelia after Grandpa divorced her. It appeared to me that the relationship was conveniently developed to benefit both of them. My suspicion was subsequently reinforced when I read the comment made by one of the psychologists who voiced her final opinion on this bizarre alliance: 'Based on written materials you two had provided me with and my personal inquisition during many hours you had spent in my office, I have arrived to only two plausible intertwined explanations.

Aamir is mentally insane and his former sister-in-law Amelia had to find a convincing way to counterbalance the blunders she committed prior to the divorce.' Grandma, I have taken note of what I have read. Before returning to school for the second semester, I will have a few free days that I can use to do some calm reflection and rational mental analysis of all that I have learned from my reading. Hope to see you again right after school commencement."

Martine entered the house first after Azalee disarmed the security system then loudly called out, "Mom and Dad, are you home?"

Not hearing a human response except the regular sound of the grandfather clock in the living room, both carefully looked at every single room in the house. Suddenly, Azalee turned to Martine. "Grandma, I almost forgot to relate to you one more noteworthy impression I got out of the reading of your files of documents. Undeniably, there was a strong bond between Uncle Yasir and Grandpa, especially during the first three years they lived alone, before you became a part of their life. This was the result of Uncle Yasir's need of love, expressed on a daily basis through words and deeds, from the only person he was sharing his lonesome life with during that period. There was a mutual dependence of action and influence between them. Grandpa had seen in Uncle Yasir a loving, well-behaved, mild-mannered, and intelligent youth who loved him unconditionally. And Uncle Yasir recognized without any doubt, especially during his preteen years, the sacrifices made by his father in order to give him a sound upbringing based on a solid religious foundation, enabling him to have a bright future. In my humble opinion, what was the most touching aspect of this father-son relationship, despite a change of heart on the part of Uncle Yasir seven years after he left his father's home, was Grandpa's reflection on his younger son's personality, Grandpa's unwavering love for Uncle Yasir from the time the latter was born, and it remained steadfast until he died."

In the last part of his memoir, when his insurmountable fatigue caused by leukemic anemia made him bedridden, Abd tried to explain to himself and also to his offspring how his young son—leaving aside his older son whose indisputable motive for disowning his father was already mentioned previously—was overwhelmed by irresistible intense external pressure to disconnect with him. Undoubtedly, this remark made by Abd had profound influence on Azalee's feeling toward her grandfather unjustly shunned by his two sons. Furthermore, in the same paragraph, Abd raised the following question to be addressed by future generations of his offspring: "Who has the brightest idea to explain to me if there is a difference between having a still living father with whom his children have totally severed the relationship and having a father who had died years ago? If anyone of you can tell me that there is indeed a difference, please evoke my soul and let it know of your answer." Then he went on to write, "They [his two sons] must believe in the old thirteenth-century adage 'Out of sight, out of mind.'"

Finally, with a sadness of expression on her face, Martine embraced her loving Azalee and asked her to securely lock the door, and then she left.

Even though she had been visited by her brothers and sisters monthly or bimonthly, Martine led a lonely life at the nursing home since she returned from the burial of her husband. Every weekday at around four o'clock in the afternoon, she slowly pushed her walker to the indoor mailbox, hoping to receive a letter from Azalee. Month after month went by, but the only contact she had with her step-granddaughter was occasional brief phone calls made by the latter from Carcassonne. She suspected that Azalee's reconnection with her was still kept in secrecy.

Finally, after three and a half years, Azalee's promised note to Grandma expressing her calm reflection had arrived. With some trepidation but mainly with emotion that brought tears to her eyes, Martine went over her step-granddaughter's long cursive handwritten paragraphs:

Dear Grandma Martine,

How have you been? Has your doctor successfully managed to regulate your heartbeats with medicines? I worry about your health, Grandma. After I finished reviewing the notes I took with me, I spent most of my time during the weeks preceding my return to Carcassonne thinking about family issues you and I are confronted with. I have been, and still at this point, overwhelmed by the events and circumstances that constitute my mental maze. In a corn maze, with some patience and perseverance, I should be able to eventually find the exit, but here in this intangible structure, I feel I am mentally and emotionally bulldozed by too many unanswered questions I have raised. I am finding no way out. I am convinced that the main cause of the problem was the result of poor communication, use of wrong words or wrong expressions, mistrust, wrong assumption...; and that these negative elements that had initiated disharmony from within the family unit or from external sources could be put to rest if we decide to start a dialogue among ourselves to find the way to return to a peaceful unity and love. God is always in us and ready to cleanse our sins for us. Grandma, I have been racking my brain trying to find answers to the numerous questions I have raised since I finished reading your entire thick folder of documents. Instead of going over all issues, please let me bring into question just a few that bother me the most and appear rather irrational, senseless, bizarre, and even childish. Please allow me to be specific in discussing these issues. I came to realize that somehow the question about 'churchgoing' Grandpa had asked me on that school Grandparents' Day when I was eleven years old was interpreted as an act of premeditated privacy infringement and 'a deliberate intention on your (Grandpa's) part to use a day with her (me) for your own (Grandpa's) gain but entirely at Azalee's expense.' I am wondering whether I had played a catalytic role in the conflict and whether I was the straw that broke the camel's back, giving the immaturity of my conduct at the age of eleven. I feel guilty thinking that I might inadvertently have caused the rift between two sets of people I love dearly. It is not uncommon for a religious grandparent to inquire whether his grandchild has been going to church, synagogue, or mosque on a regular basis. It is not a crime that deserves a severe punishment of the total disconnection with that grandparent. I think you are right when you wrote, 'It is another excuse to build his (my dad's) case.'

The shunning of Grandpa is on top of the list of my infinite unanswered questions. Since it was the final outcome of many years of conflict between members of two generations of the same family, I would like to analyze it in depth in order to find an explanation for this drastic measure taken by those who were supposed to remain grateful to the person(s) who had saved them from sinking into the most destitute parental post-divorce environment and who singlehandedly took care of them while they were still preteens. Adult children should unconditionally acknowledge the sacrifices made by the parent who had chosen to remain single after the divorce in order to concentrate his/her effort on the care for the children until they had finished their education, enabling them to be financially self-sustaining and emotionally competent enough to live independently. This was not the case here unfortunately.

Now let us discuss about the decision taken by grown-up children to unilaterally disconnect themselves permanently from their aging parents when the latter are in their eighties. In my opinion, this extreme form of estrangement equates with a condemnation of their seniors to a premature death. This comparison sounds too harsh, but please let me explain to you how I had arrived to think that way.

Grandma, please ask yourself what would remain for a senior couple to dream on after the postponement of their retirement for many years due to the financial insecurity and after spending every dime they could earn while still working and still had a huge bank loan to pay for the education of their children thereafter? Would not the joy of seeing their children successful and the anticipation of spending a lot of leisure time with the grandkids after retirement be considered as the only remaining compensation for many sacrifices the seniors had made? What would be left for the latter if they were cut off from their grown-up children and their family? Grandma, you can realize now that the unilateral disconnection with the seniors in this scenario constitutes a death sentence. Indeed, nothing was left for their remaining years except old age illnesses and eventual dementia.

Grandma, you know by now that I have a very analytical mind like Grandpa, right? So please let me try to bring up all factors that had led my parents and Uncle Yasir to shun Grandpa and you. It is not difficult for me to put all pieces of puzzle together and arrive to an explanation by using extrapolation, exclusion-inclusion concepts, and sound rationalization.

I noted that the relationship between my parents and you two deteriorated gradually several years after my Afghan paternal great-grandmother Elaha, the matriarch, died, and the family bond started to dwindle about the time when Aamir and my paternal grandmother Amelia reconnected after they had met only once two decades earlier. This was followed by Uncle Yasir's unusual disrespectful behavior toward you two. The earlier meeting of my father and Grandpa many years ago at the city park had revealed for the first time that my father and Uncle Yasir had not wanted to bring back for discussion any issue that had "connection with the past" and that anything that had to do with Grandma Amelia was considered as a sacred cow. No wonder their meeting had miserably failed and subsequently their relationship got much worse than before. The bond between you two and your adult stepchildren became no more than just occasional sit-down-for-a-meal contacts on a few particular occasions like birthday, Christmas, or New Year. The cold relationship between you, Grandma, and my mom, starting after my birth, as you had in detail documented a few times in your handwritten notes, had certainly transformed the natural family bond into a superficial and casual relationship for the sake of familial peace. It must be heartbreaking for you and Grandpa to be shunned by the very people you loved and continue to love despite enormous personal sacrifices you had made to put them back on the right track of life after they were severely affected by their parental separation.

Now please let me dissect Uncle Yasir's comportment from the time he had decided to live with Grandpa Abd after the divorce until the time period when he joined in with his brother to take the 180-degree turn vis-à-vis the relationship with you two around five to six years after he left his father's home to be on his own. I recall, from reading your notes, Uncle Yasir had already shown to be a person with a good heart and a mild manner at an early age. He loved his father and constantly worried about his father's health during the post-divorce years when he was living alone with his old man. But all these virtues were about to change over the next few years. Chronologically, here is how he had come up with explanations why he had decided to become his father's second estranged son. Again, around the time when his uncle Aamir reached out to his mother, my grandma Amelia, he strongly objected each time Grandpa Abd reminded him and his brother that they were their own judges and that they had decided on their own, without being coerced, to pack up and go with their father immediately after the parental separation. Then he became repeatedly insolent on the phone because his father had been "repeating over and over" the same arguments. As his telephone contacts with Grandpa and you were becoming scantier, he came up with the "nothing left to talk about" as the explanation of his deliberate disengagement on his part for the next couple of years. Then came a bombshell—he accused his father of having "forbidden" him from traveling through South American nations known for their high crime rate during his world solo bike trip. But he couldn't give an answer when you and Grandpa asked him, "If it was true that his father had forbidden him to do so, why had he accepted the 1,200 French francs as a gift to partially defray his travel expenses before he started the trip?" He continued to insist that his father had verbally "forbidden" him to travel through Chile even after you two had pointed out to him the universal common knowledge that parents have no say once the grown-up children leave their parents' home and are on their own; and therefore, accusing his own father for having used this command was frivolous.

The next jolt Uncle Yasir came up with was his contention that I was verbally abused by Grandpa when I was five years old and was playing on the floor with toys I received during Christmas Eve. Truly, I don't remember that Grandpa had ever said an unkind word to me. I believe you when you wrote these words to Uncle Yasir: "Ënerod didn't want me in the kitchen so I stayed next to your father in the living room delightfully watching Azalee playing on the carpeted floor, and I didn't hear even a single harsh word from him. I think your memory has failed you." Grandma, I still remember that I was sitting between you and Grandpa that evening on the dark-green upholstered couch facing my Christmas toys lying on the floor. You two took turns reading children's books with me while waiting for dinner. Furthermore, as you had questioned him, why Grandpa had to pick a fight with his five-year-old granddaughter on a Christmas Eve and yet you two, living then less than half an hour by car from us, were granted to see her no more than a couple of times a year? I still vividly recollect those moments when I was allowed at the age of three to jump on your queen-sized bed while each of you was standing at the bedside with your arms stretched out, ready to catch me in case I fell. Being a certified internist/pediatrician, Grandpa was very conscious of safety for children. To this day, I still clearly see him standing against the walls of your home, ready to catch me in case I missed my step and fell while dancing on the long hallway Oriental rug lying over the slippery, shiny wood floor. I was then seven years old. He was watching every movement I made, every word I said. But now he is gone... Grandma, I miss him...

Still, there weren't enough accusations made by Uncle Yasir. Here is another one. On one page, you wrote, "He [Yasir] reproached Abd for having interfered with his life by calling several schools for information on his contemplated study for a master's degree." Then you added, "I don't understand why he [Yasir] had the nerve to pointlessly accuse his father for interference. Knowing that Yasir was extremely busy with his research projects during the day and overwhelmed by his evening classes, his father had consulted with Emal before he made several calls to a number of French universities that had a teaching curriculum on subjects included in the evening courses he was taking, enabling him to get additional credits toward his master's degree. During the same period, Abd contacted a half dozen governmental organizations and private companies dealing with soil and water pollution to find out whether these had openings for employment while offering scholarships for advance degrees on research in their related field. Because he had wanted to keep the inquiry strictly confidential, he assured Emal that he was going to use my maiden name and the given name of one of my brothers when he started to establish contact with all these institutions. Emal didn't see any reason why his father couldn't lend a hand to Yasir." Grandma, I don't understand why Uncle Yasir was so angry against his father. Grandpa had been very careful not to mention the name Yasir Rasulov during the entire process of information gathering. In my opinion, what Grandpa did was totally innocuous. If I were in Uncle Yasir's shoes, instead of having an accusatory attitude, I would be very grateful to Grandpa for being always ready to help. After all, after the divorce, Grandpa had managed to singlehandedly start a new life from scratch with my dad and Uncle Yasir. He put them through expensive education until they graduated from college. He diligently pursued the new path of his life with determination, while ignoring much toil, privation, and personal sacrifices in order to keep his two sons from sinking into the depression and

*despair caused by the post-parental divorce phase.
I concurred with your fourth psychologist when he
wrote his last note to you and Grandpa: "There are
no adequate words for the boys to truly express their
gratitude for the immense self-sacrifice made by the
doctor."*

*Grandma, you brought up another issue Uncle
Yasir had with Grandpa. If I understood correctly,
he told one of the psychologists you two had worked
with that "Grandpa's problem lies with his childhood" and that his psychotherapist didn't want him
to be "specific" about it. So I had decided to scruti-
nize Grandpa's childhood through reading of your
written documentation and talking about growing
up with Charlotte and with my parents. The latter
had been rather evasive about this subject, probably
because they were afraid to reveal the source of several fabricated unfounded rumors, one of which was
the false story that my great-grandfather Haashim
Rasulov had an affair with the aunt of his wife (my
great-grandmother Waida) during the evacuation
from war-torn Bamyan. Apparently, Grandpa had
mentioned to you that he himself and a cousin of
my great-grandma Elaha fell in love when they were
around twelve years old. If Uncle Yasir had considered that childhood romantic first love as a criminal
act, he is wrong. According to my friend Charlotte
who has a PhD degree in psychology and two quotes
from prominent psychologists she handed to me, this
"puppy love" is a natural process preteens and teenag-
ers are going through before reaching adulthood.[12, 13]
During that phase of development, many boys and
girls start to explore then discover their own body
and that of the opposite sex. Therefore, hugging and
kissing were considered by the majority of educators*

to be a part of the normal human development, which is perfectly acceptable.

The last statement Uncle Yasir, at age thirty-eight, had made to you in person, in the absence of Grandpa, who was away on humanitarian medical mission abroad, when you asked him whether in retrospect he would have preferred to live with his mother and her boyfriend Jean-Marie after the divorce instead of joining his brother and his father to move to another city, was in my opinion very troublesome. If his response, "I had a second thought about it," meant that he had regretted having made a wrong decision at age eleven in the court chamber when the judge gave him the opportunity to have the last word, I think an internal conflict was still boiling in him; and I am glad, per my parents, he had been seeing his therapist on a regular basis for at least three years. Grandma, perhaps you might be surprised by what my instinct is telling me: Uncle Yasir is fundamentally a good person with a heart of gold, and he will eventually come around to realize that he had falsely accused Grandpa. But for the time being, he remains very ambivalent: on one hand, he still loves his father, but on the other, he is constantly influenced by unending coercion from his brother, his mother, his uncle Aamir, and perhaps his sister-in-law to remain vague about the real reason for his disconnection with you two.

I am closing this long note with the following questions and comments. While leaving out details and concentrating only on the outcome and the aftereffect, I am very troubled by the unusual relationship between Grandma Amelia and Aamir Rasulov and wonder whether this man was indeed the main cause, directly or indirectly, of the total disconnection in question that had led to my com-

plete forced separation from you two starting almost a decade ago. Please let me go over a few questions I came up with while reading your file of documents.

Let's start with my dad. The reason was quite obvious to me why my dad, whose contacts with you two since my early childhood had been meager at best, had to stop at a gas station on his way from work and used the public phone each time he wanted to place his rare calls to you two, instead of waiting until he was back at his bureau at home. It must be quite clear to you why he had also chosen to make these skimpy calls from the airport, while waiting for his flight departure, instead of from home. I still remember the only phone call he had made from home to you two on a Saturday when my mom was out shopping. Grandma, in order to assure myself of a benefit of doubt, I carefully scrutinized every page of your two files of documents, hoping to find other possible reasons to explain the unusual relationship between my dad and Grandpa from the time my dad married my mom. Grandpa's conduct toward my parents was flawless until the day when my dad called and talked to Grandpa about the election of the new French president, who happened to be of mixed African race. I was then nine years old. Since my mom is a newly converted liberal, and my dad, who claims to be independent politically even though he was a member of the conservative French political party, they have diametrically opposite opinions on the election result with Grandpa. My dad, according to your note, "became at least unpleasant" on the phone. Grandpa's reaction during that brief telephone encounter was rather unfortunate. He referred to my mom at one point as "that woman of yours." However, on further reflection, I can understand why Grandpa had made that mistake. He was so frustrated, not much by the election result, but more so by the way you two were treated during the preceding period of over a decade by my parents. Thereafter, Grandpa felt sorry for having used those words and had apologized.

But the most troublesome to me was Aamir Rasulov's behavior. Why did Aamir defy public opinion and normal social code of conduct by siding with a woman his own brother had divorced? Why did he refer to himself as a "black sheep" when he dealt with his three older brothers he despised? For what reason had he spread the false rumor through his family tree book that he wrote himself that his father had committed adultery? What was his motive for lying about Grandpa having borrowed money from a destitute poor niece whom Grandpa had been for years sending regular financial assistance? Why did he lie about Grandpa forbidding my father and Uncle Yasir from having contact with him for almost three decades? And last, but not least, why in secrecy had he had Grandma Amelia's maiden name engraved on the flat stone at the head of an empty tomb several years after she was divorced from Grandpa? I remember I read several excerpts from my grand-uncle Zekirullah's letters to his brothers and his children calling Aamir a "professional liar." In the copy of a letter addressed to elders in Tuti Koshteh that I found in your file, the latter had made a comment about his brother Aamir: "His success was blemished by no pangs of conscience and remorse. He considered himself as irreproachable, and with his tranquil conscience, he continued to carry his head high." I am very thankful to Charlotte for having initially suspected this extraordinary involvement of an extended family member into the life of children recovering from the destructive effect of parental divorce. However, I am profoundly saddened by the unexplained unilateral disconnection my parents and Uncle Yasir have made with you two and the deprivation of the well-known joy the majority of retired grandparents have, through close contact with their offspring during the remaining years—the so-called golden years—of their life.

Grandma, my outlook of the human interaction at this point of my life is rather bleak. Everywhere I looked, I saw predominantly signs of conflict and hardly any trace of peace and harmony. The struggle starts with "inner turmoil" within the individual person. It is also recognized within the family unit with spousal discord leading to separation, within the nation, between different political factions breeding corrupt and self-serving leaders. Struggles in the form of warfare are not uncommon between nations and are often due to economic or theocratic reasons. In our case, since my parents, jointly with Uncle Yasir, steadfastly refused to give the reason(s) after pronouncing the verdict against Grandpa, circumstantial evidences had led all your four psychotherapists to the same conclusion: a secretive quid pro quo financial deal. Since I have not been able, even with my friend Charlotte's help, to come up with a plausible explanation for the necessity from their part of shunning Grandpa, sadly I have to admit to you that I ended up believing in your therapists' conclusions. It is depressing, when you think about all these troubles, isn't it? However, there is an eternal and unshakeable consolation—the domain of God.

Hope to pay you a visit this summer. I love you, Grandma.

Azalee

Azalee was caught between the devil and the deep blue sea. On one hand, she wanted to remain respectful and loving to her parents as well as to her Uncle Yasir, whom she loved dearly; but on the other, she could not tolerate the injustice they caused to her shunned set of grandparents. Reader will find out in the end how she managed not to choose between these two equally unacceptable choices.

EPILOGUE

bdulai (Abdulah or Abd) died of complications of chronic myelogenous leukemia in his midseventies and was buried near his birthplace. On a few occasions, he mentioned in his memoir the main burden of his life: the estrangement leading to complete disconnection with his two sons for almost two decades prior to his death. He believed that this deliberated shunning, which caused severe stress on him, had a detrimental effect on his health, as the words "my impaired immune system function" or "progression to the development of my leukemia" were found in the last few pages of his narrative. A few decades later, it has become evident that Abd's suspicion turned out to be a human biological proven reality.[14, 15]

Martine, the step-grandmother of Azalee, slowly showed signs of dementia a couple of months after her seventy-eighth birthday. Afraid of her frequent falls and lack of adequate nutrition, her close relatives moved her to a nursing home in La Rochelle to be near them. She passed away seven years later. Before moving from Grenoble to La Rochelle, Martine had her meager asset of less than one-half million French francs legally willed to a French humanitarian organization for the future construction of a day-care building somewhere in the township of Tupchi near Bamyan in memory of her husband. In her will, she instructed the director of the nursing home to have all her written communications with the family members of her deceased husband forwarded to "the author or the author's substitute." Undoubtedly, before she died, she continued to count on Hans Reinberg or his wife Shelly to complete the writing of Abd's memoir.

Amelia and her husband *Serge*, in their late eighties, remained in Foxeline and continued to visit yearly with Maurina, whose husband Biorn succumbed to surgical complications at a private rehabilitation center in Stockholm a few years earlier.

Dr. Zekirullah, the oldest son of the Haashim Rasulov family, died of old age in Tuti Koshteh. He had never left Afghanistan after returning from Sweden with a doctorate degree in general medicine. In association with his mentor, Dr. Faisal, he provided the state-of-the-art care he had learned from having spent his years of training in one of the best Western countries known for their advance in medicine. His being raised from the childhood in Third World poverty to the position of minister of health in a war-torn country was remarkable.

Faiz managed to cope with his attention-deficit hyperactive disorder (ADHD) throughout his life and continued to work as a farmer until one morning he was found drowned in a shallow pond while still holding his workhorse by the reins. The circumstance of his death was not well-known to the town where he spent his entire life.

Ali, the most intelligent of the six Rasulov children, married to an Afghan refugee lady who turned out to have schizophrenia. He stayed with her and singlehandedly took care of his four children until she prematurely died of stomach cancer. His dream of becoming a science teacher in high school had evaporated upon the discovery of his wife's illness. He took a few evening courses in advanced chemistry, physics, and mathematics for a few years, but because of the family's distressed situation, eventually he had to resign his vocation for the career of a pharmaceutical representative covering the southern Austrian region. He died at the age of seventy-seven of abdominal aneurysm rupture while being operated on.

Aamir, retired at the age of sixty-eight from his prosperous computer chip-making business, remained in Aix-en-Provence and was still making frequent trips to Foxeline to visit with Amelia and Serge. After the death of all three of his older brothers, occasionally he returned to Bamyan area where he became, to the eyes of poor local villagers, the idol of the Rasulov family. He wasn't too happy when elders in Tuti Koshteh turned down his significantly large financial compensation in exchange for the replacement of Abdulah's tombstone by a new one with the words "Amelia Englund" put back on it. The popularity of Aamir among his compatriots in exile or as refugees in Europe had suffered severely since word were spreading that he was not the person he had made them to believe. In the end, only a handful of his countrymen were still in contact with him, but he continued to tightly associate with former warlords living abroad.

Nabeela and Feda: With the regular financial assistance from Abd and Zekirullah, Nabeela arrived to finish her four-year pharmacy study, as she had wished, and became a certified pharmacist. Her husband, Feda, graduated from the same school. Both eventually opened their own pharmacy. They had a very successful business for over thirty years until they retired in a suburb of Paris.

Omira, after Faiz's tragic death, took over the house in which the Rasulov siblings grew up and cohabitated with a war-orphaned distant cousin that Haashim brought home four years to the day before he died. She never married. At one point, when she knew that none of the Rasulov siblings still living abroad would return and live in Afghanistan, she asked them whether one of her own relatives could squeeze in another house on the premise. Abdulah initiated the idea of giving the entire property to the grown-up war orphan instead. He sent a reply to Omira with signatures of all still living Rasulovs, rejecting her request. Instead, they cited that the house and land should remain the sole property of future descendants of the Rasulov clan. Reportedly, Omira was not at all happy with Abdulah's proposition, which was unanimously endorsed by his siblings, and thereafter she became more dependent on and friendly with Aamir, who used his wealth to win her support in order to alienate further his relationship with Abdulah. She developed "severe senility" and died in her late seventies with the orphan woman at her bedside.

Emal and Ënerod: Emal, whose contact with the senior couple had been rather scanty after his marriage, was not too eager to show his indebtedness to Martine and Abd. Approximately six years after shunning his father, while on a business trip in Moscow, Emal learned from his brother that his father had an acute brain hemorrhage precipitating to a stroke of unknown cause (cryptogenic isch-emic stroke). On the same day, he called Martine, who related to him his father's course of illness. He asked Martine whether he "should interrupt his trip and fly home." But the estrangement with his father and his stepmother subsequently remained uninterrupted, and he did not learn of his father's death until several years later when one of his college classmates sent him a cut-out page from a medical news-letter on which a brief but lofty eulogy of his father, pronounced by a colleague, was listed in the "In Memoriam" section. The couple moved to Switzerland and retired at the Lugano Lake area.

Yasir, still a bachelor at age of forty-seven, left his job in Paris and moved out of the country. Subsequently, nobody seemed to know where he went and why he didn't want anybody to know where he was. Undoubtedly, Amelia, Emal, Ënerod, and Uncle Aamir knew everything about Yasir but wanted to keep quiet. Rumor had it French tourists had seen him in Perth, Australia.

Because the true maternal love for her stepson remained immense and unwavering, Martine, with the help from a family friend, managed to locate Yasir exactly where he lived a few years after her husband's death. Then Yasir consented to keep in touch with her. Through occasional postal mail, he remained in contact with her until she was placed in the assisted-living facility and was no longer able to communicate with the outside world. During that period, Martine purposely wanted to share with him news on his father's declining health, then the man's posthumous legacy, but Yasir showed no interest. The two brothers Emal and Yasir had never wanted to reveal to their stepmother Martine the reason for which they unilaterally disconnected with their father. Yasir had expressed a few times his gratitude toward her and her deceased husband Abdulah for the care he received solely from the latter after the divorce until he graduated from college. Neither Emal nor Yasir was present at their stepmother's burial ceremony.

Azalee: Since Azalee's last visit with Martine over a year and half ago, she called her step-grandmother twice to inquire about her health and to find out whether the thick file of documents had ever been shown to her parents and/or to Uncle Yasir. She was bewildered when Martine replied that she had indeed offered to them at least twice the full access to all the filed documents; but neither of the three had any interest in her offer. During these two brief phone conversations, Martine sensed that Azalee's bewilderment was accompanied by some sort of restraint in terms of judgment *vis-à-vis* the disconnection of the relationship between her parents and the old Rasulov couple. Martine was totally surprised when she learned from Azalee that she had switched her two major subjects, from arts and music to the biological branch of natural sciences and humanities (the study of human condition) when she began the first semester of her college sophomore year. In addition, she picked religion as her minor subject. Martine couldn't figure out why Azalee had made such a drastic change. However, she knew for sure that the high school valedictorian non-blood-related granddaughter could do well in the study of any subject taught in college. She hoped that Azalee still wanted to pursue her interest in arts and especially in music after the switch of college major subjects.

Azalee had been in touch with Grandma Martine at least twice a year either by phone from school or by letter during the next four years. In one of her birthday cards to Martine, Azalee wrote,

> I am sorry for not being able to pay you a visit during the last twenty-one months. Things have not been going as well as I had hoped, but I am sure you have an idea why. When I learned of Grandpa's passing, I mourned his departure for weeks. Can you imagine a granddaughter's deepest sorrow for having been prevented from having contact with her grandfather from the time she was still a preteen until her second college year to suddenly find out that she will never see him again? Grandma, I am still mourning…too sad to continue dwelling on this subject. So, let's move on to something else that broke my heart. Every time I tried to bring up the issue of severance of relationship, my parents, especially my mother,

345

advised me either to "stay out of it" or to con-
sider it as "a thing of the past." Since they love me
so much, I don't want to disappoint them. I love
and respect my parents, even though occasionally we have contradicting opinions, especially
since my first visit to your house seven years ago.
I sense that my father and Uncle Yasir don't want
to preserve that natural bond with their father.
The two main issues that I had gathered from my
reading of your filed documents have been bothering me every time I think about them. Often, I
ask myself why my parents and Uncle Yasir continue to ignore your and Grandpa's request for an
explanation of the disconnection of relationship
and why my father and Uncle Yasir have become
so ungrateful to Grandpa for having singlehandedly taken care of them not only after the divorce
but already during the preceding years when the
union of their parents took a turn for the worse. In
my opinion, they have nothing to lose by remaining at least polite, correct, and in sporadic contact
with you two, even after they knew that Grandma
Amelia had willed a whopping asset to be distrib-
uted between them after her death. Disagreement
between two generations is not uncommon, but
it is not an excuse to permanently disconnect
with one's own father and stepmother without
cause. It is incomprehensible to me. I also cannot
understand why Uncle Yasir, so nice to everybody
and who loves me so much, could be so mean to
you; I am referring to your encounter with him
in the hotel room in Paris. I feel bad that neither
of them had sincerely—by action and not just
talk—expressed their gratitude also to you, who
have done so much for both, from the time you
married Grandpa until after they finished their

college education and beyond. Grandma, please join me in our prayers for a divine miracle that will reunite all of us. Happy birthday to you, Grandma. I love you. Take good care of yourself.

Azalee

Martine could not hide her emotion after she finished reading the handwritten note. That was her seventy-sixth birthday, and her health started to decline. In the meantime, Azalee continued to do well in college and in her two-year premed study. She managed to pay Grandma Martine two more brief visits without her parents' knowledge and to keep secret contact with the old lady even after the latter was placed in the nursing home in La Rochelle. She finally realized that her beloved grandma was gradually becoming more incapacitated mentally and physically. The telephone communication between them became more laborious, as Martine was progressively hard of hearing. A couple of years after entering the nursing home, Martine had been indeed transferred to the section of assisted living.

Three more years had gone by. There was absolutely no contact between the two sons of Abdulah's first marriage and his second wife Martine. Abdulah's death did not bring the rapprochement one would have expected. Instead, the elderly lady was leading a lonely life within the four confining walls of the nursing home. Alternate weekly visits from her two younger brothers and the occasional letter from Azalee remained the only communication with the outside world. Fortunately, one bright day in June, Martine was still mentally alert enough to rejoice in the announcement that her beloved step-granddaughter had been awarded the degree of medical doctorate at the same university medical school in Paris where her husband had spent his academic years and that the young lady was going to pursue her medical profession by spending a total of four more years in combined internal medicine and infectious disease fellowship.

Martine's health continued to decline further as she was reaching her eighty-fifth birthday. For the last ten days or so, the in-house doctor had been coming to see her almost daily. She refused to swallow food and water and quickly became bedridden, then gradually was sinking into comatose. A letter envelope postmarked "So. Cota—— [the last four letters being illegible], The Philippines" was delivered to Martine's room the week preceding her death; and the letter, still stayed wide-open, was lying at the side of the envelope on her night table. It read:

Dear Grandma Martine,

How have you been? I am truly sorry for not having been able to see you in person or to write you sooner. The last few years have been very hectic for me. I have been trying to fulfill my role of the only grandchild by equally spreading my time between two sets of families besides my fellowship training to become a medical specialist, my required religious evening study, and—to your big surprise—to profess my vows as a Catholic nun. Materialistically speaking, I had a wonderful life until now, but spiritually I was deprived. Human suffering has been in my mind since my senior year in high school when I first joined the school's International Amnesty support group. False accusation followed by erroneous condemnation that ends in torture then final execution of innocents happens too often. This and just vague allegations of misconduct or even casual insinuation among members of a family causing the fragmentation of the bond between kinsfolk was the main source of my concern that had led me to search for God's forgiveness. It is now time for me to pay back to humanity the privilege extended to me since I was born by serving the underprivileged and the poor. I think often of your and Grandpa's several medical mission trips to developing countries during the later years of his life. I am living now in the southern part of the Philippine Islands, and my ultimate goal of dedicating my entire life to serve God has been reached. I joined the order of the Holy Rosary Sisters and arrived here in the southern part of the Philippine Islands two weeks ago. I will be installed as the vice director of a fifty-bed hospital this coming Sunday. I will give you more details of my vocation next time I return to France. I pray every day for you, Grandpa, my parents, Uncle Yasir, and my other two sets of grandparents. I am at peace with God and with myself. Please pray for a better understanding between those we love. I love you, Grandma.

Azalee (Sister Marie-Thérèse)

In addition to this last long communication with Martine, Hans Reinberg received from the nursing home in Larochelle additional odds and ends of written materials related to the Rasulov family. Among those, he found a ragged piece of paper loosely tucked in between page 1 and page 2 and folded over page 3 of Azalee's letter. It read:

Martine,

I know you have not been sentimentally recipro-cated for your maternal care and love that Emal and Yasir received since you became the partner in starting a new chapter of my life. I want you to know how much I appreciate your personal sacri-fice in order to guide them not only through the hardship of the post-parental separation phase, but also to give them the moral support they needed during the subsequent years until they decided to leave the parental nest for a life on their own and beyond. You must be frustrated with the unfair way they treated you. Since they were brought up in an environment where fairness, justice, toler-ance, and morality formed the cornerstone of the family unit, and since both had completed their catechism study and had received the certificate of Confirmation from the Lutheran Church, I am convinced that they are basically good-natured persons reinforced by a solid religious education. My instincts are telling me that they will come around sometime in the future—very likely after I am gone—and decide to change their opinion about us, realizing that the materialistic aspect of life will never in the end make anyone happy. Furthermore, I am at peace with God and with myself, knowing that God will forgive "them" and therefore, I should do likewise. Knowing that God's love is boundless and endless, I continue to love my two sons—and their family—as much as I have since they were born.

Abd

Interestingly, the piece of paper fitted perfectly well into the missing part of the last page of Abd's diary mentioned earlier.

No one at the nursing home knew for sure whether Martine was able to read and comprehend Azalee's last message to her before she went into comatose.

Approximately a year after Hans started writing the memoir, he received from Martine's youngest sister the following handwritten note by Yasir. Apparently, the note was found at the bottom of Martine's safety box, and it was not discovered until her family decided to dispose all of its contents.

Perth, Australia, Dec 19, 1981

Dear Martine,

How have you been lately? Azalee wrote me last week, informing me that you are now living in a nursing home. With this short but sincere note, I want to express my deep regret for having wrongly accused Dad of his misconduct when he was growing up without giving him a specific reason, and for having totally disconnected with him during the entire period preceding his death. I learned from Azalee that the accusation Emal and I had made was based solely on hearsay and false story fabrications made by Uncle Aamir and his protégés. Furthermore, I came to realize that I was very ungrateful to Dad. Now, I feel guilty for not being able to ask for his forgiveness in person. Martine, I am deeply sorry; and my remorse is immense. I also want to apologize to you for my insolence when I met with you and Dad at the Parisian Hotel Bourbillon, Quartier Latin, several years back. I am not at peace, neither with God nor with myself. I beg you to include Dad's soul and mine in your daily prayers.

Love,
Yasir

During the two years preceding her death, Martine had sent at least four letters to Yasir offering unconditional reconciliation with her step-son; but the latter ignored them completely and none of those letters returned undelivered.

REFERENCES

1. "Communism and the Family," first published in *Komunistka*, no. 2, 1920, and in English in *The Worker*, 1920. Source: *Selected Writings* by Alexandra Kollontai, translated by Alix Holt (Allison & Busby).
2. Wikipedia, "May 1968 Events in France," http:// en.wikipedia.org/wiki/May_1968_events_in_France, updated 2016-05-27T09:01Z.
3. Peter Schwarz, "The General Strike and the Student Revolt in France, 1998," World Socialist Website (28 May 2008).
4. Stephen W. Lockley and Russell G. Foster, *Sleep: A Very short Introduction* (Oxford University Press, 2012.)
5. Stapleton A. E., Nudelman E., Clausen H., Hakomori S., Stamm W. E., "Urinary Tract Infection (UTI): Binding of Uropathogenic *Escherichia coli* R45 to Glycolipids Extracted from Vaginal Epithelial Cells Is Dependent on Histo-Blood Group Secretor Status," *Journal of Clinical Investigation* (1992): 90, 965–972.
6. Wikipedia, "Family Estrangement," June 2014.
7. Christian Frei, *The Giant Buddhas (Salsal & Shamama Statues)*, a film (2006).
8. Carolyn Gregoire, "How Being an Oldest, Middle or Youngest Child Shapes Your Personality," *The Huffington Post*, May 13, 2015, updated May 15, 2015.
9. National Institute of Diabetes and Digestive and Kidney Diseases, "Drug Record: Protein Kinase Inhibitors" (United States National Library of Medicine, 2015).

10. Mayo Clinic, "Chronic Myelogenous Leukemia: Treatment" (Minnesota: May 26, 2016).

11. Stefan Faderl, Moshe Talpaz, Zeev Estrov, and Hagop M. Kantarjian, "Chronic Myelogenous Leukemia: Biology and Therapy," *Ann Intern Med.*

12. American Academy of Pediatrics, "Theme 8: Promoting Healthy Sexual Development and Sexuality," in *Bright Futures: Guidelines for Health Supervision of Infants, Children and Adolescents*, 3rd ed. (Elk Grove Village, IL), 169–76.

13. "Normative Sexual Behavior in Children: A Contemporary Sample, *Pediatrics*, 101 (4), E9.

14. J. I. Webster Marketona and R. Glaser, "Stress Hormones and Immune Function," *Cell Immunology* (2008 Mar–Apr): 252 (1–2): 16–26. doi: 10.1016/j.cell imm. 2007.09.006. E-pub 2008 Feb 14.

15. Judy L. M. McCoyd and Carolyn Amber Walter, *Grief and Loss Across the Lifespan. A Biopsychosocial Perspective*, 2nd ed. (Springer Publishing Co.), 3–5.

ABOUT THE AUTHOR

The principal author, an MD with two subspecialties, has used a pen name for the sake of strict privacy.

Additionally, his philosophy about medical success is not centered on financial achievement, but rather on providing the best care possible and on how to provide that care on a benevolent basis. This is already alluded to in the "About the Author" on the back cover.

CPSIA information can be obtained
at www.ICGtesting.com
Printed in the USA
LVHW050124291220
675237LV00010B/1488